Causes o
Civil Law and Social Justice

The Final Report of the First LSRC Survey of Justiciable Problems

Pascoe Pleasence

and

Alexy Buck
Nigel Balmer
Aoife O'Grady
Hazel Genn
Marisol Smith

ISBN 0 11 703327 8

First published 2004

Printed in the United Kingdom for The Stationery Office
CR: 154737

Contents

Foreword

I welcome the opportunity to contribute a foreword to this important publication. In building upon Professor Hazel Genn's groundbreaking *Paths to Justice* study it presents a unique insight into the relationship between 'justiciable' problems and deprivation and demonstrates the important role of advice and legal services in the fight against social exclusion.

As Secretary of State for the new Department for Constitutional Affairs, I have stressed through my manifesto the importance of justice for all so that particularly those who are most vulnerable are able to exercise their rights effectively. This study makes evident the grave social, economic and health consequences of a failure to enable people to achieve justice. It therefore reveals the extent to which access to justice supports the Government's broad social policy objectives. It also strengthens the case for greater collaboration between the work of my Department and other Departments of State.

I have been struck by three key findings of the study in particular. First, that many individuals and families do not experience one isolated justiciable issue, but often clusters of inter-related issues, sometimes stemming from a single 'trigger' problem. The emerging details of trigger problems and problem clusters will be of enormous value in targeting public support for advice and legal services. Secondly, that in respect of nearly one in five justiciable problems no action is taken, often because people do not believe anything can be done, or sometimes because they are simply too scared to act. The need to raise awareness of individual rights and the processes that can be used to give effect to them is clearly a vital challenge for the future. Thirdly, that where people are unable to obtain advice from first advisers they may give up trying to resolve problems if there is no clear direction to an appropriate alternative source of advice. The need for signposting and referrals systems that enable people to navigate the 'advice maze' is manifest.

Taken together, the findings from the survey will be of particular relevance in informing the ongoing development of the Community Legal Service. This is key if we want genuine access to justice for all to become a reality rather than an aspiration.

ii

I am therefore most grateful to the authors for all the work they have done to bring about this publication and to the National Centre for Social Research for undertaking the fieldwork for the national and temporary accommodation surveys. I am pleased that the national survey is to be developed and periodically repeated over the years ahead, as this will, for the first time, provide the opportunity to evaluate civil justice policy over the long-term. It will also provide the opportunity to build a progressively deeper understanding of justiciable problems and the difficulties people face in resolving them, which will in turn provide the evidence base for innovation in policy making.

The Right Honourable Lord Falconer of Thoroton
Secretary of State for Constitutional Affairs and Lord Chancellor
February 2004

Acknowledgements

The completion of this study would not have been possible but for the contributions of, literally, thousands of people. We could not hope to detail them all here, but we would none the less like to formally acknowledge at least some of them. Specifically, we would like to thank Peter Lynn, Paddy Costigan, Debbie Collins and Kirby Swales, who worked within the National Centre for Social Research to help finalise the survey questionnaires and manage the survey fieldwork, along with the many fieldworkers of the National Centre for Social Research who conducted survey interviews and, most importantly, the 5,808 people who gave up their time for no personal reward to be interviewed about sometimes very personal and life-changing experiences.

We would like to thank the many past and present staff members of the Legal Services Commission and Department for Constitutional Affairs who worked to make this study and this publication a reality, and in particular Clare Dodgson, Steve Orchard, Roger Hamilton, Richard Buxton, Chris Smith, Catherine Max, Helen Perkins, Derek Hill, Robert Gill, Howard Thomson, Alan Cogbill, Phil Staker, Tony Donaldson, Lesley Hopcraft, Penny Innes and Stephen Gascoigne. We would also like to thank Donald Franklin of H.M. Treasury for contributing ideas during the development of the survey questionnaire. We are also most grateful for the immense contribution we received from the many members of the Legal Services Commission's Regional Planning and Partnership Teams and the many members of Community Legal Service Partnerships throughout England and Wales with whom we discussed our provisional findings and from whom we obtained many ideas as to how to best interpret them and further develop our analyses.

We would like to thank Kathryn Green of the Legal Services Research Centre for her diligent proof reading of the text and for assisting in drawing up the notes to the text, and also Ash Patel for his generous assistance.

We would also like to thank Spencer Caston of The Stationery Office for managing the publication process, and recognise the special contribution of Patrick Bos Coe in designing and preparing the cover for publication.

Finally, we would like to thank the Nuffield Foundation for having supported the earlier *Paths to Justice* study, without which this study may never have been undertaken.

1

Introduction: Civil Law and Social Justice

The problems to which the principles of civil law apply are not abstract 'legal problems'. They are not problems familiar only to lawyers, or discussed only in tribunals and civil courts. They are in most part the problems of 'everyday life'[1] – the problems people face as constituents of a broad civil society. Today, following the establishment over the last thirty years of an extensive range of rights and obligations related to child support, education, employment, debt, health, housing, and welfare benefits, these problems involve numerous issues of basic social well-being.[2]

This does not mean that legal process provides the best, a good, or even a sensible means through which to resolve particular 'justiciable'[3] problems. Many alternative means of resolution exist. Some of these, such as complaint and negotiation, often occur with reference to the law – in the 'shadow of the law'[4]. Others, though, such as Lewis's DIY solution for housing disrepair, invariably occur without any reference to law at all.[5] Also, resolutions may be brought about through governmental, rather than individual, action. However, the existence of a defining framework of civil law applicable to many problems of everyday social life and social well-being, and the possibilities for utilising legal services and process to reach solutions to such justiciable problems, mean that the infrastructure of civil justice today plays an important role in realising social justice.[6] Also, especially as those who experience justiciable problems 'often experience a problem more than once *and* more than one type of problem,'[7] this infrastructure plays an important role in efforts to tackle 'social exclusion' – the 'shorthand term for what can happen when people or areas suffer from a combination of linked problems such as unemployment, poor skills, low incomes, poor housing, high crime, bad health and family breakdown'.[8]

This link between the infrastructure of civil justice – which comprises courts, tribunals, professional and lay legal services, 'problem noticers',[9] and professional

2

and public legal education – and social exclusion is becoming increasingly recognised. Explicit reference was made to it in the 1998 government white paper *Modernising Justice*.[10] The white paper heralded the Access to Justice Act 1999 and the establishment of a Legal Services Commission with responsibility to strategically develop a Community Legal Service focused on the issues that affect the everyday lives of the 'disadvantaged and socially excluded'.[11] The Legal Services Commission's corporate plan refers to the Community Legal Service as being 'a component of a wider government programme aimed at creating a fair and inclusive society.'[12] A recent joint publication of the government and Law Centres Federation stated that 'lack of access to reliable legal advice can be a contributing factor in creating and maintaining social exclusion.'[13] It then went on to explain that 'poor access to advice has meant that many people have suffered because they have been unable to enforce their legal rights effectively, or have even been unaware of their rights and responsibilities in the first place.' Also, away from government it has been argued that 'legal advocacy and advice for the poor and excluded is an effective engine of social inclusion and fighting poverty through insuring and expanding rights to critical benefits and services, and giving a voice to grievances and empowering people and communities.'[14]

Despite this increasing recognition, though, little research has been undertaken to identify those people most vulnerable to justiciable problems, to establish how such problems impact on people's lives and communities, or to expose how such problems contribute to social exclusion. Prior to the mid-1990s, few attempts were made even to assess the prevalence of justiciable problems,[15] and little was known about the strategies people adopt to deal with them, the range of sources from which people seek advice, the way in which people use dispute resolution processes, people's objectives in addressing problems, and the extent to which resolutions match objectives. Since the mid-1990s, a number of important and innovative studies have investigated the prevalence of problems and the strategies to deal with them. However, despite Genn's *Paths to Justice* and *Paths to Justice Scotland* surveys, and similar surveys conducted in the United States and New Zealand,[16] little is known about how people progress through the maze of advice services they utilise, and what the infrastructure of civil justice actually 'delivers',[17] either for individuals or society at large.

In this book, drawing on data collected through the first Legal Services Research Centre (LSRC) national periodic survey of justiciable problems and a parallel survey of people living in temporary accommodation, we move on from *Paths to Justice,* and set out in detail the irregular experience and impact of justiciable problems, the pitfalls people face when navigating the advice maze, and the degree to which legal services and processes facilitate problem resolution and prevention. In so doing, we illustrate and underline the important links between justiciable problems and social exclusion, and between civil law and social justice.

THE LSRC NATIONAL PERIODIC SURVEY OF JUSTICIABLE PROBLEMS

The first LSRC national periodic survey of justiciable problems, conducted between July and October of 2001, constitutes the baseline survey in a long-term project to provide a broad empirical base for civil justice policy development. It was designed to establish the nature, pattern and impact of people's experience of justiciable problems across England and Wales, and detail the use and success of different problem resolution strategies. The periodic nature of the survey is intended to overcome the dangers of using different studies to compare changes in experience and processes over time,[18] and thus allow the impact of government policies to be assessed and progress against Public Service Agreement (PSA) targets to be measured.[19]

The first survey is the most extensive of its kind so far undertaken, and builds upon a tradition of surveys dating back to the recession at the United States' Bar in the 1930s.[20] The methodology drew heavily from the *Paths to Justice* survey; adopting the same approach to identifying justiciable problems, including the same 'triviality threshold', and featuring the same limitation to 'private individuals'.[21] It also incorporated a questionnaire developed from that employed in Genn's earlier survey. Important refinements were made, though, to address problems that arose with the earlier survey (such as in determining sources of financial assistance to those seeking redress), to shift the balance of questions away from rare events (such as the use of formal process) towards early stage decision making, and to provide comprehensive social and demographic data in relation to *all* survey respondents. The survey reference period was also reduced from five-and-a-half to three-and-a-half years to echo the interval between surveys.

All respondents completed a screen interview, in which they were asked if they had experienced 'a problem' since January 1998 that had been 'difficult to solve' in each of 18 distinct justiciable problem categories: discrimination; consumer; employment; neighbours; owned housing; rented housing; homelessness; money/debt; welfare benefits; divorce; relationship breakdown; domestic violence; children; personal injury; clinical negligence; mental health; immigration; and, unfair treatment by the police. To assist recall and allow some assessment of the relative incidence of the different types of problem falling within these categories, for 12 of them respondents were presented with 'show cards' on which were set out detailed lists of constituent problems, and then asked to indicate which of them, if any, matched their own problems.[22] So, for example, constituent problems relating to employment included unfavourable changes being made to terms and conditions of employment the work environment being unsatisfactory or dangerous, and being sacked or made redundant; constituent problems relating to rented housing included difficulties in getting a landlord to make repairs, difficulties in obtaining repayment of a deposit, and eviction; constituent problems relating to money/debt included difficulties getting someone to pay money that they owe, disputes over bills, being threatened with legal action to recover money owed, and mismanagement of a pension fund; constituent problems relating to children included difficulties fostering or adopting children, difficulties with children going to a school for which they are eligible, and children being unfairly excluded or suspended from school; and, constituent problems relating to mental health included unsatisfactory treatment or care in hospital, unsatisfactory care after release from hospital, and difficulties obtaining a discharge from hospital.[23]

In addition, respondents were asked whether, apart from anything already reported, they had had legal action taken against them, had been threatened with legal action or had started or considered starting any court proceedings. These problem categories are similar to those used in the *Paths to Justice* survey, but with the inclusion of mental health and homelessness categories, and the exclusion of the renting out property category. Also, no *separate* neighbours, welfare benefits, domestic violence, clinical negligence, immigration or unfair treatment by the police categories were included in the earlier survey.

For the two most recent problems identified in each category, respondents were asked what help they had tried to obtain to resolve them, whether and what formal dispute resolution processes had been utilised, whether and when the problems concluded, and if nothing was done to deal with them, why this was so. Respondents were also asked for a range of details about themselves and the household in which they resided. On average, screen interviews lasted 15 to 25 minutes, depending on whether problems were identified.

If respondents reported at least one problem in the screen interview (excluding neighbours problems[24]), they progressed to a main interview, which addressed a single problem in depth.[25] Areas covered by the main interview included: the sources of advice and information that respondents considered using; the obstacles faced in obtaining advice; the nature and extent of assistance provided by advisers; respondents' use and experience of courts, tribunals and alternative dispute resolution (ADR) processes; respondents' objectives in taking action; the impact and outcome of problems and resolution strategies; respondents' regrets about resolution strategies; sources of financial assistance; and, general attitudes to the civil justice system. On average, main interviews lasted around 25 minutes.

All interviews were conducted face-to-face in respondents' own homes and were arranged and conducted by the National Centre for Social Research. Respondents were drawn from a random selection of 3,348 residential household addresses across 73 postcode sectors of England and Wales. 92 per cent of adult household members (over 18 years of age) were interviewed, yielding 5,611 respondents.[26] The household response rate was 57 per cent (66 per cent where successful contact was made with an adult occupant), and the cumulative eligible adult response rate was 52 per cent. This compares to other large-scale social surveys, such as the Family Expenditure Survey (59 per cent in Britain and 56 per cent in Northern Ireland for 2000/01[27]), Family Resources Survey (65 per cent for 2000/01[28]) and General Household Survey (67 per cent for 2000/01[29]). Of the 5,611 respondents, 1,623 completed both a screen and a main interview.

Unless indicated otherwise, all figures and analyses reported below are weighted for non-response using 2001 census data, so as to be generalisable to the adult population of England and Wales. Weighting also includes a factor to reverse the effect of oversampling in three postcode sectors.[30]

PARALLEL SURVEY OF PEOPLE LIVING IN TEMPORARY ACCOMMODATION

In parallel with the first LSRC national survey of justiciable problems, a separate survey was conducted of 197 adults in 170 households living at 47 temporary accommodation addresses (i.e. hostels, boarding houses, bed and breakfast lodgings and hotels) in 7 local authority areas. The parallel 'temporary accommodation' survey was not intended to be representative of all adults living in this type of temporary accommodation. Instead, it was intended to provide an indication of the particular experience of one group of people normally excluded from national surveys – due to the difficulty of constructing an inclusive sample frame – and contrast it with that of the 'national' survey population. Living in such temporary accommodation is not only symptomatic of a broad range of social (and justiciable) problems, it can also have 'a hugely negative effect on the health, educational, welfare and social development of children,'[31] and consequently increases the likelihood of further justiciable problems. In light of this, the current government sees the reduction of families living in Bed and Breakfast accommodation as a priority and established a Bed and Breakfast Unit in the Homelessness Directorate (now within the Office of the Deputy Prime Minister) in November 2001. The 2001 census estimated that of the 934,263 people living in 'communal establishments', 38,366 were living in hotels and hostels (excluding medical and care establishments).[32] This represents one-tenth of 1% of the adult population of England and Wales;[33] a small percentage, but nonetheless a considerable number.

As with the national survey, all interviews were conducted face-to-face and were arranged and conducted by the National Centre for Social Research. A technical report of both surveys has been published by the National Centre for Social Research.[34]

STRUCTURE OF THE BOOK

Chapter 2 sets out the pattern of experience of justiciable problems across England and Wales. It provides a detailed analysis of how differences in life circumstances entail differences in vulnerability to problems, and why different rates of problem incidence are therefore associated with differently constituted population groups, both in general terms and within individual problem categories. In doing so, it describes the vulnerability of certain population groups to problems that can be constituent elements of social exclusion, and the particular vulnerability of socially excluded groups to the experience of justiciable problems. It then explains how some types of justiciable problem are experienced commonly in combination, and how certain problems are more likely to lead to others, or to other social, economic and health problems. As a part of this, it reveals how, by reinforcing the disadvantage of those who are vulnerable to justiciable problems, the experience of problems has an additive effect – meaning that each time a person experiences a problem they become increasingly likely to experience additional problems. Moreover, it demonstrates how people who experience multiple problems become disproportionately more likely to experience some of the problems that play a direct role in social exclusion.

Chapter 3 sets out the ways in which people deal with justiciable problems. It highlights the sense of powerlessness and helplessness often experienced by those who face them, and confirms there is a general lack of knowledge about obligations, rights and procedures on the part of the general public. It reveals that inaction is common in relation to some serious problem types, and also more likely among some disadvantaged population groups. In describing the problems in relation to which people most often obtain advice, it demonstrates that advice is more likely to be obtained in relation to more serious problems, but also explains how decisions on whether or not to obtain advice influence the way later problems are resolved. The chapter then details the many sources from which people attempt to obtain advice, the difficulties they experience in doing so, and the nature of the advice and additional help received by those who are successful in doing so. Through this, it illustrates how people's choices of advisers, although often logical and apposite, can also be desperate and unpromising. It also illustrates how people's choices can be undermined by the provision of services in manners that do not fit into people's lives. In addition, it exposes the phenomenon of referral fatigue, whereby the more times people are referred on to another advice service by an adviser, the less likely they become to act on a referral. The chapter thus highlights the importance of equipping those from whom people initially seek advice with the means to quickly and effectively refer them on to the most appropriate adviser when necessary. The chapter also demonstrates the relative infrequency of court, tribunal and alternative dispute resolution processes being used as part of the process of resolving problems. Lastly, it details the people and organisations that pay for advice, and in doing so, it confirms that most advice is provided free at the point of delivery, and that advice is commonly paid for by legal aid, trade unions, legal expenses insurance and private individuals.

Chapter 4 sets out the range of objectives that motivate people to act to resolve justiciable problems. It illustrates the different objectives associated with different problem types, problem resolution strategies, advisers and population groups. In doing so, it describes how objectives vary along with the consequences of problems, and confirms that certain problems are more likely to lead to others. It then details the ways in which problems conclude, and the extent to which people obtain their objectives. It points to evidence that those who are represented before courts and tribunals fare better than those who are not, and also that objectives are more often met in relation to the most important problems. It also explains that, because the problems in relation to which people obtain advice are fundamentally different from those they resolve on their own, it is not possible to compare the outcome of these two sets of problems. Nevertheless, it suggests that it is evident that advice is beneficial to the problem resolution process. The chapter then explains how the duration of problems varies by problem and adviser type, and also, seemingly, by seriousness. Lastly, it shows that although people can greatly benefit from taking action to resolve justiciable problems, the resolution process can be stressful and even bring about ill-health.

Chapter 5 highlights the principal findings of the LSRC survey and parallel survey of people living in temporary accommodation, and draws together the various threads running through the discussion in previous chapters. It also sets out the implications of our improved understanding of the nature and experience of justiciable problems, people's strategies and difficulties in dealing with them, the reach of public funding of legal services and the impact of problems, attempts to deal with them and their resolution.

2

The Experience and Impact of Justiciable Problems

This chapter sets out the pattern of experience of justiciable problems across England and Wales. It provides a detailed analysis of the different rates of problem incidence associated with differently constituted population groups, both in general terms and within individual problem categories. In so doing, it describes the vulnerability of particular population groups to problems that can be constituent elements of social exclusion, and the particular vulnerability of socially excluded groups to the experience of justiciable problems. It also explains how some types of justiciable problem are experienced commonly in combination, and how certain justiciable problems are more likely to lead to others, or to other social, economic and health problems.

THE INCIDENCE OF JUSTICIABLE PROBLEMS

Of the 5,611 respondents to the first LSRC national periodic survey, 2,087 (37 per cent) reported having experienced one or more justiciable problems in the three-and-a-half years survey reference period; 2,017 (36 per cent) if 'trivial'[35] problems are excluded. These reporting rates are similar to those of the *Paths to Justice* survey (40 per cent and 34 per cent respectively[36]), but higher than those of the *Paths to Justice Scotland* survey (24 per cent and 23 per cent respectively[37]) and lower than those of surveys conducted recently in the United States (49 per cent[38]) and New Zealand (51 per cent[39]). The higher reporting rates in the United States and New Zealand surveys are at least in part attributable to the inclusion of a broader range of problem categories.[40] Also, the United States survey was of households, rather than individuals; thus entailing a greater chance of problems being reported in each instance. However, neither focus nor method can account for the much lower reporting rate in Scotland. The *Paths to Justice Scotland* survey used the same methodology and questionnaire as the earlier *Paths to Justice* survey and shares, therefore, the earlier survey's similarities to our own.

In *Paths to Justice Scotland* Genn and Paterson 'discounted the possibility that there is actually a lower incidence of justiciable problems in Scotland, and instead suggested explanations for a substantial reporting difference between the population of England and Wales and that of Scotland'. The lower rate in Scotland was ascribed to a 'greater sense of fatalism' and more 'community-orientation' on the part of the Scottish population. These would lead, it was argued, to systematic under-reporting of problems and a lesser likelihood of them being perceived as 'individual matters rather than collective problems'[41]. Certainly, attitude may lie behind some of the difference. However, real differences in underlying experience north and south of the Scottish border cannot be discounted. There are significant geographical and demographic dissimilarities between Scotland and England and Wales,[42] and these dissimilarities will be reflected in real differences in life circumstances. In turn, as we will illustrate in later sections, differences in life circumstances entail differences in vulnerability to justiciable problems. Genn and Paterson themselves observed a substantial difference in reporting rates as between 'urban' (28 per cent) and 'rural' (23 per cent) Scottish regions.[43] Our findings go on to indicate clearly that the rate of incidence of justiciable problems can vary considerably between other differently constituted population groups.

Although 37 per cent of LSRC survey respondents reported one or more justiciable problems, their experience of problems was far from randomly distributed across the survey population. We used binary logistic regression to test the influence of a range of social and demographic predictors on the likelihood of reporting one or more justiciable problems. Technical details are set out at Appendix B. A number of predictors were found to be significantly influential: health/disability status; family type; tenure type; housing type; age; economic activity; income; qualifications.[44]

Long-standing ill-health or disability was the most influential predictor of justiciable problems being reported. So, whereas 43 per cent of respondents who reported long-standing ill-health or disability also reported having experienced one or more justiciable problems,[45] only 35 per cent of the remaining respondents did so.

The type of family in which respondents lived also influenced strongly whether justiciable problems were reported. Thus, whereas 41 per cent of single respondents reported one or more problems, only 36 per cent of married or co-habiting respondents did so. Providing even more of a contrast, whereas 66 per cent of lone parents[46] reported problems, just 33 per cent of married or co-habiting respondents without children did so.

As with type of family, the type of home in which respondents lived had a strong influence on whether justiciable problems were reported, both in terms of tenure and physical structure. Those living in the rented sector and those living in flats or terraced houses were more likely than others to have reported problems. Accordingly, whereas 46 per cent of respondents who were renting in the private or public rented sector reported one or more problems, 40 per cent of those with mortgages and just 25 per cent of those who owned their home outright did so.[47] Similarly, whereas 52 per cent of respondents living in flats and 40 per cent of respondents living in terraced houses reported one or more problems, only 34 per cent of those living in detached or semi-detached houses did so.

The reporting rate of justiciable problems also varied with age; problems being reported most frequently by respondents in their thirties, with a peak at the age of 38. As with other surveys, the reporting of problems then declined consistently as age increased.[48] So, whereas 45 per cent of respondents aged between 25 and 44 reported one or more problems, just 18 per cent of respondents aged 75 or over did so. Younger respondents were also less likely to report problems, with only 34 per cent of respondents aged between 18 and 24 doing so.

Also, respondents in different economic circumstances reported problems at different rates. Unemployed respondents and those unable to work through sickness reported problems more often than others. Whereas 54 per cent of unemployed respondents reported one or more justiciable problems,[49] 39 per cent of the remainder of respondents of working age did so. Likewise, whereas 46 per cent of respondents in receipt of welfare benefits reported one or more problems, only 35 per cent of others did so.[50] Demonstrating the complexity of patterns of vulnerability, though, and mirroring the findings of the United States survey,[51] those with higher incomes were found to report problems more often than those with lower incomes. 41 per cent of respondents earning in excess of £50,000 per annum reported one or more problems, compared to 35 per cent of those earning between £4,000 and £10,000 per annum.

However, we also found that those on very low incomes were more likely than others to report problems. 48 per cent of respondents with an income less than £4,000 per annum reported one or more problems.[52]

Finally, as the New Zealand survey found, respondents with academic qualifications were more likely to report justiciable problems than those without.[53] To some extent this reflected a link between academic qualifications and age, with older respondents less likely to possess them. Thus, when we included an interaction term linking academic qualifications and age in our regression model academic qualifications moved from being the second most influential significant predictor to being the eighth (of eight) most influential.

Certainly, some of these findings in part reflect differences in understanding, perception and attitude towards what constitutes 'a problem' that is 'difficult to solve'. It would be unrealistic to believe a survey such as ours could completely bypass 'socially stratified differences in lay perceptions'[54] of justiciable problems. Because our social and demographic data relates only to the time of interview, differences in reporting rates also reflect in part the social, economic and health impact of justiciable problems. In the sections that follow, though, we will illustrate clearly how reporting patterns of all types of problem reflect real underlying patterns of vulnerability.

As with the *Paths to Justice* surveys,[55] we did not find any differences in the overall problem reporting rates of male or female respondents, white or black and minority ethnic respondents,[56] or respondents receiving or not receiving welfare benefits. However, as we will also illustrate, there were significant differences in the types of problems reported by respondents in these population groups.

INCIDENCE AMONG THOSE IN TEMPORARY ACCOMMODATION

Given the findings in the previous section, it is no surprise that respondents to the parallel survey of people living in temporary accommodation – being much more often lone parents (30 per cent, compared to 4 per cent),[57] substantially younger (43 per cent aged under 25, compared to 8 per cent),[58] less economically active (25 per cent in employment, compared to 60 per cent),[59] on very low incomes (median income less than £6,000 per annum, compared to £20,000),[60] and not living in their own homes – reported justiciable problems much more often than LSRC survey respondents. Overall, 84 per cent of temporary accommodation survey respondents reported one or more justiciable problems;[61] more than two and a quarter times the rate of incidence in the LSRC survey. If 'trivial' problems are excluded, the figure reduces slightly to 83 per cent.[62]

THE INCIDENCE OF PROBLEMS OF DIFFERENT TYPES

The reported incidence of problems of different types varied greatly in the LSRC survey. As with the United States, New Zealand and first *Paths to Justice* surveys, consumer problems were reported most frequently (13 per cent of respondents), and immigration and nationality problems least frequently (1/3 per cent of respondents).[63] Other commonly reported problems were those relating to noisy or anti-social neighbours (8 per cent), money and debt (8 per cent), employment (6 per cent), housing (owned or rented) (6 per cent[64]), personal injury (4 per cent), and family breakdown (4 per cent[65]). Other rarely reported problems were those relating to unfair treatment by the police (2/3 per cent), homelessness (2/3 per cent), and mental health (1/2 per cent). Details are set out in Table 2.1.

The frequency of reporting of different problem types in large part reflects the frequency of experience of the 'defining circumstances' from which they can arise. The most common problems arise from circumstances routinely experienced across the adult population. Consumer problems arise from transactions for goods and services. Problems with noisy or anti-social neighbours arise where people live in proximity. Money and debt problems arise from financial dealings. Employment problems arise from being employed. Rare problems, on the other hand, arise from circumstances that people experience much less frequently. Immigration problems arise from people changing their country of abode, residence status or citizenship. Mental health problems arise from people suffering or appearing to suffer from mental illness. Clinical negligence problems arise from people receiving clinical treatment.

Of course, the reporting rates of different problem types also reflect other things. The likelihood of justiciable problems arising from defining circumstances varies between problem types, as does the likelihood of problems arising that are 'difficult to solve'. Accordingly, reporting rates in part reflect these likelihoods. This explains why, despite the fact that twice as many respondents owned as rented their home, 50 per cent more people reported problems relating to rented housing than reported problems relating to owned housing.

Table 2.1

Reported Incidence of Problem Types

Problem Type	%	N
Consumer	13.3	748
Neighbours	8.4	471
Money/debt	8.3	465
Employment	6.1	344
Personal injury	3.9	217
Rented housing	3.8	215
Owned housing	2.4	135
Welfare benefits	2.3	127
Relationship breakdown	2.2	124
Divorce	2.2	122
Children	1.9	108
Clinical negligence	1.6	92
Domestic violence	1.6	88
Discrimination	1.4	80
Unfair treatment by the police	0.7	38
Homelessness	0.6	36
Mental health	0.5	26
Immigration	0.3	18

Weighted base=5,611

In addition, the reporting rates of different problem types in part reflect the propensity of respondents to recall and then disclose details of them. The similarity, frequency and salience of problems all influence the propensity of respondents to recall them[66] – a matter we explore further in Appendix C. Beyond recall, though, disclosure of the details of some problems may involve social embarrassment or shame, and may also raise concerns of privacy, confidentiality, and personal safety. Domestic violence, mental health and debt problems might all be expected to be underreported to some degree in consequence.[67]

PATTERNS OF VULNERABILITY AND THE IMPACT OF JUSTICIABLE PROBLEMS

The fact that justiciable problems arise from defining circumstances entails that experience of them varies between different population groups. Those people who most often experience the defining circumstances of a particular type of problem will also, all else being equal, most often experience problems of that type. However, all else is not always equal. People's physical make-up, experience, resources and disposition will also affect their vulnerability to experiencing problems – especially problems that are 'difficult to solve'. Justiciable problems, and particularly those that are difficult to solve and are the subject of this study, do not therefore strike indiscriminately.

We used binary logistic regression to test the influence of a range of social and demographic predictors on the likelihood of individual problem types being reported. Technical details are set out at Appendix B. Drawing on those predictors found to be significantly influential in relation to the reporting of one or more problem types, we are able to determine the likely basic features of patterns of vulnerability to those problems studied. Some of the predictors also give indication of the substantial impact that justiciable problems can have on people's lives. Because our social and demographic data relates only to the time of interview, we are not always able to conclude whether particular situations contributed to or followed from individual problems. In many instances, though, this is readily apparent, and where it is not we are able to draw upon other studies to support our analysis.

Stages of Life

As people move through life their circumstances change and expose them to different types of justiciable problem. Respondents' ages had a significant influence in predicting 14 of the 18 problem types studied: consumer, neighbours, money/debt, rented housing, welfare benefits, relationship breakdown (i.e. disputes over assets, maintenance, and residence and contact), divorce, children, domestic violence, discrimination, unfair treatment by the police, homelessness, mental health, and immigration.

The youngest respondents were most likely to report rented housing, unfair treatment by the police, homelessness and mental health problems. This reflects the fact that younger people are less economically independent, more mobile,[68] live in poorer standard accommodation,[69] are most likely to be involved in criminal activity (and are therefore most likely to have contact with the police),[70] and are at increased risk of psychiatric disorder.[71] The difference in simple numerical reporting rates of rented housing and homelessness problems between 18 to 24 year old respondents

16

and older respondents was compounded by the fact that over 80 per cent of them lived in the rented housing sector, compared to just 30 per cent of older respondents.

Consequently, whereas 11 per cent of 18 to 24 year old respondents reported rented housing problems, just 3 per cent of older respondents did so. Likewise, whereas 3 per cent of 18 to 24 year old respondents reported homelessness problems, fewer than one-half of 1 per cent of older respondents did so (Figure 2.1).

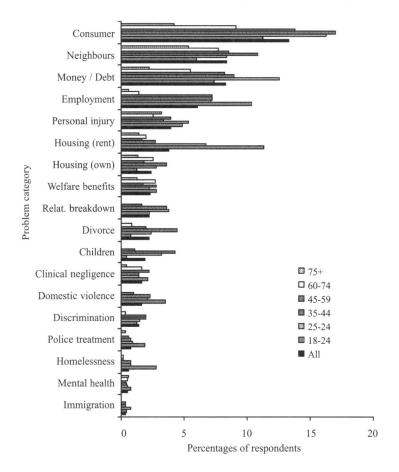

Figure 2.1
Reported Incidence of Problem Types by Age

All else being equal, 25 to 34 year old respondents were most likely to report immigration, consumer, money/debt and domestic violence problems. The likelihood of reporting immigration problems peaked at 30, reflecting a pattern of migration in which young people of working age are most likely to migrate to or seek asylum in the United Kingdom[72] Consumer problems and money/debt problems peaked at 32 and 33 respectively, echoing increasing personal expenditure and use of debt as people become economically independent and commence acquiring major assets - such as houses. However, although 13 per cent of 25 to 34 year olds reported money/debt problems, compared to 7 per cent of respondents in other age groups, clear differences were observable in the ages of respondents reporting different types of money/debt problems. Thus, whereas problems with debt peaked at 29, problems relating to recovering money and financial services did not peak until 42 and 43 respectively. Domestic violence problems also peaked at 33, with increasing numbers of people living with partners while still at an age where violent conduct is prevalent.

As people move on through their thirties and early forties, the great majority will live with a partner, and the number of households containing children will reach its highest. This paves the way for peaks in the number of divorces, problems ancillary to relationship breakdown, and problems relating to children.[73] So, twice as many divorces and problems ancillary to relationship breakdown were reported by those between 35 and 44 as by others. However, whereas disputes over assets peaked in the early forties, disputes over residence and contact peaked earlier, in the early thirties, reflecting an interaction between the age of children and the accumulation of equity. Problems relating to welfare benefits peaked at 39, coinciding with a peak in the take-up of working families tax credit. Discrimination problems peaked at 40.

As people move into their late forties and fifties their children start to leave home and the number of family problems subsides appreciably. By this age rented housing problems are also in steep decline, and problems relating to homelessness and unfair police treatment are very rarely experienced. Homelessness problems, for example, were reported by fewer than one-fifth of 1 per cent of respondents aged over 44. Of course, those people who become homeless later in life may be less able to escape from the predicament, which would result in underreporting by people in standard residential accommodation.[74] Contrasting with other problem types, consumer, money/debt, and welfare benefits problems remain prevalent at this age, and neighbours problems only come to peak at 50; this late peak in neighbours problems perhaps reflecting a greater sensitivity to them on the part of older people. It may also, though, reflect greater periods of time spent in the home.

18

Respondents aged over 59 reported ever fewer problems of all types, except those relating to mental health; the increase in problems relating to mental health reflecting an increasing risk of depression, anxiety disorder and dementia among older people.[75] Also, although in general rented housing problems were much less frequently reported by older respondents, problems with unsafe or unsatisfactory rented housing were frequently reported by retired respondents; perhaps reflecting a greater reliance on others to maintain the upkeep of their accommodation, in both physical and economic terms.

Decreasing reporting rates of other problem types among older respondents do not necessarily reflect an equal decline in the prevalence of the defining circumstances of problems. As already suggested, people will find problems easier to deal with as they become more familiar with them. People's sensitivities and senses of importance will also change over time. In addition, some of the decreased reporting rates of respondents of retirement age may reflect ignorance of circumstances, compounded by the frequent growing isolation of old age. For example, the decrease in welfare benefits problems reported by those aged 75 or over may reflect lack of knowledge of the availability of benefits. It may also reflect a reluctance to engage with the benefits system.

Although age was not found to be a significant predictor of employment or money/debt problems being reported, retirement status was. Retired respondents, 94% of whom were aged 60 or over, were substantially less likely to report employment problems than other respondents, as a consequence, of course, of their greatly reduced levels of employment. Accordingly, the reporting rate of employment problems can be seen in Figure 1.1 to drop considerably after the age of 59. In contrast, retired respondents were more likely than others to report money/debt problems.

Gender

Gender had a significant influence in predicting 3 of the 18 problem types studied: domestic violence, clinical negligence and unfair treatment by the police. Female respondents were much more likely than male respondents to report being victims of domestic violence. 24 per cent of reported victims of domestic violence were men. Both the overall incidence of domestic violence reported through the LSRC survey and the proportion of male victims are therefore much lower than reported through the British Crime Survey. The 1996 British Crime Survey, using a computer assisted self-interviewing (CASI) method, indicated that 5 per cent of adults had been the victim of a domestic assault or frightening threat of such assault.[76] There was no difference in the reporting rates of assault (4 per cent) between female and male respondents, though female respondents more often reported threats. The difference between the results of the 1996 British Crime Survey and the LSRC survey can be explained in large part, though, by differences in the method of interview used and the fact that the LSRC survey included only problems that were regarded as 'difficult to solve'. Just 32 per cent of female and 9 per cent of male respondents who reported domestic violence through the 1996 British Crime Survey CASI questionnaire also reported it through standard interviews. So, far fewer male than female respondents would be expected to report domestic violence through the LSRC survey. Also, female respondents to the 1996 British Crime Survey were twice as likely as male respondents to report violence that resulted in injury, and four times as likely to report having been upset or frightened by it.[77] So again, fewer male than female respondents would be expected to report domestic violence through the LSRC survey.

Female respondents were also more likely than male respondents to report clinical negligence problems, reflecting greater use of health services by women and the unique risks associated with childbirth.[78] So, whereas 2 per cent of female respondents reported such problems, just 1 per cent of male respondents did so. Male respondents on the other hand, were much more likely than female respondents to report unfair treatment by the police; accounting for 74 per cent of all such problems. As was the case with young respondents, this reflects the greater male involvement in criminal activity and proportion of men therefore becoming the subject of police interest.[79]

Although gender was found to be a significant influence in predicting only 3 general problem types, it was also found to be a significant influence in predicting narrower defined problems relating to obtaining maintenance payments; a continuing symptom of the economic imbalance between women and men in this country.

Also, there were disproportionate reporting rates between women and men associated with a further 4 general problem types, identified using a simple χ^2 test: employment,[80] personal injury,[81] neighbours[82] and rented housing.[83] These associations were not highlighted by multivariate regression analysis as they are linked to other aspects of vulnerability that provide a better explanation of variance.

So, although more male than female respondents reported employment and personal injury problems, this was a consequence of the influence of, among other things, employment patterns, which in turn vary greatly between women and men. Similarly, although more female than male respondents reported neighbours and rented housing problems, this was a consequence of, among other things, patterns of household composition, that also vary greatly between women and men.

Ethnicity

Ethnicity also had a significant influence in predicting 3 of the 18 problem types studied: divorce, discrimination and immigration. White respondents were more than twice as likely as black and minority ethnic respondents to report a divorce, less than one-quarter as likely to report discrimination, and less than one-tenth as likely to report an immigration problem. Indeed, just one-tenth of 1 per cent of white respondents reported immigration problems, compared with 3 per cent of black and minority ethnic respondents.

Also, although in general rented housing problems were reported equally by white and black and minority ethnic respondents, white respondents were only one-third as likely to report problems relating to unsafe or unsatisfactory rented housing, perhaps reflecting their lesser likelihood of living in a high density urban environment.[84]

However, echoing Smith's findings in relation to the criminal justice system,[85] our analysis reveals that it is inadequate to distinguish merely between white and black and minority ethnic respondents in an investigation into differences in the experience of diverse ethnic populations. There are important differences in the experience of different black and minority ethnic groups, and these are masked when black and minority ethnic groups are amalgamated. We therefore undertook our analysis using both binomial (white, black and minority ethnic) and multinomial (white, Asian, black, mixed, other) 'ethnicity' variables.[86]

The results of our analysis using the multinomial variable indicated that Asian and mixed-ethnicity respondents were much more likely to report discrimination than either white or black respondents. In contrast, black respondents were much more likely to report immigration problems than either white or Asian respondents, and 'other' ethnicity respondents were much more likely to do so than black respondents; reflecting changing patterns of immigration to the United Kingdom. For example, the number of people immigrating from outside of the Old and New Commonwealths and the European Union more than doubled between 1997 and 1999.[87]

Analysis using the multinomial variable also suggested, though our findings were not statistically significant, that Asian respondents were least likely to report domestic violence. This is in line with the findings of the 1996 British Crime Survey.[88] It is also consistent with the suggestion that Asian respondents were least likely to report problems relating to their children's education or problems ancillary to relationship breakdown, which we have shown elsewhere to be more likely where there is domestic violence in a family.[89] A lower rate of education problems also concords with differing patterns of educational attainment associated with different ethnic groups in the United Kingdom.[90] There may also, though, have been underreporting of domestic violence problems by Asian respondents as a consequence of cultural and religious attitudes to problems occurring within the family.[91]

Economic Circumstances

Aspects of respondents' economic circumstances[92] had a significant influence in predicting all types of justiciable problem studied, apart from divorce and domestic violence. Unlike age, gender and ethnicity, though, economic circumstances can change as a result of the experience of justiciable problems. To some extent, therefore, we are looking here not only at patterns of vulnerability to problems, but also at their economic impact.

As regards patterns of vulnerability, respondents on higher incomes were more likely than those lower down the income scale to report consumer problems, presumably in consequence of their greater consumer activity. So, respondents earning in excess of £30,000 per annum reported consumer problems twice as often as those earning less than £10,000, and problems with builders and holidays three times as often. Respondents receiving welfare benefits were also, though, more likely than others to report consumer problems; a finding perhaps explained by the greater relative value to them of routine consumer transactions. This might lead to them finding routine consumer problems more 'difficult to solve'. This explanation is consistent with the finding that respondents receiving welfare benefits reported a disproportionate number of low value consumer problems, including, for example, problems relating to unfit food products and small electrical purchases.

Respondents on higher incomes were also more likely to report problems with investment services, such as mismanagement of pensions, and problems to do with owned housing, echoing their greater opportunities to utilise such services and purchase their own home(s).

Respondents on lower incomes, on the other hand, were more likely than those higher up the income scale to report problems relating to unsafe or unsatisfactory rented housing and homelessness. Indeed, respondents earning less than £10,000 reported problems relating to unsafe or unsatisfactory rented housing ten times as often as those earning in excess of £30,000, and homelessness problems nine times as often, reflecting their lesser range of housing options and economic independence.[93] Again, those on lower incomes were more likely to report problems relating to their children's education, owing possibly in part to their lesser ability to choose the schools their children attend and, once more, their lesser range of housing options – which makes them less able to move to the catchment areas of better performing schools.[94] Reflecting higher rates of benefit receipt, those on lower incomes were also more likely to report problems relating to welfare benefits.

In addition to consumer problems, and independent of income, respondents receiving welfare benefits were more likely than others to report homelessness and debt and severe money management problems, again reflecting lesser economic independence. They were also more likely to report rented housing problems; although this did not extend to problems relating to unsafe or unsatisfactory housing. Moreover, respondents receiving welfare benefits more often reported problems relating to unfair police treatment.[95]

Presumably as a simple consequence of their spending more time at home, respondents who described themselves as 'looking after the home or family' and respondents who were unable to work because of illness were more likely than others to report problems to do with neighbours. Naturally, those respondents who were looking after the home or family also reported fewer employment problems, along with the self-employed. They were also more likely to report problems ancillary to the breakdown of a relationship, reflecting their enhanced child care role and their lack of income through employment.

Respondents in full-time employment were more likely than others to report personal injury problems, possibly as a consequence of their greater exposure to industrial, construction and other workplace accidents. Respondents in part-time employment, on the other hand, were more likely to report money and debt problems of all descriptions, and, along with the self-employed and those unable to work because of illness, were also more likely to report problems of clinical negligence. However, in the latter case, the employment status of respondents is more likely to have resulted from the clinical negligence reported, than to have contributed to its experience.

The self-employed and those unable to work because of illness were also more likely to have reported problems relating to mental health. However, although the latter of these has a clear link to the experience of mental illness, it is not immediately apparent what the association is between self-employment – which encompasses a heterogeneity of forms of work[96]– and problems relating to mental health. Indeed, the results of the EUROSTAT ill-health module of the 1999 Labour Force survey indicated that the self-employed were less likely than employees to report conditions such as work-related stress.[97] Possibly, though, those with mental health problems, facing discrimination and difficulties in adapting to employment, are more likely to become self-employed.

Finally, employment problems were most likely to be reported by the unemployed, demonstrating the immediate economic impact that can be brought about by justiciable problems of this type.

Housing and Tenure Types

The type of housing in which respondents lived and their form of tenure, both linked to their economic circumstances, had a significant influence in predicting 16 of the 18 problem types studied: consumer, neighbours, money/debt, employment, personal injury, rented housing, owned housing, welfare benefits, relationship breakdown, divorce, children, domestic violence, discrimination, homelessness, mental health, and immigration. Indeed, it is probably a further reflection of economic circumstances that saw respondents who owned their own homes more likely than others to report consumer problems and less likely than others to report problems relating to homelessness. Economic factors may also have been behind respondents living in detached and semi-detached houses having been less likely to report problems relating to rented housing and immigration, and respondents in the rented housing sector having been more likely to report problems relating to money and debt (especially debt and severe money management problems)[98] and welfare benefits.

Respondents who lived in detached houses were also less likely to report problems relating to personal injury, reflecting their lesser likelihood of working in heavy labour jobs. Again, they were also less likely to report problems with neighbours, possibly as a consequence of their having fewer neighbours to have problems with.

Respondents living rent free in a household were more likely than others to report problems relating to mental health and discrimination, suggesting that the incidence of mental illness may be higher among this population group. We are not able, though, to verify this. In fact, such respondents were less likely than others to report long-standing ill-health or disability.[99]

Indicating the impact of relationship breakdown, described in detail below, respondents in detached houses were less likely to report problems ancillary to relationship breakdown, divorce, domestic violence and problems relating to children. Likewise, respondents in the private rented sector were more likely to report divorce and problems ancillary to relationship breakdown.

Justiciable Problems and the Family

The type of family in which respondents lived had a significant influence in predicting 10 of the 18 problem types studied: neighbours, employment, rented housing, owned housing, relationship breakdown, divorce, children, domestic violence, discrimination, and mental health.

As is indicated by Figure 2.2, for every one of these problem types, except employment, lone parent respondents were more likely to report having experienced them than respondents living in other types of family, a matter of particular concern given the steady increase over the past thirty years in the number of lone parents. Lone parent households now account for 22 per cent of all households with dependent children.[100]

Unsurprisingly, lone parent and other single respondents were more likely than married or co-habiting respondents to report divorce and problems ancillary to relationship breakdown;[101] although, reflecting the greater likelihood of a significant past relationship and the presence of children, lone parents were more likely than other single respondents to do so, and much more likely to report problems relating to maintenance payments and the division of assets. Again unsurprisingly, lone parents were more likely to report having experienced domestic violence; the violence no doubt having played a part in the breakdown of an abusive relationship. However, the change in personal circumstances that results from relationship breakdown, especially for those with whom any children of the relationship come to reside, leaves lone parents particularly vulnerable to a range of further problems, many of which can constitute elements of social exclusion.

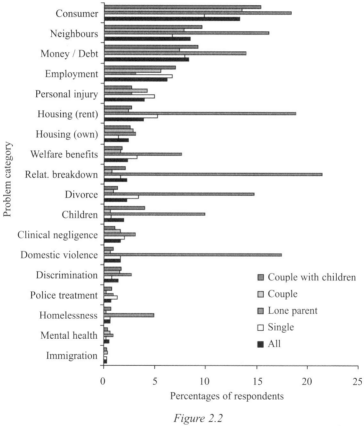

Figure 2.2
Reported Incidence by Family Type

For example, a report by the National Council for One Parent Families and the homelessness charities Crisis and Health Action for Homeless People stated,

> Lone parenthood is associated with downward mobility in the housing market.
> One-parent families are more likely than others to be in public-sector housing
> or lower standard private housing.[102]

Consequently, we found that lone parent respondents were more likely than others to report problems to do with both owned and rented housing, especially problems to do with unsafe or unsatisfactory rented housing. Indeed, 11 per cent of lone parents reported problems concerning unsafe or unsatisfactory rented housing, compared to fewer than 1 per cent of other respondents.

The finding that lone parent respondents reported more problems relating to owned housing than respondents living in any other type of family went against the general trend of married and co-habiting respondents reporting more such problems; reflecting their greater earning potential. However, the problems lone parents reported were different from those reported by married and co-habiting respondents, relating more often to communal repairs and conveyancing and not at all to planning matters. Also, no lone parent reported a problem relating to repossession of the family home.

As with quality of housing, the general standard of living of lone parents has been reported as being much lower than that of rest of the population.[103] Thus, although this was not highlighted by multivariate regression,[104] lone parents disproportionately reported money/debt problems.[105] This drop in living standard relates in part to the obstacles faced by lone parents in gaining employment,[106] resulting in considerably lower rates of employment (although as a consequence of the New Deal for Lone Parents the gap is starting to narrow)[107]. Accordingly, lone parent respondents were more likely to report discrimination problems and less likely to report employment problems. Also, lone parents are far more likely to receive welfare benefits than the rest of the population. In 2001 it was estimated that half of lone parents in Britain were receiving income support and one-third Working Families Tax Credit.[108] Thus, although again this was not highlighted by multivariate regression, lone parents disproportionately reported welfare benefits problems.[109]

There was, though, a difference between female and male[110] lone parent respondent employment patterns. Female lone parents were less likely to be working (42 per cent, compared to 50 per cent)[111] and more likely to be receiving welfare benefits (90 per cent, compared to 67 per cent)[112]. They were also considerably more likely to be in part-time employment if they were working (26 per cent, compared to 6 per cent).[113] In consequence, female lone parents reported welfare benefits problems more frequently than male lone parents (8 per cent, compared to 6 per cent), although the difference was not statistically significant.

As a result of the 'major emotional'[114] impact of relationship breakdown, and the fact that many lone parents are unable to work, have no partner to share responsibilities or 'engage in reflective dialogue regarding parenting issues',[115] have limited financial resources and live in unsuitable housing, lone parents can be susceptible to experiencing psychiatric and other health problems.[116] It is not surprising, therefore, that lone parents were more likely to report justiciable problems relating to mental health than those living in other types of family.

Finally, as would be expected, lone parents, along with other respondents with resident children, were more likely than others to report problems relating to children.[117] They were also both more likely than others to report problems relating to neighbours, probably reflecting the greater amount of time spent in the home.

Long-Standing Ill-Health And Disability

Health and disability status had a significant influence in predicting 14 of the 18 problem types studied: consumer, neighbours, money/debt, employment, personal injury, rented housing, owned housing, welfare benefits, relationship breakdown, clinical negligence, domestic violence, discrimination, homelessness, and mental health.

It has been said that 'of all the disadvantaged groups in society, the disabled are the most socially excluded,' and that as a consequence 'life opportunities remain severely restricted for many.'[118] Disabled people and those with long-standing ill-health often experience disadvantage in the labour market,[119] and the consequent economic hardship suffered means that poverty is a 'key factor in the modern constitution of disability'.[120] Thus, we found that respondents who reported long-standing ill-health or disability were far more likely than others to report discrimination problems. Indeed, no fewer than half of all the discrimination problems reported through the LSRC survey concerned disability discrimination. Respondents who reported long-standing ill-health or disability were also more likely to report problems concerning employment, money and debt and welfare benefits. So, for example, whereas more than 4 per cent of such respondents reported problems relating to welfare benefits, fewer than 2 per cent of others did so.

Disabled people and those with long-standing ill-health are also prone to being 'selected out'[121] of home ownership and, despite the system of prioritisation for social housing, are 'often relegated to housing of poorer standard'.[122] Consequently, respondents who reported long-standing ill-health or disability were more likely to report problems relating to rented housing. They were also more likely to report problems relating to homelessness.

Again, people with physical or mental incapacities are 'at greater risk of all forms of abuse and violence than are the general population,'[123] and because of their greater exposure to clinical procedures are at greater risk of being further injured or disabled through clinical intervention. Thus, respondents who reported long-standing ill-health or disability were much more likely to report problems relating to domestic violence and clinical negligence. In fact, ill or disabled respondents reported domestic violence twice as often, and clinical negligence four times as often as others.

Respondents who reported long-standing illness or disability, which includes mental illness or impairment, being much more exposed to the defining circumstances of justiciable problems relating to mental health, were also much more likely to report problems of this type.[124] In addition, being more exposed to the activity of neighbours, as a consequence of being more likely to spend longer periods of time at home, they were more likely to report problems to do with neighbours.

Of course, illness and disability not only increase vulnerability to the experience of justiciable problems. Justiciable problems can also cause, or exacerbate pre-existing illness and disability.

Clearly, negligent accidents, clinical negligence and domestic violence can do so – and, as well as the immediate physical consequences of the latter, such violence can also have serious psychological effects, manifesting as, for example, post-traumatic stress disorder and battered wife syndrome.[125] Likewise, housing in a state of disrepair[126] and overcrowded households can bring about physical and psychological ill-health.[127] Also, problems relating to discrimination[128] and employment[129] can lead to psychological ill-health, as can (frequently related) problems to do with debt.[130]

As well as domestic violence, non-violent justiciable problems relating to the family, such as divorce and disputes ancillary to relationship breakdown can also cause long-term psychological ill-health, both on the part of adult and child family members – particularly as they become more acrimonious.[131] Thus, respondents reporting disputes ancillary to relationship breakdown were much more likely than others to report a long-standing illness or disability; especially if disputes related to the division of assets. However, we did not observe a link between illness and disability and divorce on its own, consistent with the idea that people cope better with less problematic separations.

Further, a secondary analysis of data from the British Household Panel Survey has found that mortgage indebtedness adversely impacts on health and increases the likelihood that men will visit general practitioners.[132] Consequently, it was recently suggested that 'the stress caused by mortgage arrears and repossession needs to be viewed as a major health issue.'[133] Consistent with this, we found respondents who reported long-standing ill-health or disability were more likely than others to report problems relating to owned housing, and were also more likely to report problems relating to repossession.

THE INCIDENCE OF PROBLEMS AMONG THOSE IN TEMPORARY ACCOMMODATION

Given, as described above, that respondents to the parallel survey of people living in temporary accommodation were much more often lone parents, substantially younger, much less economically active and on considerably lower incomes than their LSRC survey counterparts, it is not surprising that they reported a very different pattern of experience of the different types of justiciable problem studied (Figure 2.3).

Given that complications with housing will have been the reason for many respondents to the parallel survey having come to live in temporary accommodation, it is not surprising that they were far more likely than LSRC survey respondents to report problems relating to rented housing (52 per cent, compared to 4 per cent).[134] However, aside from this inherent difference, the reporting rate of such problems would have been expected to be much higher among a sample with such a young profile, and including such a high proportion of lone parents.

The high proportion of lone parents did not translate into a significantly higher reporting rate of children related problems, although such problems were reported more frequently by respondents to the parallel survey. However, there were in fact similar numbers of households containing children in the two surveys, only whereas

30

almost all children within households included in the parallel survey were in lone parent families, the great majority of children within households in the LSRC survey were in two parent families.

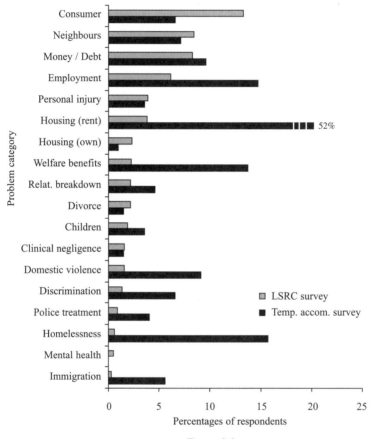

Figure 2.3
Comparison of Problem Incidence between Surveys

Again, as more than half of respondents to the parallel survey were black and minority ethnic,[135] it is not surprising that the reporting rates of problems relating to immigration and discrimination were much higher than those in the LSRC survey.[136] Likewise, as almost three times as many respondents to the parallel survey as to the LSRC survey reported being in receipt of welfare benefits, a much higher incidence of justiciable problems relating to welfare benefits was inevitable.[137] The reporting rate of employment problems was also higher among respondents to the parallel survey,[138] perhaps linking to the higher unemployment rates they also reported.

Although most problem types were reported more frequently by respondents to the parallel survey, consumer problems were reported considerably less frequently by them, reflecting their substantially lower incomes and consumer activity.

THE EXPERIENCE OF MULTIPLE PROBLEMS

Respondents to the LSRC survey reported 4,214 justiciable problems; 4,050 if trivial problems are excluded.[139] This equates to an average of just over 2 problems per respondent who reported a problem. Problems were not, though, reported in equal numbers by those who had experienced them (Figure 2.4). Experiencing justiciable problems has an additive effect. Each time a person experiences a problem they become increasingly likely to experience additional problems. So, of the 37 per cent of respondents who reported one or more justiciable problems, 46 per cent reported two or more, and of those 47 per cent reported three or more. This pattern continued as the number of problems increased, culminating in 88 per cent of respondents who reported 8 or more problems reporting nine or more.[140]

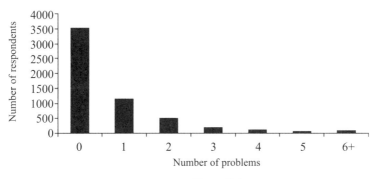

Figure 2.4
Number of Justiciable Problems Reported

As certain population groups – including people with a long-standing illness or disability, lone parents and those receiving welfare benefits – are more vulnerable than others to a range of justiciable problems, and as the experience of justiciable problems can itself increase such vulnerability – through, for example, bringing about illness or disability,[141] lone parenthood[142] or unemployment[143] – the proportion of

32

respondents in vulnerable groups increased as the number of problems reported increased. So, as can be seen from Figure 2.5, whereas 27 per cent of respondents who reported just one problem also reported a long-standing illness or disability, the figure rose to 38 per cent among those respondents who reported six or more problems. Likewise, while just 24 per cent of respondents who reported one problem were in receipt of welfare benefits, the figure rose to 52 per cent among those who reported 6 or more problems, and for lone parenthood the figures were 4 per cent and 24 per cent respectively. Univariate analysis of covariance (ANCOVA) confirmed that respondents in these population groups, along with those living in high density housing and in the private rented sector, were significantly more likely to report multiple problems than were others. Technical details are set out at Appendix B.

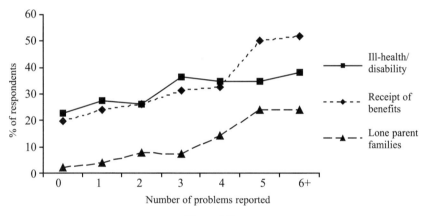

Figure 2.5
Multiple Problems and Personal Circumstances

Also, as people experience multiple problems, they become increasingly likely to experience problems that play a direct role in social exclusion. So, for example, whereas just one-fifth of 1 per cent of respondents who reported one problem reported a problem relating to homelessness, 9 per cent of respondents who reported six or more problems did so. Whereas 4 per cent of respondents who reported one problem reported a problem relating to unsafe or unsatisfactory rented housing, 29 per cent of those who reported six or more problems did so. Also, whereas 3 per cent of respondents who reported one problem reported a divorce, 20 per cent of those who reported six or more problems did so (Figure 2.6).

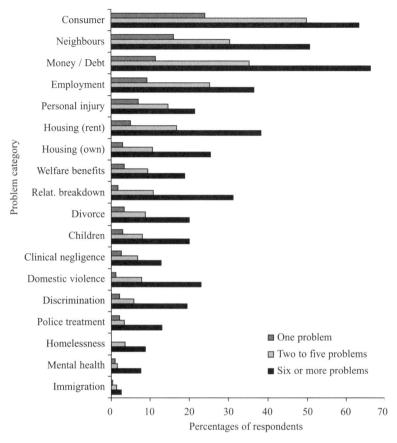

Figure 2.6
Pattern of Problems as Number Experienced Increases

To a large extent these differences in reporting rates reflect the general increased incidence of problems among those who experience many of them. However, some problem types become more prevalent as the number of problems increases.

To establish which problem types become more prevalent, observed and expected relative proportions of each problem type were calculated as problems reported increased, and straight lines fitted to observed and expected data using linear regression. Technical details are set out at Appendix B. The results indicated that the relative likelihood of respondents reporting domestic violence, problems ancillary to relationship breakdown and problems relating to homelessness increased significantly along with the number of problems reported. So, as illustrated by Figure 2.6, these three problem types were relatively unlikely to have been reported in isolation.

In contrast, the relative likelihood of respondents reporting problems relating to personal injury, clinical negligence, welfare benefits, neighbours, employment and immigration decreased significantly as the number of problems reported increased. Demonstrating the complexity of incidence patterns, though, this does not mean that these problem types were necessarily more likely than others to be reported in isolation; only that they were unlikely to be reported along with many other problems. In fact, immigration problems were the fourth least likely type of problem to be reported in isolation, and problems relating to welfare benefits were less likely to be reported in isolation than was divorce.

TRIGGER PROBLEMS

It is no surprise that domestic violence was reported relatively frequently by respondents who had experienced multiple problems. Domestic violence is symptomatic of dysfunctional relationships and can lead directly to separation and divorce.[144] These in turn can entail disputes regarding maintenance and the division of property. Also, the need for one or both parties to move home, along with changes to income and expenditure patterns following separation, can bring about problems relating to homelessness, suitability of accommodation and financial hardship. Moreover, if there are children involved, these problems can be exacerbated by the parent with primary care responsibilities having additional difficulties in obtaining or retaining employment, and a consequent increased likelihood of dependency on maintenance, child-support and welfare benefits.[145] Domestic violence can also stem from other justiciable problems. For example, losing a job can increase the likelihood of abusing a partner.[146]

Again, it is no surprise that homelessness was reported relatively frequently by respondents who had experienced multiple problems. The fact of homelessness is itself 'evidence of multi-dimensional problems',[147] and as well as often being preceded by social, economic and/or mental health problems,[148] some or all of which may be justiciable, it can also increase vulnerability to further problems. Living on the streets, for example, increases contact with the police, increases the likelihood of physical assault, increases the likelihood of alcohol and substance abuse, reduces employment opportunities and increases dependency on welfare benefits.

As well as domestic violence, relationship breakdown and homelessness problems, other justiciable problem types have been suggested as being comparatively more likely to either cause further, or follow on from earlier, problems. For example, *Paths to Justice* documented how personal injury and work related ill-health may lead to unemployment or diminish employment opportunities; especially where a victim experiences a substantial degree of residual disability.[149] This in turn can lead to an increased risk of experiencing problems relating to welfare benefits and debt,[150] even if compensation is obtained in relation to the original injury or illness.[151] Serious personal injury and work related ill-health can even lead to other members of a victim's household having to give up work to become carers.[152] Evidently, also, personal injury can be caused by unsafe working conditions.

The above findings in relation to vulnerable populations also suggest a broader causal link between employment problems and money/debt and welfare benefits problems; reflecting the financial hardship that can follow from becoming unemployed. Indeed, all justiciable problems that lead to a reduction in income or diminish employment opportunities would seem likely to increase vulnerability to money/debt and welfare benefits problems. Thus, clinical negligence, mental health and immigration problems might also be expected to do so.

To confirm the justiciable problem types most likely to act as triggers of other problems, we used a repeated measures General Linear Model to compare the number of justiciable problems reported as occurring before and after instances of each individual justiciable problem type. In addition, having transformed problem orders to a range from zero (first in sequence) to one (last in sequence), we used a median test[153] to establish whether problems were more likely to be found at the beginning or end of reported sequences of problems.

As anticipated, marginal means from the General Linear Model showed more problems were reported to follow than precede the three problem types relating to dysfunctional relationships: domestic violence, divorce and relationship breakdown problems.[154] Also, divorce and relationship breakdown problems were significantly more likely to have been reported towards the beginning than towards the end of a sequence of justiciable problems.[155] In fact, 61 per cent of divorces reported as occurring in sequences of four or more problems were reported as being the first problem in the sequence.[156] In contrast, just 15 per cent were reported as being the last problem.[157] Domestic violence, too, often occurred at the beginning of such sequences, with 43 per cent of instances reported as being first in a sequence.[158] However, while 35 per cent of relationship breakdown problems were reported as being the first problem in such sequences, they were more often reported towards the middle, reflecting the greater likelihood of other family problems preceding them.[159] Thus, when we used the McNemar test, a nonparametric test for two related dichotomous variables, to establish which problem type in each pair of problem types was more likely to occur first when both were reported, we found that divorce was more likely to occur before relationship breakdown problems,[160] and that domestic violence was more likely to occur before divorce.[161] We also found that domestic violence, divorce and relationship breakdown problems were all more likely to be reported as occurring before money/debt problems, reflecting the increased likelihood of experiencing financial difficulties following the breakdown of a relationship.[162] Domestic violence and divorce were also more likely to be reported as occurring before consumer problems, although this may reflect in large part the tendency of respondents to report only recent consumer problems. An analysis of the reliability of autobiographical memory in relation to the different types of justiciable problems is set out at Appendix C. In addition, divorce was more likely to be reported as occurring before problems relating to rented housing and children; reflecting again the financial impact of relationship breakdown, the need for sometimes speedy relocation, and the impact of relationship breakdown on children's education.[163]

Also as anticipated, more problems were reported to follow than precede personal injury problems, though the difference was not statistically significant.[164] Personal injury was, though, significantly more likely to have been reported as occurring first than last in a sequence of four or more problems.[165] However, because of the small number of instances of some problem types and the size of the effect observed here, it was not possible to establish any likely knock-on problem types – although again personal injury was more likely to be reported as occurring before consumer problems.

In addition, there was some indication that more problems followed than preceded problems relating to homelessness, mental health and immigration, although our findings were not significant.[166]

Finally, as already indicated, consumer problems were more likely to have been reported to follow on from than precede other problems,[167] and be reported at the end than the beginning of a sequence of justiciable problems.[168]

PROBLEM CLUSTERS

Problem types do not have to cause or follow on from one other in order for there to be a connection between them. Connections can also stem from coinciding characteristics of vulnerability to problem types, or coinciding defining circumstances of problem types. Thus, a connection between owned housing and consumer problems was reported in *Paths to Justice* that we can now attribute to both problem types being most likely to be experienced by those on higher incomes, living in larger houses and with a greater number of academic qualifications. In some instances, connections may stem from patterns of causation and vulnerability and coincidence of defining circumstances (e.g. problems relating to children and the care and control or financial support of children).

We used hierarchical cluster and factor analysis to establish general and underlying connections between different problem types. Technical details are set out at Appendix B. Then, by reference to the position of problems in sequences of problems within individual clusters, we determined the typical ordering of problems associated with each of the main clusters identified.

The results of the hierarchical cluster analysis are summarised in a dendrogram set out in Figure 2.7. As anticipated – given that family type problems appear to follow on from each other, are each most frequently reported by people aged between 25 and 44, and all have substantially overlapping defining circumstances – a distinct cluster of family problems is evident, comprising domestic violence, divorce, relationship breakdown and children problems. This same cluster was also revealed by a secondary hierarchical cluster analysis of the *Paths to Justice* data (Figure 1.9), and factor analysis. In fact, almost half of all family problems were reported as having occurred in combination with one or more other family problems.

38

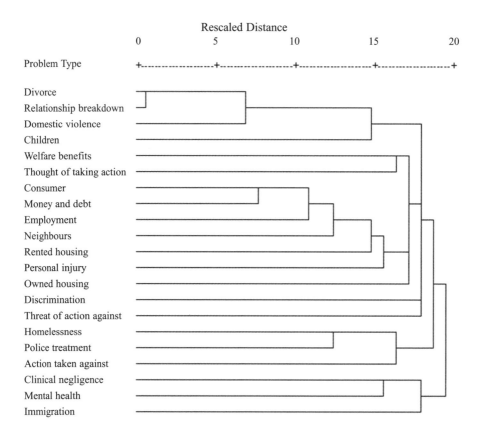

Figure 2.7

Dendrogram using Average Linkage (Between Groups)

As we have reported elsewhere,[169] indicated above,[170] and as is suggested by Figure 2.8, domestic violence, which occurred in combination with one or more other family problems in just over half of all instances, often lay behind the experience of those other family problems. Thus, if domestic violence was reported in combination with a divorce, it generally occurred first, and its existence increased substantially the likelihood of problems ancillary to the divorce being reported.[171]

Outside of divorce, violence was equally likely to occur before or after relationship breakdown problems, and if before, not as long before as in the case of divorce; suggesting that domestic violence is tolerated for longer within marriage. However, violence still appeared to be strongly linked with such relationship breakdown problems, being reported in one-third of all instances.

The existence of domestic violence also increased substantially the likelihood of problems relating to children being reported. So, whereas 14 per cent of respondents who reported domestic violence also reported children related problems (mostly concerning education)[172], just 2 per cent of other respondents did so.[173] Moreover, 29 per cent of respondents who reported domestic violence and problems ancillary to the breakdown of a relationship reported children related problems, compared to 2 per cent who reported neither.[174] Children related problems were generally experienced at the end of sequences of problems within the 'family' cluster.

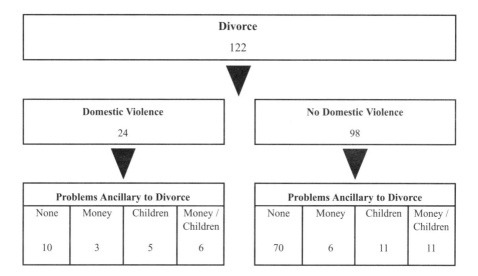

Figure 2.8

Family Problems Relating to Divorce

Hierarchical cluster analysis also indicated a problem cluster involving homelessness, unfair treatment by the police, and action being taken against the respondent. Again, factor analysis revealed the same cluster. It also suggested, however, that problems relating to rented housing form an additional element of it. In fact, over half of all homelessness problems were reported in combination with a rented housing problem, and the expanded cluster principally embodies a cycle of rented housing and homelessness problems.

Rented housing problems relating to unsafe and unsatisfactory accommodation were disproportionately reported by respondents reporting homelessness, and very much characterise the route into and out of homelessness. Rented housing problems were consequently reported at the beginning and end of sequences of problems within this 'homelessness' cluster.

The inclusion of problems relating to the police in the homelessness cluster stems from both problem types being most often experienced by young people in receipt of welfare benefits, and the increased vulnerability to police related problems that accompanies extended periods of time being spent on the streets and the social problems associated with the homeless population (e.g. alcohol and drug abuse). Possibly this latter connection explains why police related problems apparently occurred at any stage in sequences of problems within the cluster. On the other hand, action being taken against the respondent clearly occurred late on in sequences of problems within the cluster. Apart from the generally grievous situation of people who become homeless, however, it was not clear what the connection was between these problems and others within the cluster.

A third cluster identified by hierarchical cluster analysis involved clinical negligence, mental health and immigration problems. Again, factor analysis revealed the same cluster. Again, though, it also suggested the inclusion of an additional problem type, namely problems relating to welfare benefits.

As already observed, mental health problems increase vulnerability to clinical negligence, as mental illness increases the likelihood of people receiving clinical treatment. Indeed, 20 per cent of all respondents reporting justiciable problems relating to mental health also reported a problem relating to clinical negligence. However, there was relatively little overlap of the other problem types in this cluster, apart from in relation to welfare benefits, and it is best characterised as being made up of pairs of problems, generally including welfare benefits problems. For example, 39 per cent of immigration problems were reported in combination with a welfare benefits problem, but not one of these pairs of problems was reported in combination with another problem within the 'health and welfare' cluster.

In terms of ordering, welfare benefits problems generally occurred at the same time as problems relating to mental health and clinical negligence, but after the onset of immigration problems.

A fourth cluster identified by hierarchical cluster analysis involved a broad range of problem types including those relating to welfare benefits, consumer transactions, money/debt, employment, neighbours, rented housing, personal injury, and owned housing. Within this cluster were then further more defined clusters, most particularly a core cluster incorporating consumer, money/debt, neighbours and employment problems, and at another level, rented housing and personal injury problems.

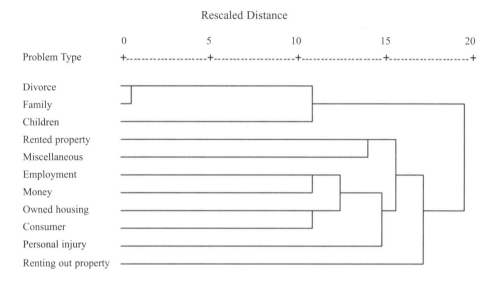

Rescaled Distance

Figure 2.9

Dendrogram Derived from Secondary Analysis of Paths to Justice Data

Unlike the family cluster, the structure of which also clearly emerged from a secondary analysis of *Paths to Justice* data, the structure of this broad cluster differed somewhat to the equivalent cluster drawn from the *Paths to Justice* data. For example, the dendrogram set out in Figure 2.9 suggests more of a connection between owned housing and consumer problems, and less of a connection between consumer and money/debt problems. This may, though, be due to the different composition of the owned housing and money categories within the *Paths to Justice* dataset. For example, owned housing problems included problems relating to neighbours in the *Paths to Justice* study, and money problems included problems relating to welfare benefits. Nevertheless, factor analysis also revealed more of a connection between owned housing and consumer problems, although it placed consumer problems in two distinct clusters – an option not available with hierarchical cluster analysis.

However, these relatively minor differences aside, a reasonable degree of connection between the six problems that make up the core cluster just described was evidenced by both factor analysis and (as far as is possible) secondary analysis of *Paths to Justice* data.

The connections between employment and personal injury problems have been described above, as have those between employment, personal injury and money/debt problems. Where these problems occurred in combination, personal injury generally came first, and money/debt problems last.

In addition, money/debt problems can lead to downward mobility in the housing market, along with general difficulties relating to mortgage and rental payments; thus increasing vulnerability to rented housing problems. As a result, as we demonstrated above,[175] respondents in the rented housing sector were more likely to report money/debt problems than were others. Also, of the six problems in this 'economic' cluster, money/debt problems most often overlapped with consumer problems, perhaps reflecting the overreaching economic activity of some of those who face money/debt problems. Over one-third of respondents who reported money/debt problems also reported a consumer problem.[176] However, because of the common experience of consumer problems, over one-fifth of respondents who reported each of the other cluster problems also reported consumer problems; as did significant numbers of respondents reporting non-cluster problems, with the single exception of problems relating to homelessness.[177]

Reporting of neighbours problems did not overlap substantially with reporting of any of the other economic cluster problems. However, neighbours problems are associated with high density housing – which is more common in the rented housing sector (leading to respondents in the sector being more vulnerable to such problems[178]) – and with extended periods being spent at home, a possible consequence of both employment and personal injury problems. Interestingly, though, factor analysis suggested that where consumer and neighbours problems occur in combination, it is unlikely that employment and personal injury problems will also occur, and vice versa.

PROBLEM CLUSTERS AND PATTERNS OF VULNERABILITY

As with individual problems, experience of multiple problems falling within identified problem clusters does not uniformly affect people across the population. We therefore used binary logistic regression and analysis of covariance (ANCOVA) to enable us to determine which population groups are most vulnerable to experiencing multiple problems within each of the problem clusters set out above. For the binary logistic regression, the dependent variable was based on experience of two or more problem types within the relevant cluster. For the analysis of covariance, the factor scores produced by the factor analysis described in the preceding section were used as dependent variables. Technical details are set out at Appendix B.

As with each of the four types of family problem, and reflecting the impact of such problems, lone parents were most likely to report multiple problems within the family cluster. In contrast, respondents who were living with a partner at the time of interview were least likely to do so. Again reflecting the impact of family problems, respondents living in the rented housing sector and in high density housing were more likely than others to report multiple family problems. Also, binary logistic regression suggested that those respondents who reported long-standing illness or disability were more likely to report family cluster problems, demonstrating again their considerable health impact, as well as the greater vulnerability of the ill and disabled to them. In all, 80 respondents reported multiple family cluster problems.

Reflecting the economic disadvantage of those people experiencing problems within the homelessness cluster, respondents receiving welfare benefits were more likely than others to report multiple homelessness cluster problems, as were respondents without their own mechanised transport. Unsurprisingly, there was also evidence that those living in the rented housing sector were more likely than others to report multiple such problems, although this finding fell short of being statistically significant. In addition, binary logistic regression suggested that respondents who reported long-standing illness or disability were more likely than others to report multiple problems within the homelessness cluster; perhaps in part reflecting the 'relegation' of those with a long-term illness or disability to poor quality housing. Consistent with our findings relating to homelessness, binary logistic regression also suggested that younger respondents were more likely to report multiple problems within this cluster. In all, 30 respondents reported multiple homelessness cluster problems.

As problems relating to clinical negligence and mental health are included within the health and welfare cluster, it is no surprise that it too was associated with respondents reporting long-standing ill-health or disability, as well as, according to analysis of covariance, respondents who were unable to work because of sickness. As the cluster includes immigration problems, it is also no surprise that black and minority ethnic respondents were more likely than others to report multiple problems within it. This was particularly so in relation to those in the black and 'other' ethnicity categories. Evidently, as the cluster includes welfare benefits problems, respondents in receipt of welfare benefits and living in rented housing were also more likely than others to report multiple problems within it. Also, both binary logistic regression and analysis of covariance indicated that those living with a partner, but without children, were more likely than others to report multiple problems within it. In all, just 16 respondents reported multiple health and welfare cluster problems, reflecting the rarity of the constituent problems.

Finally, reflecting the broad range of problems encompassed by it, the social and demographic associations with the economic problem cluster were similar to those found for the experience of justiciable problems in general. Thus, lone parents, those living in high density housing and the rented sector, those reporting long-standing ill-health or disability, and those on higher incomes (reflecting in large part the incidence of consumer problems) were more likely than others to report multiple problems within the economic cluster. However, unlike more generally, male respondents were also more likely to report multiple problems within the economic problem cluster. In all, 514 respondents reported multiple economic cluster problems.[179]

SUMMARY

Over one-third of LSRC survey respondents reported having experienced one or more justiciable problems during the preceding three-and-a-half years. Evidently, such problems are common. However, the experience of problems was far from randomly distributed across the survey population. Experience reflected not only chance, but also underlying differences in life circumstances that entailed differences in vulnerability to problems. In general terms, those who reported long-standing ill-health or disability, lone parents, those living in the rented housing sector and in high density housing, those who were unemployed and on very low incomes, and those aged between 25 and 44 were most likely to report problems. Thus, although there was also a tendency for those on very high incomes to report problems at higher than average rates, and although there were instances of problems being reported by respondents from all walks of life, it is clear that 'socially excluded' groups are particularly vulnerable to experiencing justiciable problems. This was starkly illustrated by the fact that more than four-fifths of temporary accommodation survey respondents reported one or more problems during the same three-and-a-half years time period.

Of course, the reported incidence of individual problem types, and the population groups most vulnerable to them varied greatly. So, common problems, such as those that arose from consumer transactions, arose from 'defining' circumstances routinely experienced across the adult population. In contrast, rare problems, such as those that arose from a change of country of abode, residence status or citizenship, arose from defining circumstances far from the routine. Those who most often experienced the 'defining' circumstances of individual problem types were, all else being equal, also most vulnerable to experiencing the problems themselves. However, all else was not always equal. Physical make-up, experience, resources and disposition were also observed to influence patterns of vulnerability.

Age was found to be a significant influence in predicting all problem types except those relating to employment, owned housing, personal injury and clinical negligence. In addition, gender was found to be a significant influence in predicting problems relating to domestic violence, clinical negligence and unfair treatment by the police, and ethnicity was found to be a significant influence in predicting problems relating to divorce, discrimination and immigration.

Also, aspects of respondents' economic circumstances had a significant influence in predicting all problem types except those relating to divorce and domestic violence. However, unlike age, gender and ethnicity, economic circumstances can change as a result of the experience of justiciable problems. Our findings in this regard therefore reflect not only patterns of vulnerability to justiciable problems, but also their economic impact. So, for example, employment problems were most likely to be reported by the unemployed. Similarly, the type of housing in which respondents lived and their form of tenure, both linked to economic circumstances, had a significant influence in predicting problem types except those relating to clinical negligence and unfair treatment by the police.

In large part indicating the impact of relationship breakdown, the type of family in which respondents lived had a significant influence in predicting 10 problem types: neighbours, employment, rented housing, owned housing, relationship breakdown, divorce, children, domestic violence, discrimination, and mental health. For all but one of these problem types, many of which can constitute elements of social exclusion, lone parent respondents were more likely than others to have reported experiencing them. The change in personal circumstances that results from relationship breakdown, especially for those with whom any children of the relationship come to reside, can thus be seen to be instrumental in bringing about or consolidating social exclusion. In addition, lone parents disproportionately reported money/debt and welfare benefits problems, although this was not highlighted by multivariate regression.

Lastly, respondents who reported long-standing ill-health or disability were more likely than others to report all problem types except those relating to divorce, children, immigration and unfair treatment by the police. Such respondents were particularly vulnerable to a whole range of justiciable problems associated with social exclusion. Not only did half of all the discrimination problems reported through the LSRC survey concern disability discrimination, but ill and disabled respondents also had a much greater tendency than others to report employment, money/debt, welfare benefits, rented housing and homelessness problems. As well as ill-health and disability increasing vulnerability to justiciable problems, they can also be brought about or worsened by such problems. This is obviously so in relation to negligent accidents, clinical negligence and domestic violence. However, there is also evidence that housing in a state of disrepair and overcrowded households can bring about physical and psychological ill-health, and problems relating to discrimination, employment, debt and relationship breakdown can lead to psychological ill-health.

As respondents to the parallel survey of people living in temporary accommodation were much more often lone parents, younger, much less economically active and on considerably lower incomes than their LSRC survey counterparts, they, unsurprisingly, reported a very different pattern of experience of problems. This included increased rates of reporting rented housing, employment, welfare benefits, discrimination, and immigration problems.

Reinforcing the disadvantage of those who are vulnerable to justiciable problems, the experience of such problems has an additive effect. So, each time a person experiences a problem they become increasingly likely to experience additional problems. As certain population groups – including people with a long-standing illness or disability – are more vulnerable than others to a range of justiciable problems, and as the experience of justiciable problems can itself increase such vulnerability – through, for example, bringing about illness or disability – the proportion of respondents in vulnerable groups increased as the number of problems reported increased. Also, as respondents experienced multiple problems, they became increasingly likely to have experienced problems that play a direct role in social exclusion. Of course, to a large extent this is simply a consequence of their experiencing increasing numbers of problems. However, some problem types, such as those relating to homelessness and domestic violence, became more prevalent as the number of problems increased. In contrast, some problem types, such as those relating to personal injury and welfare benefits, became less prevalent as the number of problems increased.

Although the experience of problems has an additive effect, not all problem types were associated with the same risk of additional problems being experienced. Domestic violence, divorce, relationship breakdown, and personal injury problems, though, all appeared more likely to trigger additional problems. This is unsurprising. Domestic violence, for example, has been shown to be symptomatic of dysfunctional relationships and can lead directly to separation and divorce, which, in turn, can lead to disputes regarding maintenance and the division of property. Also, the changes in living arrangements and economic circumstances following separation can bring about, for example, problems relating to housing and financial hardship. Again, *Paths to Justice* has documented how personal injury and work related ill-health can diminish employment opportunities and lead to unemployment, which, in turn, can lead to problems relating to welfare benefits and debt, even if compensation is obtained in relation to the original injury or illness.

Of course, problem types do not have to cause or follow on from one other in order for there to be a connection between them. Connections can also stem from coinciding characteristics of vulnerability to problem types, or coinciding defining circumstances of problem types. Hierarchical cluster and factor analysis identified four principal problem clusters. The most distinct, a 'family' cluster, was comprised of domestic violence, divorce, relationship breakdown and children problems. This same cluster was also revealed by a secondary hierarchical cluster analysis of the *Paths to Justice* data. A 'homelessness' cluster comprised problems relating to rented housing, homelessness, unfair treatment by the police, and formal action being taken against the respondent. A 'health and welfare' cluster comprised problems relating to clinical negligence, mental health, immigration and welfare benefits. Lastly, an 'economic' cluster comprised problems relating to consumer transactions, money/debt, neighbours and employment problems, and at another level, problems relating to rented housing and personal injury.

As with individual problems, experience of multiple problems falling within identified problem clusters is not randomly distributed. Respondents who reported long-standing illness or disability were more likely to report multiple problems within all four clusters. Lone parents, those living in the rented housing sector and those living in high density housing were also more likely than others to report multiple problems within the family cluster. Respondents receiving welfare benefits, those without their own mechanised transport, and younger respondents were also more likely than others to report multiple problems within the homelessness cluster. Black and minority ethnic respondents, those in receipt of welfare benefits, those living in rented housing, and those living with a partner, but without children were also more likely to report multiple problems within the health and welfare cluster. Finally, lone parents, those living in high density housing and the rented sector, those reporting long-standing ill-health or disability, and those on higher incomes (reflecting in large part the incidence of consumer problems) were more likely than others to report multiple problems within the economic cluster.

3

Inaction and Action:
Responses to Justiciable Problems

This chapter sets out the ways in which people deal with justiciable problems. Using information obtained from screen interviews, it highlights the sense of powerlessness and helplessness often experienced by people who face such problems, and examines the different rates of action and use of advice services associated with different problem types and population groups. As part of this explanation, it reveals how people's problem resolution strategies can become entrenched. Using information obtained from main interviews, the chapter then details the many sources from which people attempt to obtain advice, the difficulties they experience in doing so, and the nature of the advice and any additional help received by those who are successful in doing so. Through this, it illustrates how people's choices of advisers, although often logical and apposite, also can be desperate and unpromising. It also illustrates the phenomenon of referral fatigue, whereby the more times people are referred on to another service by an adviser, the less likely they become to act on a referral.

INACTION AND ACTION

Not everyone who experiences a justiciable problem will take action to resolve it. As Felstiner, Abel and Sarat depicted in their influential model of disputing behaviour, before action can be taken a problem must be recognised as such.[180] People faced with the constituent elements of a justiciable problem will not always regard them as problematic. As suggested in the preceding chapter, sensitivity as well as vulnerability to problems varies between differently constituted population groups. People's perceptions of specific sets of circumstances are influenced by, for example, their familiarity with them, understanding of them, and general expectations. These, in turn, are influenced by, for example, their age, education, economic situation and physical, social and cultural environment. So, for instance, as expectations of standards of behaviour vary between people of different ages, young people are less likely to regard 'neighbour nuisance' as problematic.[181] Also, as physical strength and the experience of physical violence vary between people of different gender, men are less likely to regard an assault by a partner as upsetting or frightening, and consequently as problematic.[182]

As the Hughes Commission noted, if the constituent elements of a justiciable problem are regarded as problematic, action to resolve it will still be unlikely if it is believed that nothing can be done to effect a satisfactory resolution.[183] Of course, as was observed in *Paths to Justice*, people who take no action to resolve a problem because they think nothing can be done make this judgment without the benefit of advice and, therefore, without the benefit of an opportunity to identify solutions they are not personally aware of.[184] As few people are familiar with the complexities of the framework of civil law that bears on everyday life, the existence of unidentified solutions is no doubt commonplace. Thus, the Hughes Commission advocated that education and the provision of general information regarding rights and obligations and the means available to effect them is essential to the promotion of just solutions to justiciable problems.

Furthermore, even if people believe that something can be done to resolve a problem, action may yet not be taken because of concerns about the physical, psychological, economic or social consequences of doing so;[185] such inaction perhaps constituting a simple personal preference, reflecting the inherent cost of taking action, or, alternatively, perhaps reflecting structural failings in the civil justice infrastructure.

In all, no action was taken in relation to 19 per cent of problems reported through the LSRC survey. The most common reason provided was that respondents 'did not think anything could be done' (31 per cent; 6 per cent of problems overall),[186] supporting findings elsewhere and confirming a 'profound need for knowledge … about obligations, rights, remedies, and procedures' for resolving justiciable problems.[187] Other common reasons included problems not having been sufficiently important to warrant action (12 per cent[188]), there having been no 'dispute' and nobody who was regarded as having been in the wrong (10 per cent[189]),[190] action having become unnecessary as a result of activity on the part of others (9 per cent[191]), and the potential damage action might have caused to an on-going relationship (8 per cent[192]).

Concerns about the potential cost of action were reported as a reason for inaction on only relatively few occasions (4 per cent[193]); as were concerns about the time it might take to reach a resolution (6 per cent[194]). In fact, being 'scared to do anything' was more often a reason for inaction than were concerns about cost (6 per cent[195]; 1 per cent of problems overall).

Just over half of those respondents who took no action to resolve problems discussed their situation with friends and relatives, particularly partners, before reaching a final decision on the matter.[196] However, 32 per cent of friends and relatives who had been consulted had actually recommended action be taken. In contrast, just 4 per cent had recommended no action be taken. Respondents' reasons for inaction in the face of a contrary recommendation by friends or relatives were similar to reasons in general, but with the virtual absence of lack of importance or dispute. This suggests that problems were more likely to be discussed if there was a greater interest in action being taken. It also suggests that support in taking action is sometimes important in overcoming doubts about its utility.

In *Paths to Justice* it was commented that the reasons for failure to take action provided by 'lumpers'[197] conveyed, on the whole, 'a rather negative and powerless quality.'[198] We observed this to be most acute in respect of those problems in relation to which respondents reported combinations of reasons for not acting. For example a profound sense of powerlessness and helplessness was indicated by respondents who reported that they did not act because they were both scared to do so and believed that, in any event, nothing could be done (1 per cent) – particularly as their problems appeared serious and chronic (relating to their employment, relationships, or living environment).

Consistent with findings elsewhere, reasons for inaction varied significantly by problem type.[199] As is suggested by Figure 3.1, on examining standardised Pearson residuals to assess the source of the overall significance,[200] we found that respondents who did not act were most likely to believe nothing could be done to resolve mental health (64 per cent[201]) and discrimination (52 per cent[202]) problems, and least likely to believe nothing could be done to resolve personal injury problems (23 per cent[203]); perhaps reflecting the proliferation of advertising of no-win no-fee personal injury claim services. Respondents were, though, most likely to regard personal injury problems (22 per cent[204]) as not being sufficiently important to warrant action, and least likely to regard divorce (0 per cent[205]) in such a manner. They were also most

52

likely to regard there as having been no dispute involved in personal injury problems (36 per cent[206]), although in relation to this reasoning divorce was also more likely than other problem types to be regarded similarly (47 per cent[207]). Problems relating to neighbours (2 per cent[208]), consumer transactions (3 per cent[209]) and rented housing (0 per cent[210]) were least likely to have been regarded as involving no dispute.

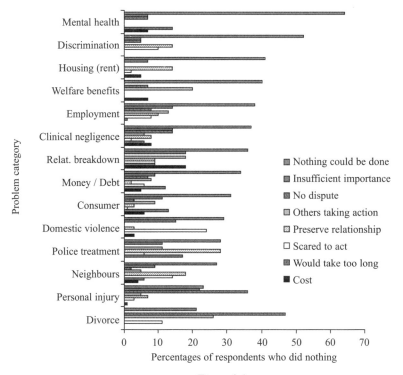

Figure 3.1
Reported Reasons for doing Nothing to Resolve a Problem

Those who took no action in relation to divorce were, additionally, more likely than others to report action as unnecessary as a result of activity on the part of others (26 per cent[211]), as were those who took no action to resolve welfare benefits problems (20 per cent[212]). Conversely, those who took no action to resolve problems relating to domestic violence were least likely to point to activity on the part of others (0 per cent[213]), reflecting the intransigent nature of such problems.

Respondents who took no action in relation to problems relating to unfair treatment by the police (28 per cent[214]) and neighbours (18 per cent[215]) were most likely to express concerns about the damage that action might have caused to on-going relationships; relationships that were doubtless often unsatisfactory to start with. Those who took no action in relation to money/debt problems were least likely to express such concerns (2 per cent[216]).

Those who took no action to resolve problems relating to neighbours (14 per cent[217]), along with those who took no action in relation to domestic violence (24 per cent[218]), were also most likely to report that they had been scared to act. Unsurprisingly, those who took no action to resolve consumer problems were least likely to do so (1 per cent[219]).

Concerns about the time that it can take to resolve problems were most likely to be reported by those who took no action to resolve consumer (16 per cent[220]) and money/debt problems (10 per cent[221]), and least likely to be reported by those who took no action in relation to personal injuries (0 per cent[222]).

Lastly, concerns about the cost of action were most likely to be reported by those who did nothing to resolve problems ancillary to relationship breakdown (18 per cent[223]), and least likely to be reported by respondents who took no action to resolve employment problems (0 per cent[224]). As will become clear below, cost concerns in relation to problems ancillary to relationship breakdown reflect a general perception that such problems should be dealt with through a solicitor. Respondents who considered getting advice from a solicitor, but did not go on to do so, cited cost concerns on many more occasions than those who considered getting advice from other types of adviser, but did not go on to do so.[225]

PATTERNS OF INACTION

As with the reasons given for taking no action to resolve problems, the proportion of occasions on which no action was taken varied by problem type. In addition, it varied between differently constituted population groups. We used binary logistic regression to test the influence of problem type, previously used problem resolution strategies, and a range of social and demographic predictors on the likelihood of respondents having taken action to resolve a problem. Technical details are set out at Appendix B. Problem type was the most influential predictor. Those faced with problems relating to mental health or clinical negligence were much less likely than others to take action

54

to resolve them;[226] a legacy of the common belief that nothing could be done to help, exacerbated by the frequent and substantial imbalance of knowledge, standing[227] and institutional support between the parties. So, as is shown in Figure 3.2, although action was taken to deal with 81 per cent of problems overall, inaction was more common than action for mental health and clinical negligence problems.

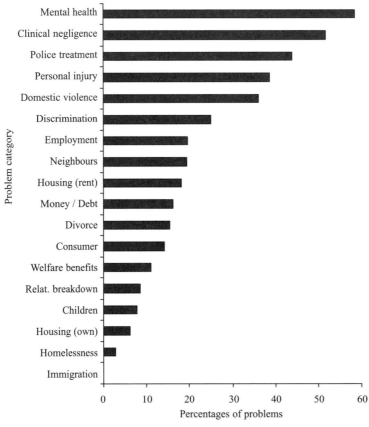

Figure 3.2
Percentage of Problems Where No Action Was Taken

Those who faced problems relating to unfair treatment by the police were also less likely than others to act to resolve them (57 per cent), again in part a consequence of the above imbalances. Likewise, those who experienced domestic violence were less likely than others to take action (64 per cent).[228] Here, though, physical, economic and emotional imbalances between the parties would likely have been of greater importance. Lastly, those faced with personal injury problems were less likely than others to take action (61 per cent), although, as is clear from above, this was principally a result of these problems being much more often regarded as insufficiently important to warrant action or as involving no dispute.[229]

Respondents faced with problems relating to homelessness were most likely to take action to deal with them. In fact, just one such respondent took no action. Those faced with family related problems, other than domestic violence, were also more likely than others to act (89 per cent), as were those faced with problems relating to owned housing (94 per cent), welfare benefits (89 per cent) and consumer transactions (86 per cent).[230]

Beyond problem type, it appeared that those respondents who were in work, particularly the self-employed, were less likely than others to act to resolve problems, perhaps indicating difficulties faced in making time available to do so. Also, as we explain below, many advice services operate only during normal working hours, making them more difficult to access for those who work such hours.

The relationship between economic circumstances and inaction was, though, complex. For example, while those in work were less likely than others to act, those who owned their own home were more likely than others to act. Also, if tenure was removed from the analysis, then, as was reported in both *Paths to Justice* and *Paths to Justice Scotland*, those on higher incomes were seen to be more likely than others to act.[231] So, while working seems to make it more difficult for people to act to resolve problems, this difficulty appears to be somewhat offset by greater economic independence. Those in low income occupations, therefore, are particularly unlikely to take action to resolve problems.

Gender and ethnicity also influenced the likelihood of respondents having taken action to resolve problems. Male respondents were less likely than female respondents to have done so. So, whereas 21 per cent of men facing problems took no action to resolve them, the same was true of only 17 per cent of women. Also, black and minority ethnic respondents were less likely than white respondents to have taken action to resolve problems. Accordingly, whereas 23 per cent of black and minority ethnic respondents facing problems took no action, the same was true of slightly less than 19 per cent of white respondents. Among black and minority ethnic respondents, Asian respondents were the least likely to take action, taking no action on 27 per cent of occasions, compared to just 14 per cent of occasions for 'other' minority ethnic respondents.[232]

Although there was some indication that black and minority ethnic respondents who did not act were more likely than their white counterparts to think that nothing could be done to help them (39 per cent, compared to 31 per cent), this finding was not statistically significant.[233] There was, though, evidence of significant differences between black and minority ethnic and white respondents in the frequency of their reporting having been scared to act, with black and minority ethnic respondents having done so more often.[234]

PATTERNS OF ACTION

When action was taken to resolve justiciable problems, 63 per cent of respondents (51 per cent overall) reported that they sought formal advice to assist them in the resolution process. The remainder handled their problems alone, without ever seeking such advice (37 per cent; 30 per cent overall). In handling problems alone, these respondents most often simply talked or wrote to 'the other side' involved in a dispute, and attempted to negotiate a solution.[235] Of course, the fact they did not seek formal advice did not mean they sought no information or support at all in taking action. On one-twelfth of occasions they obtained information from a self-help guide (one-sixth) and/or an internet site (one-seventh), and on one-third of occasions they discussed their situation with friends or relatives prior to or whilst acting.[236]

A small number of respondents who handled their problem alone went beyond the normal practice of negotiating direct with 'the other side' and commenced proceedings in a court or tribunal (2 per cent), though they did so far less often than those who had sought formal advice in dealing with problems (11 per cent).[237] The extent to which this difference is a consequence of the types of problems they faced, the preferred methods of advice providers, or the relative seriousness of problems is discussed below.[238]

Also, on a few occasions those who handled problems alone utilised an Ombudsman or a mediation service (2 per cent and 1 per cent respectively). Again, though, this was less often than those who sought advice (3 per cent and 7 per cent respectively).[239]

Again, we used binary logistic regression to test the influence of problem type, previously used problem resolution strategies, and a range of social and demographic predictors on the likelihood of respondents who took action to deal with problems having sought advice while doing so. Technical details are set out at Appendix B.

Problem type was again found to be the most influential predictor. However, different problem types were associated with seeking advice, as compared to simply taking action. So, for example, whereas those faced with consumer problems were more likely than others to take action to resolve them, they were less likely than others to seek advice once they took action. As is shown in Figure 3.3, those who took action to resolve consumer problems sought advice less often than they handled problems alone. Only those who took action to deal with problems relating to mental health were less likely to seek advice (22 per cent). Conversely, whereas those faced with problems relating to domestic violence or personal injury were less likely than others to take action in the first instance, they were more likely than others to seek advice once they did (88 per cent and 84 per cent, respectively).

Also, those who took action to resolve money/debt problems were less likely than others to seek advice (49 per cent), and those who took action in relation to problems relating to homelessness (94 per cent), owned housing (79 per cent), divorce (96 per cent) or problems ancillary to relationship breakdown (87 per cent) were more likely than others to seek advice.[240] In addition, there was evidence that respondents who took action to resolve rented housing problems were more likely to seek advice if the problem concerned unsafe or unsuitable accommodation, which was shown in the last chapter to be a defining element of the homelessness problem cluster.[241]

Unsurprisingly, owing to constraints on their time, respondents in full-time employment, as well as having been less likely than others to have acted to resolve problems, were also less likely than others to have sought advice when they did act (57 per cent). However, this was not the case in relation to those who were in part-time employment, and the self-employed were actually the most likely to seek advice (72 per cent). Also contrary to our findings in relation to bare action and inaction, those living in the rented sector appeared more likely than others to have sought advice when they acted.

In addition, those with no academic qualifications were more likely than others to have sought advice when they acted, perhaps indicating a lesser confidence as to the options available to them. A closer examination of qualifications revealed that those with a degree were the least likely to have sought advice.[242]

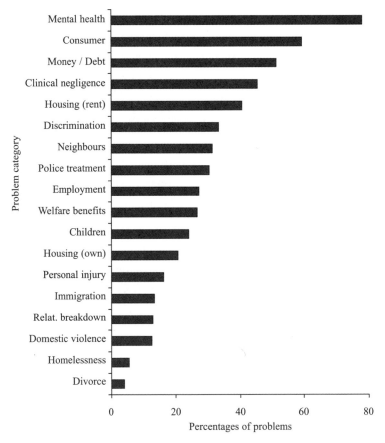

Figure 3.3
Percentage of Problems Where No Advice Was Sought
Despite Action Having Been Taken

Lastly, it was evident that respondents were more likely to handle problems alone if they had previously done so. Thus, whereas 53 per cent of those who had previously handled a problem alone did so in relation to the problem in question, the same was true of just 36 per cent of others.[243]

There were no significant differences in the likelihood of advice being sought by those who took action to deal with problems between respondents on different incomes, white and black and minority ethnic respondents, or female and male respondents.

Overall, though, female respondents who acted to resolve problems sought advice more often than their male counterparts (65 per cent and 60 per cent respectively).[244] Also, if those who sought advice were compared to those who either handled their problems alone or took no action to deal with them, then there was a significant difference between the strategies adopted by women and men.[245] Our findings therefore reflect those in the health field, where women appear more likely than men to utilise medical services – at least from adolescence onwards.[246]

White and black and minority ethnic respondents who acted to resolve problems sought advice at almost identical rates.[247] Again, though, there was a more pronounced difference when respondents who sought advice were compared to those who either handled their problems alone or took no action to deal with them. Overall, white respondents who had experienced problems sought advice more often than black and minority ethnic respondents (51 per cent and 48 per cent respectively). However, this finding was not significant. Again, though, it reflects findings in the health field, where white people appear more likely than black and minority ethnic people to utilise medical services.[248] In England this has been found to be especially so where black and minority ethnic people are unable to speak English,[249] and it also appears that culturally rigid health care services act as a barrier to health care.[250] Some studies of advice services, too, have highlighted the need for translation services and cultural empathy to lower barriers to comprehensive service provision, and there is evidence that some black and minority ethnic people consider that 'seeing an adviser from another cultural identity would cause difficulties'.[251]

ADVICE AND SERIOUSNESS

In addition to the above, there was evidence that the likelihood of respondents having sought advice increased along with the seriousness of the problems they faced. Respondents were, for example, more likely to describe problems in relation to which advice was sought as having been 'very important to sort out' (86 per cent compared to 75 per cent).[252] Also, as is illustrated in Figure 3.4, when respondents' objectives in acting concerned money, the likelihood of them having sought advice increased along with the amount.[253] So, whereas advice was obtained in relation to just 56 per cent of problems involving sums less than £100, it was obtained in relation to 92 per cent of problems involving sums of £5,000 or more, and in relation to all problems involving sums of £25,000 or more.

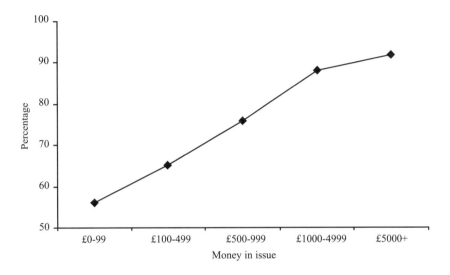

Figure 3.4
Percentage of Problems Where No Advice Was Sought
by Sum of Money Involved

As we explain in Appendix C, the relative likelihood of instances of particular problem types that occurred early on in the survey reference period being recalled by respondents provides a further indication of their seriousness. In short, problems that are forgotten quickly are likely to be less serious than those that take longer to forget.

To establish whether problems that respondents attempted to resolve on their own were forgotten more quickly than problems in relation to which respondents sought advice, we fitted simple exponential decay functions, using non-linear regression, to the number of problems starting in each of fourteen time periods that together made up the LSRC survey reference period as a proportion of the highest number of problems starting in any time period. First, we did this for problems that respondents attempted to resolve on their own, and then for problems in relation to which advice had been sought. In both cases, the functions fitted the data well.[254]

As can be seen from Figure 3.5, problems in relation to which advice had been sought appeared to be forgotten less quickly than those that respondents attempted to resolve on their own. The decay coefficients were 0.07 and 0.13 respectively. Even with the relatively small number of time periods, the confidence intervals for these coefficients did not overlap, indicating significant differences.[255] Also, when problem types were ranked according to similarly derived decay coefficients there was a significant correlation between that ranking and the ranking of problem types according to the likelihood of advice being sought.[256] Again, then, it appears that the likelihood of respondents having sought advice increased along with the seriousness of the problems they faced.

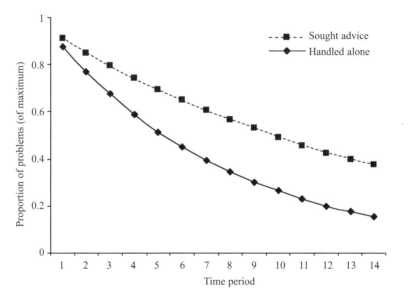

Figure 3.5
Proportion of Problems Recalled for Each of Fourteen
Time Periods Making Up the Reference Period (Fitted)

PHYSICAL BARRIERS TO ADVICE

Supporting previous findings, from both the United Kingdom and elsewhere,[257] information obtained from main LSRC survey interviews indicated that respondents who sought formal advice in dealing with justiciable problems did so from a wide range of types of adviser. These included solicitors' firms, Citizens Advice Bureaux and other advice agencies, local authorities, trade unions and professional bodies, employers, the police, insurance companies, health professionals, claims agencies, housing associations, social workers, court staff, churches, politicians, the media, job centres, banks and trade associations. However, 15 per cent of those who sought advice were not successful in obtaining it (8 per cent overall).[258]

Unsuccessful attempts to obtain advice were most likely to be reported in connection with problems relating to homelessness, neighbours, rented housing and welfare benefits.[259] In fact, almost half of those respondents who tried to obtain formal advice in connection with homelessness were unsuccessful in doing so.[260] Conversely, unsuccessful attempts were least likely to be reported in connection with divorce and problems relating to personal injury and consumer transactions.[261] As will become clear from the next section, these different rates of success in obtaining advice can in large part be explained by the fact that different types of advice service are commonly used in relation to different problem types. So, for example, respondents were more likely to try to obtain advice from local councils in connection with problems relating to homelessness, neighbours, rented housing and welfare benefits than in connection with other problems,[262] and unsuccessful attempts to obtain advice were most frequently reported in relation to local councils.[263] On the other hand, respondents were more likely to try to obtain advice from solicitors in connection with divorce and personal injury problems than in connection with other problems,[264] and unsuccessful attempts to obtain advice were least frequently reported in relation to solicitors.[265]

The most frequent reason given for an attempt to obtain advice having been unsuccessful was that an adviser had been unable to provide any help. It was given in relation to almost two-thirds of all unsuccessful attempts.[266] It was not, though, the most common reason given in relation to all types of adviser. Unsuccessful attempts to obtain advice from Citizens Advice Bureaux, which are general advice providers, were less likely than unsuccessful attempts to obtain advice from elsewhere to be attributed to an inability to help with the problems in question.[267] On the other hand, unsuccessful attempts to obtain advice from solicitors, who are specialist advice providers, were more likely than unsuccessful attempts to obtain advice from elsewhere to be attributed to such an inability to help.[268] Of course, respondents stating that they were unsuccessful in obtaining advice because an adviser was unable to 'help' raises some problems of interpretation. An adviser being unable to help potentially covers a range of possibilities: that the adviser was not in a position to give advice about the respondent's problem; that they did not know the answer to the respondent's questions; or, that they did not think there was anything that could be done about the respondent's problem. There may therefore have been more than a simple difference between forms of advice lying behind these differences.

The second most common reason given for an attempt to obtain advice having been unsuccessful was difficulty getting through on the telephone (16 per cent of occasions).[269] Supporting earlier findings, this was particularly so in relation to Citizens Advice Bureaux.[270] Over half the unsuccessful attempts to obtain advice from this source were reported as foundering due to problems getting through to an adviser.[271] The frustration felt by respondents in not being able to get through on the telephone was clearly evident:

"I rang them and no one answered. It was a waste of time."

"[The CAB is] inaccessible, not near to where we live and when you phone you could not get through."

Difficulties experienced in telephoning advisers were sometimes compounded by the hours of operation of many advice services. Service providers that are more focused on face-to-face advice, such as solicitors and Citizens Advice Bureaux, tend to limit delivery of their services to normal working hours – especially if they are delivered by the same individuals.[272] This poses a double problem for those who cannot get through to such services on the telephone, and cannot attend in person because, for example, they have to work during normal working hours. As one respondent said:

'Being in full-time work and having children … [There is a] lack of time to actually get [to] or telephone them.'

Respondents who sought advice from service providers that are more focused on telephone advice, such as insurance companies, reported relatively few problems contacting advice services, both by telephone and in general.[273] Dedicated telephone advice services are commonly provided on a 24-hour basis, making it easier for people to contact advisers at a time that is convenient for them. Evidently, services that are provided on a commercial basis must, to be competitive and attractive to consumers, shape their services around consumer behaviour patterns.

Although, overall, as Figure 3.6 shows, respondents reported they met face-to-face with the majority of advisers they successfully contacted, on many of these occasions initial contact was made by telephone. Thus, half of respondents' unsuccessful attempts to obtain advice were via the telephone.[274] This, along with the fact that many advisers are only ever contacted by telephone, highlights the significance of the telephone in the provision of easily accessible advice and assistance.

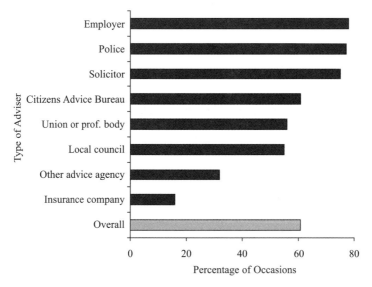

Figure 3.6
Percentage of Advisers Contacted in Person

As well as unsuccessful attempts to contact advisers by telephone, respondents also sometimes reported attempts failing because of their either having to 'wait too long' to see an adviser, or receiving no reply to a letter requesting advice (7 per cent and 12 per cent of occasions respectively).[275] Having to wait too long was most frequently mentioned in relation to Citizens Advice Bureaux and local councils.[276] Receiving no reply was most often mentioned in relation to local councils and employers.[277] However, what respondents understood and meant by 'local councils' again raises some problems of interpretation. It appears that respondents often reported the use of advice services run by local councils as if they were independent advice agencies, and tended therefore to report only the use of the normal operating or central departments of councils as use of local council services.

Only rarely did respondents complain that they had been unable to obtain advice because an adviser had been too far away.[278] It is likely, though, that there are subtle differences in this regard, that we have not been able to pick up through the LSRC survey, as between urban and rural areas. It has recently been reported that 'there is a general lack of supply of advice services' in rural areas,[279] and although there is a comparatively high level of car ownership among residents of rural areas, that makes it 'relatively straightforward' for many of them to visit geographically distant service locations, for those people without cars accessing services can be extremely difficult.[280] So, as one study of access to advice services in rural areas found, 'elderly women living on their own faced serious, almost overwhelming, problems'.[281] The continuing development of telephone and internet advice services will, of course, mitigate this problem further in the future, but the problem does still remain, and those affected by it are particularly disadvantaged within our society.

THE IMPACT OF BARRIERS TO ADVICE

Comparing the numbers of occasions on which respondents successfully obtained advice with the number of occasions on which they considered or sought advice, but obtained none, we found that respondents who considered or attempted obtaining advice from solicitors or insurance companies were more likely than those who considered or attempted obtaining advice from elsewhere to report actually obtaining it.[282] This reflects the ease of use of insurance companies' legal help lines and the geographical distribution of solicitors firms, as well as the commercial nature of both of these types of adviser. On the other hand, respondents who considered or attempted obtaining advice from Citizens Advice Bureaux were less likely than those who considered or attempted obtaining advice from elsewhere to report actually obtaining it.[283] This reflects the relatively small number of Citizens Advice Bureaux,[284] their geographical sparsity (relative to solicitors firms), their restricted opening hours,[285] and their reliance on volunteers in order to operate effectively. It also indicates that demand for their services may exceed capacity.[286]

Of course, different barriers to advice affected respondents' strategies on obtaining advice at different stages of the advice seeking process, depending upon the type of adviser under consideration. So, with Citizens Advice Bureaux and advice agencies more generally, respondents had most trouble in locating them and making initial contact. In contrast, with local councils and insurance companies, respondents had little trouble in making initial contact, but there was evidence they were more likely to be rebuffed on doing so, because these organisations were unable to provide any help. With solicitors, respondents were most likely to abandon a strategy of obtaining advice because of concerns about cost, although these concerns appeared to be based more on assumptions about the cost of solicitors' services than estimates provided by solicitors themselves.

Two-thirds of respondents who unsuccessfully attempted to obtain advice to help deal with a problem tried, in any event, to resolve it alone. The remaining one-third gave up trying to resolve it. However, important differences in behaviour were observed in relation to different problem types. So, while no respondents gave up trying to deal with, for example, rented housing, homelessness, money/debt, welfare benefits, children and relationship breakdown problems because they had been unable to obtain advice,[287] almost two-thirds and three-quarters, respectively, of those who were unable to obtain advice in relation to neighbours and employment problems subsequently did so.[288] Both of these problem types generally involve on-going and important relationships. It may therefore have been that respondents were more likely to be unwilling to further jeopardise the future by acting without the support of advice in relation to these problems.

SOURCES OF ADVICE

825 of the 1,623 respondents who completed a main LSRC survey interview successfully obtained advice. In all, advice was obtained from 1,310 advisers. That equates to an average of around one-and-a-half advisers per respondent, and therefore also per problem. 54 per cent of respondents obtained advice from only one adviser, 32 per cent of respondents obtained advice from two advisers, 11 per cent from three advisers, and the remaining 3 per cent from four or more advisers.

As can be seen from Figure 3.7, 26 per cent of advisers were solicitors, and 23 per cent were Citizens Advice Bureaux or other advice agencies (including, for example, independent advice agencies, consumer advice services and law centres). The remainder, as indicated, were of a broad range of types from which, for the purposes of analysis, we have separated out only the five most common – local councils, trade unions and professional bodies, employers, the police, and insurance companies – which together accounted for 28 per cent of advisers. No other types of organisation or person accounted for more than 2 per cent of advisers.

41 per cent of respondents who obtained advice from one or more advisers obtained advice from a solicitor at some point, 33 per cent obtained advice from a Citizens Advice Bureau or other advice agency, 11 per cent from a local council, 11 per cent from a trade union or professional body, 8 per cent from an employer, 6 per cent from the police, 6 per cent from an insurance company, and 32 per cent from another adviser.

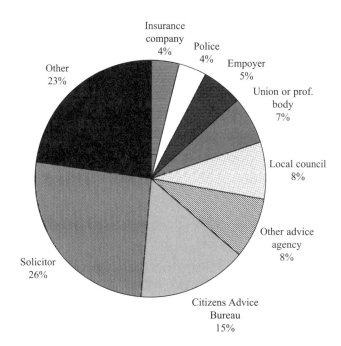

Figure 3.7
Advisers From Whom Advice Successfully Obtained

68

However, very different patterns of advisers were associated with different points in sequences of advisers, reflecting in part a progression from generalist to specialist advisers, but also apparent confusion on the part of many respondents as they tried to navigate the advice maze.[289]

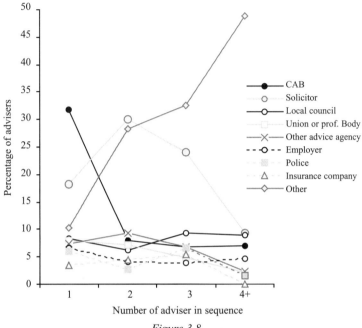

Figure 3.8
Changing Pattern of Advisers in Sequences
of Two or More Advisers

Using data relating to those respondents who obtained advice from two or more advisers to help deal with a justiciable problem, we used ordinal regression with a logit link function to determine the relative likelihood of different types of adviser being used earlier or later in sequences of advisers.[290] Technical details are set out at Appendix B. We found that Citizens Advice Bureaux tended to be used earlier in sequences than solicitors. Similarly, we found that employers, another source of general advice, tended to be used earlier in sequences than solicitors. In contrast, we found no significant difference between the point in sequences that other advice agencies, that were generally specialist in character, and solicitors were used. Thus, as is illustrated by Figure 3.8, whereas 32 per cent of first advisers in sequences of two or more advisers were Citizens Advice Bureaux, just 8 per cent of second advisers were. Conversely, whereas only 18 per cent of first advisers were solicitors, 30 per cent of second advisers were.

Also, whereas overall 40 per cent of respondents who obtained advice from solicitors had obtained advice elsewhere beforehand, the same was true of just 19 per cent of respondents who obtained advice from Citizens Advice Bureaux. Furthermore, whereas 67 per cent of respondents who obtained advice from a solicitor in the first instance obtained advice from nowhere else, the same was true of only 28 per cent of respondents who obtained advice from a Citizens Advice Bureau in the first instance.

However, not all advice seeking behaviour exhibited an orderly progression towards increasingly specialist advisers. 74 per cent of respondents who obtained advice from 'other' advisers in the first instance obtained advice from nowhere else, despite the fact that the great majority of such sources were generalist in character, and many seemed unlikely sources of good advice (e.g. a housing association in relation to a problem relating to children). Moreover, as is clear from Figure 3.8, and as was indicated by the results of ordinal regression, 'other' advisers became increasingly prominent among later advisers in sequences of advisers.

In addition, second advisers were more often friends or relatives of respondents than first advisers,[291] suggesting a degree of confusion, and even desperation, as to where to obtain advice on the part of some respondents who were unable to obtain advice from their first choice of adviser.

Some confusion and desperation is also indicated by respondents' choices of first advisers, which, confirming earlier findings, varied greatly between problem types.[292] The 'fit' of first advisers to problem type, illustrated in Figure 3.9, was generally seemingly appropriate. So, for example, respondents who had been involved in a divorce first obtained advice from solicitors (79 per cent) and advice agencies (21 per cent). Those who had faced problems relating to homelessness first obtained advice from solicitors (17 per cent), advice agencies (50 per cent) and local councils, which have a responsibility for local housing matters (33 per cent). Those who had experienced domestic violence first obtained advice from solicitors (14 per cent), advice agencies (23 per cent), local councils, which often provide shelters (9 per cent), and the police (54 per cent). Also, demonstrating the common use of appropriate specialist advice agencies, those who had experienced consumer problems, for example, often obtained advice from consumer advice or trading standards services (21 per cent), and those who had experienced personal injury problems (which often stemmed from industrial accidents) or employment problems often obtained advice from a trade union or professional body (25 per cent and 23 per cent respectively).

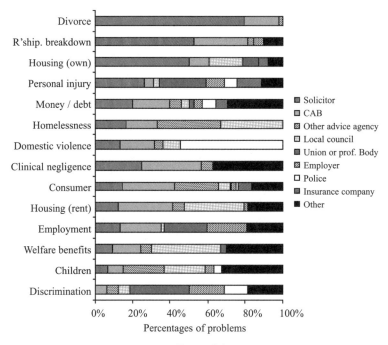

Figure 3.9
First Adviser by Problem Type

However, first sources of advice were sometimes seemingly inappropriate and unpromising. This may, to some extent, have been owing to a degree of creativity in choices, perhaps necessitated by the availability of services locally, but it seems likely that on many occasions it was, rather, uncertainty and despair that lay behind choices. For example, the extraordinary range of first advisers associated with problems relating to children indicates real uncertainty as to the most effective way of responding to them. 33 per cent of respondents who had faced such problems first obtained advice from an 'other' adviser, and although one-third of these advisers were social workers, two-thirds were made up of less likely sources of advice, such as a housing association.

Furthermore, it appears that a number of respondents may in the first instance have obtained advice from the 'other side' to disputes. For example, 22 per cent of respondents who obtained advice in relation to employment problems first obtained advice from their employers. Also, 25 per cent of respondents who obtained advice in relation to public sector rented housing problems first obtained advice from their local councils. Although it is possible that some of these respondents obtained advice from independent advice services operated by or on behalf of their employers or local councils, it seems unlikely that such services would account for all these instances. Also, although it is possible that sometimes an opposing party in a dispute might provide a person with dispassionate and valuable advice, it seems unlikely that such advice would always be as dispassionate and valuable as that potentially available from an independent adviser.

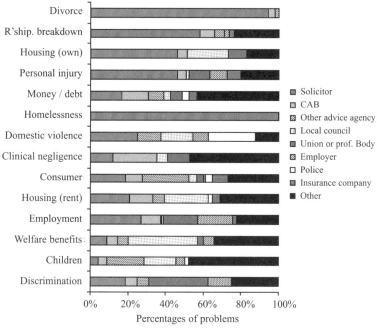

Figure 3.10
Final Adviser by Problem Type

As can be seen from Figure 3.10, respondents' final[293] advisers differed between problem types to almost as great an extent as first advisers.[294] Overall, though, final advisers were more likely to be solicitors and less likely to be Citizens Advice Bureaux, illustrating again that many respondents visited progressively more specialist advisers. Thus, whereas 25 per cent of first advisers were solicitors, and 20 per cent Citizens Advice Bureaux, 31 per cent of final advisers were solicitors, and just 9 per cent Citizens Advice Bureaux. In fact, almost all those respondents who obtained advice in relation to divorce or homelessness problems ended up obtaining advice from a solicitor (94 per cent and 100 per cent respectively).

Final advisers were also, though, more likely to be 'other' advisers, suggesting that the uncertainty and despair apparent in relation to some first advisers could remain throughout the advice seeking process. Of course, many 'other' advisers would have been perfectly appropriate sources of advice. However, many would not.

THE SUBSTANCE OF ADVICE AND ASSISTANCE

As is illustrated by Figures 3.11, 3.12 and 3.13, the substance of advice and assistance offered to respondents by different types of adviser varied greatly. In terms of the subject matter of advice, solicitors and the police most often explored respondents' legal positions, although a relatively wide range of other advisers, advice agencies in particular, also did so; demonstrating that legal advice is not, as in some jurisdictions, provided only by legal professionals.[295] Solicitors and insurance companies most often explained respondents' financial positions, reflecting the commercial nature of these adviser types. Employers and 'other' advisers most often covered other matters.

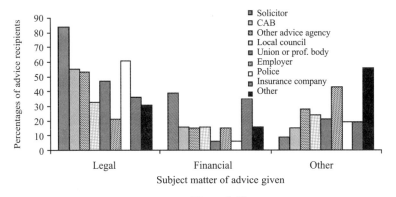

Figure 3.11
Final Advice Given by Adviser Type

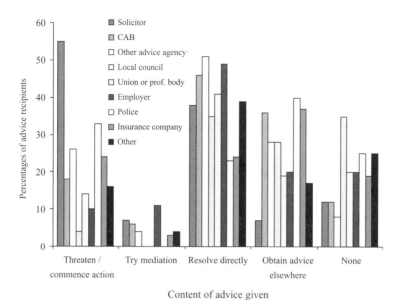

Figure 3.12
Content of Advice Given by Adviser Type

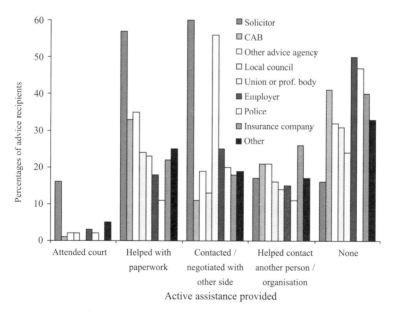

Figure 3.13
Content of Advice Given by Adviser Type

Reflecting the subject matter of advice they tended to provide, solicitors, the police and advice agencies most often suggested that respondents threaten or commence legal action. Indeed, solicitors suggested threatening or commencing legal action to over half of those to whom they provided advice, and the police to over one-third. To some extent this may have been a symptom of the predominantly legal focus of solicitors. For example, solicitors commenced legal proceedings on 24 per cent of occasions on which they were final advisers (compared to 11 per cent for other advisers),[296] and this accounted for 43 per cent of all occasions on which legal proceedings were commenced.[297] However, differences in the rates of invocation of legal processes may also have stemmed from the nature of problems that different types of adviser tended to deal with. So, as is illustrated in Figure 3.14, while solicitors suggested threatening or commencing legal action to over half their clients, and commenced proceedings for many of them, 34 per cent of their clients were facing one of the four problem types relating to relationships or children (41 per cent of those to whom the suggestion was made), and 16 per cent wished to, or were already, getting divorced (23 per cent of those to whom the suggestion was made). As divorce inherently involves formal court process, it could not be said that formal action was suggested in relation to it on account of solicitors being involved.[298] As with conveyancing,[299] therefore, it was often because formal legal process was required that respondents sought advice or assistance from solicitors, rather than vice versa. Overall, family problems accounted for 44 per cent of all instances of formal legal action.[300]

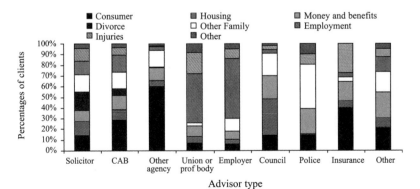

Figure 3.14
Problem Type by Adviser Type

Those occasions on which the police suggested that formal legal action should be threatened or commenced mostly involved domestic violence. It may be, however, that respondents were unclear as to the distinction between civil and criminal legal action, and thus reported suggestions or instances of criminal legal action as instances of civil legal action.

On occasion, solicitors, advice agencies and employers suggested that respondents try mediation or conciliation to resolve their problems (7 per cent, 5 per cent and 11 per cent respectively). For solicitors and advice agencies this tended to be in relation to family problems. For employers it tended to be in relation to employment problems. However, fewer than one-third of respondents to whom this was suggested went on to try mediation or conciliation, and none of them did so in relation to an employment problem. Thus, in total, mediation or conciliation was used in relation to 6 per cent of main interview family problems, and one-quarter of 1 per cent of non-family problems.[301] While the proportion of solicitors that suggested respondents try mediation is considerably higher than reported in *Paths to Justice*, our findings confirm, at least aside from in relation to family problems, where mediation has been enthusiastically promoted by the government and Legal Services Commission in recent years,[302] 'the very slight impact that [mediation and other alternatives to traditional methods of dispute resolution] have had on the thinking of advisers and, therefore, on the strategies adopted by the public for dealing with disputes'.[303]

Most types of adviser routinely suggested that respondents should try to resolve their problem by talking directly to the 'other side'. In all, 40 per cent of all advisers suggested this, and slightly more in the case of advice agencies, reflecting their common philosophy of 'empowering' clients to deal with their own problems. Only the police suggested this noticeably less often, most probably because of concerns about respondents' personal safety in relation to domestic violence.

Some advisers, particularly Citizens Advice Bureaux, the police and insurance companies also routinely referred respondents on to other advisers. This was most often to solicitors (37 per cent, 57 per cent and 55 per cent respectively), but was commonly also to specialist advice agencies (37 per cent, 21 per cent and 8 per cent respectively).

Overall, 31 per cent of all referrals were to solicitors. Consequently, 29 per cent of respondents who obtained advice from solicitors had been referred to them

76

from another adviser, and 36 per cent of those who obtained advice from advice agencies other than Citizens Advice Bureaux. The figure was just 3 per cent for Citizens Advice Bureaux, reflecting the generalist nature of their advice.[304]

Despite frequently benefiting from referrals, only 7 per cent of solicitors themselves referred respondents on to other advisers, and 40 per cent of the time this was to another solicitor or lawyer. Presumably the low referral rate associated with solicitors owes to their relative level of specialism. However, it might again indicate a relatively narrow focus on clients' legal positions; although much has been written about the fact that lawyers can spend a significant proportion of their time dealing with extra-legal matters. For example, Eekelaar, Maclean and Beinart have observed that family lawyers spend a great deal of time fulfilling the traditional roles of social worker and confidante.[305]

'Other' advisers, also, only infrequently referred respondents on (19 per cent). Given the broad range of such advisers, and the fact that many seemed unlikely sources of good advice, this is a cause for concern. It is also a cause for concern that, as can be seen from Figure 3.15, respondents referred on by 'other' advisers were the least likely to actually go on and obtain advice from another adviser. While those referred on to other advisers by Citizens Advice Bureaux, the police and local councils were very likely to obtain advice from the adviser to whom they had been

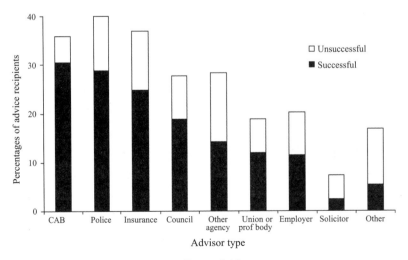

Figure 3.15
Success and Volume of Referrals by Adviser Type

referred, two-thirds of those referred by solicitors and 'other' advisers failed to obtain advice from the adviser to whom they had been referred. This may reflect in part respondents' expectations that Citizens Advice Bureaux, the police and local councils are sources of generalist *initial* advice – the place that you go when you cannot think of anywhere else to go – and that solicitors and 'other' advisers are sources of tailored and definitive advice. In the case of solicitors and 'other' advisers, respondents who were referred on may have felt they had been inappropriately 'unloaded' elsewhere. The difference in the rates of success of referrals may also reflect in part the relative experience of Citizens Advice Bureaux, the police and local councils in referring people on, or their better skill in doing so. Again, it may reflect in part the fact that advisers to whom solicitors and 'other' advisers referred respondents on to had a different profile, including more legal consultants, specialist advice agencies, and, in the case of 'other' advisers, Members of Parliament and local councillors. Finally, it may in part reflect the fact that solicitors and 'other' advisers became more prominent later on in sequences of advisers, and as Figure 3.16 illustrates, a phenomenon of referral fatigue meant that the likelihood of respondents obtaining advice from an adviser to whom they had been referred sharply declined as respondents visited more advisers.

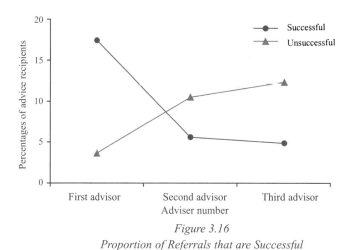

Figure 3.16
Proportion of Referrals that are Successful

The phenomenon of referral fatigue suggests a degree of exhaustion among members of the public as a result of being pushed from adviser to adviser that is consistent with the vivid descriptions reported in *Paths to Justice* of respondents having sometimes to make Herculean efforts to be seen by an adviser. It is perhaps not surprising that some respondents felt unable to maintain the necessary level of persistence and to invest the necessary amount of time to follow up repeated referrals in order to obtain the help they were looking for. In any event, the phenomenon of referral fatigue again demonstrates the importance of public education to create awareness among people of sources of help and assistance. Crucially, also, it demonstrates the importance of equipping those many individuals outside of the recognised advice sector from whom people may initially seek advice (such as health workers, social workers and politicians) with the means to effectively refer them on to appropriate advisers if necessary, both through professional education and through making appropriate advisers more accessible to those who are referred on to them.[306]

As well as providing general information and suggesting a course of action for respondents to take, many advisers also provided active assistance to them. Consistent with the concept of 'empowerment', Citizens Advice Bureaux were less likely than solicitors and other advice agencies to provide active assistance to respondents (Figure 3.13), although some active assistance was provided on around half of occasions. The same was also true of other common referring generalist advisers, such as employers and insurance companies.

Solicitors provided active assistance on 84 per cent of occasions. In particular, they took over direct negotiation or dealings with the 'other side' to a dispute and prepared, or helped in the preparation of, paperwork on the majority of occasions – especially if they were a respondent's final adviser. Trade unions and professional bodies also took over direct negotiation or dealings with the 'other side' (generally an employer) on the majority of occasions. Unsurprisingly, given the proportion of occasions on which they recommended legal action be threatened or taken, and the fact that they are legal professionals, solicitors attended court more frequently than other types of advisers. 'Other' advisers also, though, attended court relatively frequently, as well as often helping in the preparation of paperwork and with negotiations. Whether or not they had the training or experience to act as effective advisers, 'other' advisers actively supported those who sought advice from them on around two-thirds of occasions. Only solicitors, therefore, were more active in assisting respondents.

SATISFACTION WITH ADVISERS

Just over three-quarters of advisers were rated by respondents as being either helpful or very helpful. Consequently, respondents said that they would probably or definitely recommend a similar proportion of advisers to other people facing problems. However, there were differences in respondents' views of different adviser types. So, as is illustrated by Figure 3.17, whereas Citizens Advice Bureaux and solicitors were said to have been helpful or very helpful around 90 per cent of the time, employers were said to have been helpful or very helpful under 50 per cent of the time. Despite the concerns we have raised about 'other' advisers, they were regarded as having been helpful or very helpful more often than employers, local councils, insurance companies, the police and trade unions and professional bodies. This may, though, have been a consequence of the active support they frequently provided to respondents, and does not necessarily indicate that they were effective in the advice and assistance they offered. Offering help as regards the means to an end does not always equate to being helpful as regards the end itself.[307] It may be for this reason that respondents said that they would probably or definitely recommend trade unions and the police (89 per cent and 81 per cent respectively) more often than 'other'

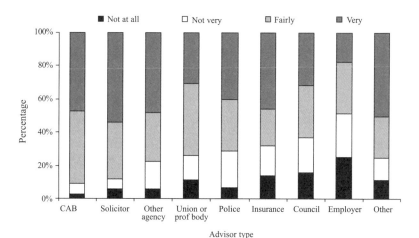

Figure 3.17
Helpfulness of Advisers

advisers (75 per cent), notwithstanding the fact that they found them to be less 'helpful'.

As well as levels of dissatisfaction, causes of dissatisfaction with advisers varied somewhat depending on the type of adviser.[308] Overall, 54 per cent of causes involved respondents regarding advisers as having not provided the 'type of help' that they 'needed', 34 per cent involved the quality of advice, 17 per cent involved respondents having been 'just sent off somewhere else', 6 per cent involved advisers having been 'not up to date', 6 per cent involved cost, and 5 per cent involved respondents having been told that nothing could be done. Local councils were most often regarded as having not provided the type of help needed (74 per cent), although this was not statistically significant.[309] In contrast, however, local councils were significantly less likely than other types of adviser to have been criticised for providing poor quality advice (16 per cent), while advice agencies (other than Citizens Advice Bureaux) were more likely than others to have been so criticised (68 per cent). Citizens Advice Bureaux, though, were more likely than other types of adviser to have been regarded as not up to date (25 per cent). Trade unions and professional bodies and insurance companies were more likely than other types of adviser to have been criticised for having told respondents that nothing could be done to resolve their problems (15 per cent and 25 per cent respectively). Solicitors were most likely to have been criticised for being too expensive (21 per cent), although insurance companies, the other main type of commercial advice provider, were also criticised for being too expensive more often than others (19 per cent).[310] Finally, solicitors were least likely to have been criticised for sending respondents elsewhere (0 per cent), reflecting their low referral rate.[311]

The position of advisers in sequences of advisers made no difference to respondents' views on their helpfulness or whether they would be recommended to others.

THE COST OF ADVICE

75 per cent of those respondents who obtained advice to deal with a justiciable problem did not have to pay any of the cost involved. Two-thirds of these respondents described the advice they obtained as 'free', and one-third described it as involving costs that were met by a range of third parties. 33 per cent of respondents whose costs

were met in full by a third party received legal aid, 26 per cent had costs met by a trade union or professional body, 18 per cent were covered by legal expenses insurance, 12 per cent had costs met by their employer, and 10 per cent obtained advice under a conditional fee agreement (although one-quarter of these respondents were unsure about this). 6 per cent had their costs met by some other person or organisation (mostly friends, partners and relatives[312]), and a similar percentage received financial assistance from more than one of the above sources.[313]

Of the 8 per cent of respondents who obtained advice and paid some of the cost involved, 40 per cent received legal aid, 13 per cent obtained advice under a conditional fee agreement, 5 per cent had the remainder of the cost met by their employer, 3 per cent were part-covered by legal expenses insurance, and the remaining 39 per cent had the remainder of the cost met by some other person or organisation. 17 per cent of respondents who obtained advice paid all the costs involved.

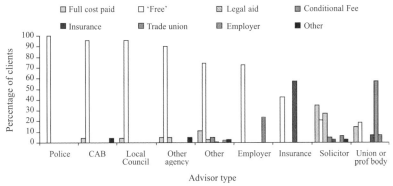

Figure 3.18
Source of Funding by Adviser Type (One Adviser Only)

As is illustrated by Figures 3.18 and 3.19, whether advice was 'free' and, if not, who ultimately met its cost varied by adviser and problem type.

Evidently, advice that was provided through charities or services funded through taxation was generally described as 'free', although legal aid funding was often recognised.[314] In contrast, advice obtained by virtue of insurance cover or union membership, where premiums or subscriptions would have been paid, was unlikely to be described as 'free'; although it was occasionally, no doubt by respondents who regarded it as a free benefit running alongside other paid services. Legal expenses insurance, for example, is often attached to general household insurance.[315]

Solicitors were sometimes described as providing 'free' advice, which most likely comprised advice provided through community 'open evenings', legal aid funded advice that was not recognised as such, and free initial consultations following which respondents went elsewhere, handled their problems alone, or took no further action.[316] They were also, though, most often described as providing services the cost of which respondents met in full (35 per cent).

Where trade unions and insurance companies were described as both funding and providing advice, it is likely that on many occasions advice was actually provided by a solicitor, either via a telephone help line or in person.[317] Respondents presumably would have regarded such solicitors, if they were aware that they were solicitors, as employees of the union or insurance company, or as 'their solicitor'.

The fact that solicitors and 'other' advisers, specifically claims agencies, occasionally provided assistance under conditional fee agreements (5 per cent and 5 per cent respectively), reflects the fact that these types of adviser commonly deal with personal injury problems (Figure 3.14). As can be seen from Figure 3.19, advice relating to personal injuries was provided under conditional fees 27 per cent of the time. This percentage will have probably risen, though, since the period covered by the LSRC survey, as it extended back to before the date that personal injury claims were removed from the scope of legal aid.[318] Also, conditional fees were only introduced in England and Wales in 1995, so the impact of their introduction on the advice and legal services market is still being felt.[319]

There were no occasions on which the cost of advice concerning a personal injury problem was reported as having been met in full by a respondent. In addition to conditional fee agreements, respondents reported their costs being met by legal expenses insurance on 31 per cent of occasions, trade unions on 13 per cent of occasions, employers on 8 per cent of occasions and legal aid on 5 per cent of occasions. They also reported receiving 'free' advice on 18 per cent of occasions, some of which may, of course, actually have been funded by one or other of the above. There were also no occasions on which the cost of advice in relation to welfare benefits problems, homelessness or mental health problems was met in full by a respondent. On 83 per cent of occasions advice about welfare benefits was described as having been 'free'; the highest percentage for any type of problem. In relation to homelessness and mental health problems, advice was either described as 'free' or as funded by legal aid. However, the numbers were very small in each case.[320]

In addition, fewer than a quarter of respondents who obtained advice relating to rented housing, consumer, children, clinical negligence, discrimination, employment, domestic violence and money/debt problems reported having met the cost of the advice they received in full. In respect of all these problem types, advice was described as 'free' more often than not.

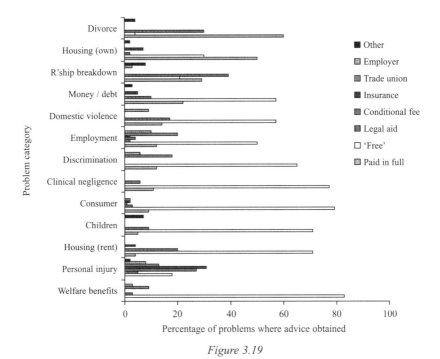

Figure 3.19
Source of Funding by Problem Type

Unsurprisingly, the cost of advice concerning employment, discrimination and welfare benefits problems, was often met by trade unions.[321] Such costs were also sometimes met by employers, as were costs incurred in relation to advice concerning family problems, reflecting the fact that general advice facilities are arranged by some employers for their employees.

Where advice concerning domestic violence was provided by a solicitor, costs were met by legal aid on one-third of occasions.

Advice obtained in relation to divorce and owned housing problems was most likely to be paid for in full by respondents (60 per cent and 50 per cent respectively), and if this was the case, advice was invariably obtained from solicitors.[322] It was also quite common for advice obtained in relation to problems ancillary to relationship breakdown to be paid for in full by respondents (29 per cent), although the cost of such advice was more often met by legal aid (39 per cent). Legal aid was also common in relation to divorce (30 per cent), rented housing (20 per cent), money/debt (10 per cent), and children problems (9 per cent).

In part reflecting the fact that both legal aid funded advice and privately funded advice were principally associated with solicitors and family problems, there was evidence that both were more likely than 'free' and otherwise funded advice to be obtained in relation to more serious problems. Solicitors were more likely than other adviser types to deal with problems involving larger sums of money, and, also, they were more likely to deal with problems that could be recalled after longer periods of time.[323] Family problems were also more likely to be recalled after longer periods of time.[324] So, legal aid funded advice and privately funded advice were more likely than 'free' or otherwise funded advice to be obtained in relation to problems involving larger sums of money[325] and problems that could be recalled after longer periods of time.[326]

We found no significant differences between the stated importance of problems funded from different sources, with the single exception of those funded by conditional fees, which were less often described as having been 'very important' to resolve.[327]

INACTION, ACTION, ADVICE AND TEMPORARY ACCOMMODATION

Respondents to the parallel survey of people living in temporary accommodation reported having taken no action to deal with problems on 28 per cent of all occasions; far more often than did respondents to the LSRC survey. However, they were much more likely to have sought advice if action was taken, with 95 per cent of them (68 per cent overall) having done so; although only around three-quarters of them were successful in doing so (74 per cent, 53 per cent overall). Because of the very different pattern of problems reported by those in temporary accommodation, and their very different social and demographic profile,[328] it is not surprising that the strategies they adopted were also different.

Again, strategy varied considerably by problem type.[329] Owing to the size of the sample of people living in temporary accommodation, it was not possible to usefully examine strategy at the individual problem type level. However, using a simple test of correlation, we were able to determine that the problem types that were associated with higher and lower rates of inaction were similar for temporary accommodation respondents and LSRC survey respondents.[330] Thus, temporary accommodation respondents very often took action to deal with immigration and homelessness problems (8 per cent and 10 per cent did nothing respectively), and very often took no action to deal with domestic violence and problems relating to unfair police treatment (55 per cent and 50 per cent did nothing respectively).

Again, also, the most common reason for respondents not acting to resolve problems was that they did not think that anything could be done. However, temporary accommodation respondents were significantly more likely than LSRC survey respondents to provide this reason (49 per cent compared to 31 per cent),[331] and this was not just a consequence of the very different pattern of problems they experienced. When we controlled for problem type the significance of the difference increased.[332] They were also significantly more likely to report that they took no action because they were scared to act (13 per cent compared to 6 per cent),[333] although in this instance the difference was not significant once problem type was controlled for.[334] Conversely, temporary accommodation respondents less often reported that they regarded problems as insufficiently important to warrant action (6 per cent compared to 12 per cent), although this finding was not quite significant,[335] and was even less so once problem type was controlled for.[336] The finding was, though, consistent with the notion, expounded elsewhere in this book, that the problems faced by respondents to the temporary accommodation survey tended to be of a more serious nature than those faced by respondents to the LSRC survey.

The problem types that were associated with higher and lower rates of advice seeking on the part of respondents who took action were also similar for temporary accommodation and LSRC survey respondents.[337] Thus, all of those temporary accommodation respondents who took action to deal with domestic violence or a divorce obtained advice, and just 30 per cent of those who took action to deal with a consumer problem obtained advice.

As regards the sources from which temporary accommodation respondents sought advice, they were much more likely than LSRC survey respondents to have obtained advice from local councils (30 per cent compared to 8 per cent); reflecting in part the disproportionately great number of rented housing and welfare benefits problems that they faced.[338] However, even when problem type was controlled for, this difference remained,[339] suggesting that temporary accommodation respondents had a tendency to regard local councils as appropriate sources of advice across a broad range of subjects, and/or that temporary accommodation respondents sought advice from local councils because they were familiar with them (perhaps because advice was obtained from them in relation to earlier housing and benefits problems). In this latter case, such behaviour could constitute another example of the entrenchment of problem resolution strategies.

Also, reflecting in part the fact that temporary accommodation respondents were much more often economically inactive, they were less likely to have obtained advice from employers (0 per cent compared to 5 per cent) or trade unions or professional bodies (1 per cent compared to 7 per cent).[340] In the case of trade unions, though, the difference was not significant once problem type was controlled for, perhaps because trade unions predominantly provided advice in relation to employment problems, which were mostly experienced by those who were economically active.[341]

Lastly, in part reflecting the disproportionately lesser number of family problems that they faced, temporary accommodation respondents were less likely to have obtained advice from a solicitor (18 per cent compared to 26 per cent).[342] However, they were also less likely to have obtained advice from a solicitor when problem type was controlled for.[343] So, it seems that those in temporary accommodation are less likely, whatever the circumstances, to obtain advice from a solicitor.

SUMMARY

No action was taken to resolve one-fifth of justiciable problems reported through the LSRC survey. Often this was because problems were regarded as insufficiently important to warrant action, because there had been no dispute involved and nobody regarded as having been in the wrong, or because action became unnecessary as a result of activity on the part of others. However, despite the fact that the judgement was made without the benefit of advice, inaction most often resulted from a belief that nothing could be done, indicating a lack of knowledge about obligations, rights remedies and procedures on the part of the general public. Of even more concern, respondents sometimes reported having taken no action because they were too scared to act. This was as common a reason for inaction as concerns about the time it can take to resolve problems, and a more common reason than concerns about cost.

Reasons for inaction varied significantly by problem type. So, for example, respondents who did not act were most likely to believe nothing could be done to resolve mental health and discrimination problems, and were most likely to report they had been scared to act to resolve problems relating to neighbours and domestic violence. Concerns about cost were most likely to be reported by those who did nothing to resolve problems ancillary to relationship breakdown. The proportion of occasions on which no action was taken also varied by problem type, with those who faced problems relating to mental health, clinical negligence, unfair treatment by the police and domestic violence having been least likely to take action to resolve them. In addition, economic circumstances, gender and ethnicity all influenced the likelihood of action having been taken.

When action was taken to resolve justiciable problems, just under two-thirds of respondents reported that they sought formal advice to assist them. The remainder handled their problems alone; although sometimes this involved obtaining information from printed literature or the internet, or support from friends and family, or, on very rare occasions, commencing proceedings in a court or tribunal, use of an Ombudsman or mediation. Again, problem type had most influence on whether respondents obtained formal advice. However, different problem types were associated with seeking advice, as compared to simply taking action. Economic circumstances, level of qualifications and previously adopted strategies also influenced the likelihood of advice having been obtained, as did the seriousness of the problems faced.

Those who sought advice did so from a wide range of types of adviser. However, over one-sixth of those who sought advice were unsuccessful in obtaining it. In part because different types of adviser were used in relation to different problem types, different rates of success were also associated with different problem types.

The most frequent reason given for an attempt to obtain advice having been unsuccessful was that an adviser had been unable to provide any help, followed by difficulty getting through on the telephone, waiting too long to see an adviser and receiving no reply to a letter. However, the reasons given for attempts to obtain advice having been unsuccessful varied by adviser type. For example, unsuccessful attempts to obtain advice from Citizens Advice Bureaux were more likely than unsuccessful attempts to obtain advice from elsewhere to be due to problems getting through to an adviser.

There was evidence that advice services operating on a commercial basis presented fewer physical obstacles to those seeking to use them. The ease of use of insurance companies' legal help lines and the geographical distribution of solicitors firms were both factors in this. However, following initial contact being made with an adviser, the picture changed somewhat, non-commercial generalist advisers were more likely to be able to provide help than, say, insurance company help lines.

Highlighting the significance of the telephone in the provision of easily accessible advice and assistance, initial contact was often made by telephone even when advice was ultimately provided face-to-face. Thus, half of respondents' unsuccessful attempts to obtain advice were via the telephone. Difficulties experienced in telephoning advisers were sometimes compounded by the hours of operation of advice services being limited to normal working hours.

Two-thirds of respondents who unsuccessfully attempted to obtain advice to help deal with a problem tried, in any event, to resolve it alone. The remaining one-third gave up trying to resolve it. Of those respondents who successfully obtained advice, around half did so from just one adviser, around one-third from two advisers, and the remainder from three or more advisers. Where respondents obtained advice from sequences of advisers, different patterns of types of adviser were associated with earlier and later points in them, reflecting in part a progression from generalist to specialist advisers, but also apparent confusion on the part of many respondents as they tried to navigate the advice maze. Confusion was, for example, indicated by the great range of advisers used by respondents facing some types of problem and, also, by the fact that three-quarters of respondents who obtained advice from 'other' advisers in the first instance obtained advice from nowhere else, despite the fact that the great majority of such sources were generalist in character, and many seemed unlikely sources of good advice. Some other first advisers also seemed inappropriate for the problem in question. In addition, confusion, and even desperation, was indicated by second advisers having been more often friends or relatives of respondents than first advisers and, also, by a number of respondents appearing to have obtained advice, in the first instance, from the 'other side' to disputes.

Despite the apparent confusion and desperation of some respondents in navigating the advice maze, the fit of advisers to problem type was generally seemingly appropriate. Indeed, in relation to some problem types respondents seemed quite clear as to the most appropriate source of advice.

The substance of advice and assistance offered to respondents by different types of adviser varied greatly. In terms of the subject matter of advice, solicitors, the police and advice agencies most often explored respondents' legal positions, solicitors and insurance companies most often explored respondents' financial positions, and employers and 'other' advisers most often explored other matters. Reflecting the subject matter of advice they tended to provide, solicitors (especially), the police and advice agencies most often suggested that respondents threaten or commence legal action. With regard to solicitors, this may to some extent have been a symptom of their predominantly legal focus. It may also, though, have stemmed from the nature of problems that solicitors dealt with. One-third of their clients were facing family type problems, which together accounted for 44 per cent of all instances of formal legal action. Overall, mediation and conciliation were suggested rarely and fewer than one-third of respondents to whom they were suggested went on to try them.

Most types of adviser routinely suggested that respondents should try to resolve their problem by talking directly to the 'other side', and some, like Citizens Advice Bureaux, routinely referred respondents on to other advisers. Although almost one-third of all referrals were to solicitors, solicitors themselves rarely referred respondents on to other advisers; presumably owing to their relatively high level of specialism. However, their low referral rate may also again indicate a relatively narrow focus on clients' legal positions. 'Other' advisers, also, only infrequently referred respondents on to other advisers, and, worryingly, more than two-thirds of those referred on by such advisers failed to go on and obtain advice from the adviser to whom they had been referred.

In analysing referral patterns we found clear evidence of a phenomenon of referral fatigue. This involved the likelihood of respondents obtaining advice from an adviser to whom they had been referred sharply declining as respondents visited more advisers. The phenomenon demonstrates the importance of equipping those from whom people initially seek advice with the means to quickly and effectively refer them on when necessary.

Specialist advice providers were more likely than generalist advice providers to provide active assistance to respondents and, unsurprisingly, solicitors attended court more frequently than other types of advisers. 'Other' advisers also, though, attended court relatively frequently. In fact, whether or not they had the training or experience to act as effective advisers, only solicitors were more active in assisting respondents than 'other' advisers.

Around three-quarters of advisers appear to have been regarded by respondents as satisfactory. However, there were differences in respondents' views of different adviser types, with solicitors and Citizens Advice Bureaux the most favoured.

Around three-quarters of respondents who obtained advice paid none of the cost involved. The majority of these respondents described the advice they obtained as 'free', and the remainder described it as involving costs that were met by a range of third parties; most frequently the Legal Services Commission, a trade union, or a legal expenses insurer. Conditional fee agreements were entered into by 10 per cent of these respondents. Fewer than one-fifth of respondents who obtained advice paid all the costs involved.

Whether advice was 'free' and, if not, who ultimately met the cost varied by adviser and problem type. Also, it appeared to vary by seriousness of problem. There was evidence that legal aid and privately funded advice were more likely than 'free' and otherwise funded advice to be obtained in relation to more serious problems.

Finally, respondents to the temporary accommodation survey reported having taken no action far more often than did respondents to the LSRC survey, and they were also significantly more likely to not act because they thought nothing could be done. Nevertheless, problem types that were associated with higher and lower rates of inaction were similar in both surveys. The problem types that were associated with higher and lower rates of advice seeking on the part of respondents who took action were also similar. However, those in temporary accommodation were more likely to obtain advice when they took action to deal with problems. Interestingly, when they did obtain advice, they were more likely to obtain advice from local councils. This may have been because local councils were familiar to them from earlier problems relating to housing and benefits. If this is so, it provides another example of the entrenchment of a problem resolution strategy.

4

The End: Objectives, and How and When Justiciable Problems Conclude

This chapter sets out the range of objectives that motivate people to act to resolve justiciable problems. Using information obtained from main interviews, it illustrates the different objectives associated with different problem types, problem resolution strategies, advisers and population groups. In so doing, it describes how objectives vary along with the consequences of problems, and confirms the triggering effect of some problem types. It then details the ways in which problems conclude, and the extent to which people obtain their objectives. It points to evidence that those who are represented before courts and tribunals fare better than those who are not, and also that objectives are more often met in relation to the most important problems. The chapter then explains how the duration of problems varies by problem and adviser type, and also, seemingly, by seriousness. Lastly, it shows that although people can greatly benefit from taking action to resolve justiciable problems, the resolution process can be stressful and even bring about ill-health.

OBJECTIVES

There is a broad range of objectives that motivate people to act to resolve justiciable problems. People can, for example, be motivated by a sense of injustice, a desire to put right something that has gone wrong or a desire to prevent something that has gone wrong from again going wrong.[344] Evidently, also, people can be motivated by money or property. Indeed, supporting earlier findings, just over half of those LSRC survey respondents who took action to resolve a problem stated, in the main interview, that they had a money or property related objective (55 per cent),[345] although one in ten such respondents had a further objective not related to either money or property. Of course, in the most part objectives are determined by problem type.[346]

We used binary logistic regression to test the influence of problem type, problem resolution strategy and a range of social and demographic predictors on the likelihood of respondents having reported a money or property related objective. Technical details are set out at Appendix B.

Problem type was the most influential predictor, and objectives in acting to resolve welfare benefits, consumer, personal injury and money and debt problems were most likely to relate to money or property. In relation to personal injury problems, our finding reflects people's general understanding that compensation is payable in relation to negligent accidents.

When objectives related to money, a lump sum was in issue on 81 per cent of occasions. However, a chi-squared test indicated that although periodic payments were rarely in issue in the case of consumer (0 per cent), personal injury (6 per cent) and money and debt problems (8 per cent), they were the norm in the case of welfare benefits problems (70 per cent).[347] They were also the most common form of monetary objective in the case of family problems (51 per cent),[348] reflecting relatively frequent disputes relating to maintenance payments. When objectives related to a lump sum of money, the sum was £100 or less on 20 per cent of occasions, £1,000 or less on 56 per cent of occasions, and greater than £5,000 on just 17 per cent of occasions.[349] However, sums varied by problem type.[350] Thus, whereas 71 per cent of consumer problems related to a sum of £1,000 or less, 87 per cent of personal injury problems related to a sum greater than £1,000, and 82 per cent of divorce and relationship breakdown problems related to a sum greater than £5,000.[351]

The fact that a justiciable problem involves a sum of £100 or less does not, of course, mean that the problem is trivial. As well as the lingering sense of injustice or betrayal of trust that can accompany justiciable problems (which can on their own introduce importance to even small value disputes), for those with little disposable income even £50 can represent a substantial loss or gain. Consistent with this, we found that the sum involved in disputes correlated with household income.[352]

Unsurprisingly, as is illustrated in Figure 4.1, rented housing (31 per cent) and consumer problems (25 per cent) most often had specific property related, as opposed to or in addition to money related, objectives.[353]

Objectives in acting to resolve problems concerning clinical negligence, children, domestic violence, divorce, discrimination, unfair police treatment and immigration were least likely to relate to money or property.[354] As regards clinical negligence, this was despite the fact that such problems are often seen as akin to personal injury problems.[355] As we have reported elsewhere, though, this supports earlier findings that suggest, at least in relation to less serious episodes of clinical negligence, that people are most concerned to understand what has happened to them, obtain remedial treatment, prevent recurrences or obtain recognition of a mistake and an apology.[356] In fact, just 2 of 36 respondents who stated their objectives in acting to resolve a problem concerning clinical negligence referred to money or property.

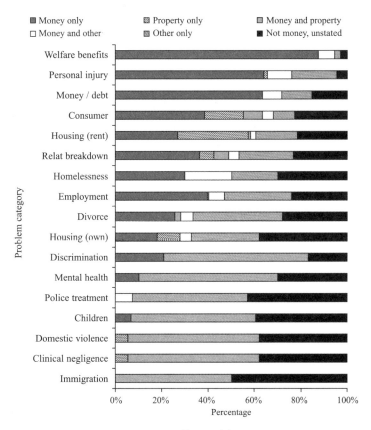

Figure 4.1
Objectives by Problem Type

Objectives that did not relate to money or property were sometimes specific to particular types of problem, reflecting the different consequences of different problem types.[357] So, for example, 73 per cent of respondents who acted to enforce, or have acknowledged, their rights had faced money/debt problems or unfair treatment by the police.[358] Over half of respondents who acted to secure job related objectives had faced employment problems, and most of the remainder had faced problems relating to discrimination, personal injury or immigration.[359] This demonstrates again the potential knock-on effect of problems such as those relating to personal injury, and supports the findings in chapter 2 that personal injury problems are linked to employment problems and, in general, increase the likelihood of additional problems. Also, over half of those who acted to prevent problems recurring had faced problems relating to personal injury or clinical negligence.[360]

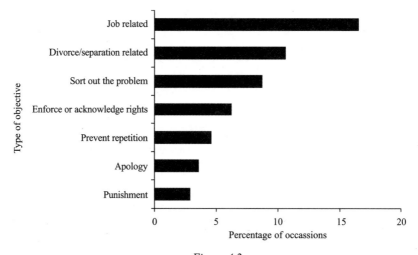

Figure 4.2
Objectives Not Related to Money or Property

As well as those who faced particular types of problem, binary logistic regression also indicated that respondents in receipt of welfare benefits, those who were lone parents and those who were seeking something from someone else, rather than having something sought from them, were less likely to act to secure objectives relating to money or property.

Furthermore, it indicated money or property related objectives were more likely among those who sought advice, as compared to those who handled their problems alone.[361] There are a number of potential explanations for this. It may be that people are less clear about how to secure money or property related objectives than other objectives. It may be that people regard advice as more effective in securing money or property related objectives. It may be that advisers introduce money or property dimensions to problems that were previously unrecognised. It may be that advisers tend to define problems in money or property terms. It may also be that people regard money or property related objectives as more important than other objectives. However, while most of these explanations are consistent with our findings, the last is not. Overall, respondents were significantly more likely to report problems that were acted upon to secure non-money or property related objectives as being 'very important' to sort out.[362]

However, not all types of adviser were associated with money or property related objectives. The likelihood of respondents who ultimately sought advice from local councils, employers or the police having had money or property related objectives was no different from the likelihood of those who handled problems alone having had such objectives. It was only respondents who ultimately sought advice from other types of adviser, especially insurance companies and advice agencies, who were significantly more likely to have had money or property related objectives than those who handled their problems alone. Interestingly, though, respondents who ultimately sought advice from solicitors, Citizens Advice Bureaux, trade unions and 'other' advisers were only observed to be more likely to have had such objectives once other factors, such as problem type, were accounted for. So, for example, overall, 46 per cent of the problems solicitors dealt with concerned money or property, compared to 45 per cent of problems respondents handled alone. Many of the problems solicitors dealt with, though, concerned family matters (34 per cent), and relatively few concerned debt or welfare benefits (10 per cent).

MANNERS OF CONCLUSION

36 per cent of problems discussed in the main interview were on-going, although respondents were continuing to try to resolve only four-fifths of them. No attempt had

been made, or an attempt had been abandoned, to resolve the remaining one-fifth of on-going problems.

Of those problems that had concluded, 64 per cent were resolved by agreement between the parties,[363] 5 per cent by adjudication,[364] and 1 per cent on their own. Seemingly, no attempt had been made (5 per cent),[365] or an attempt had been abandoned (25 per cent), to resolve the remaining 30 per cent.[366] This 30 per cent comprised problems described by respondents as having concluded without agreement or adjudication. Consistent with the fact that more of those who sought advice than those who handled problems alone described problems in this way,[367] this may sometimes have been due to respondents having had few or no grounds to pursue their objectives. One of the benefits of advice can be to prevent people from wasting time and resources in relation to problems that are unlikely to be resolved to their benefit. Thus, not all abandoned attempts to resolve problems necessarily involved injustice. However, as the problems respondents sometimes faced in obtaining advice described in the previous chapter suggest, some respondents will no doubt have abandoned trying to resolve problems simply because it became too difficult for them to continue their efforts, and injustice may have then been the consequence. There was some evidence, for example, that respondents became more likely to give up dealing with problems as the number of advisers from whom they sought advice increased. This, though, is also consistent with the possibility that some respondents sought advice from multiple sources because initial advice did not support their cause.

Raising concerns about the ability of some people to enforce adjudications in their favour, 2 respondents who 'won' in court, subsequently gave up trying to resolve their problems and described them in interview as on-going. Both problems were related to disputes ancillary to relationship breakdown.

Unsurprisingly, the manner of conclusion of problems varied by problem type.[368] For example, family problems – and particularly divorce – appeared more likely than most other problem types to be resolved by adjudication.[369] So, 11 per cent of relationship breakdown and domestic violence problems were resolved by adjudication, compared to 2 per cent of non-family problems. Consistent with the findings of *Paths to Justice*, apart from divorce, only welfare benefits problems were more likely to be adjudicated (13 per cent).[370] Consumer problems and employment problems were least likely to be adjudicated.[371]The latter were, instead, associated with the greatest likelihood that resolving action would be abandoned. Problems that respondents attempted to resolve on their own were also less likely to be resolved by adjudication.[372]

At best, 73 per cent of respondents who took action to deal with justiciable problems secured at least some of their objectives, and 54 per cent secured all their objectives. However, if it were assumed that those respondents who did not state whether or not their objectives were met and who reported that their problems concluded without agreement or adjudication were unsuccessful in securing whatever objectives they may have had, then these figures reduced to 52 per cent and 39 per cent respectively.[373] However looked at, though, those respondents who reported that their problem concluded without agreement or adjudication were far and away the least likely to secure their objectives.[374]

There was no difference in the rates at which objectives were met between problems resolved by adjudication or agreement.[375] There was evidence, though, that those respondents who were represented at a court or tribunal fared better than those who were unrepresented, although this finding was just short of being statistically significant.[376] Whereas 73 per cent of those respondents who were represented at a court or tribunal hearing at which a decision was made reported that they had 'won', only 55 per cent of those respondents who were unrepresented did so. This is in keeping with findings such as those of Genn and Genn in relation to representation before tribunals.[377] Unsurprisingly, those who 'won' at a court or tribunal were much more likely to have regarded the process as fair (92 per cent compared to 18 per cent).[378] Similarly, those who obtained their objectives through an agreement were more likely to regard the process as fair (88 per cent compared to 55 per cent).[379] Demonstrating that the process of attempting to achieve a resolution of justiciable problems takes 'quite a toll'[380] on people, the most common reasons given for respondents having entered into unfair agreements were that they would have found it 'too stressful to go on' and that they 'just wanted to bring the problem to an end' (30 per cent and 51 per cent respectively[381]).

Overall, there was no significant difference in the rate at which objectives were met between those who obtained advice and those who did not. However, as was demonstrated in chapter 2, the nature of those problems in relation to which respondents sought advice was very different to that of those problems respondents dealt with alone. This meant it was not possible to compare like with like. Also, as we were not able to objectively ascertain quality of advice, we would not in any event have been able to compare the outcome of problems in relation to which good advice was obtained and problems in relation to which no advice was obtained. It seems self-evident, though, that people are better placed to deal with problems if they have an understanding of their position and options for action, and good advice provides such an understanding.

Despite it not being possible to objectively determine quality of advice, there was evidence that respondents whose advice was funded by legal aid were more likely than others who obtained advice to secure some or all of their objectives.[382] Numbers were, though, quite small.[383]

Perhaps reflecting their greater determination, respondents who described their problem as 'very important' to sort out were more likely than others to achieve their objectives.[384] Also, there was evidence that respondents seeking non-monetary objectives were more likely to obtain them, at least in part.[385]

DURATION

While most justiciable problems conclude within a short period of time, some continue over many years. A small number may even conclude only following the death of those involved.[386] So, while 52 per cent of concluded problems reported through the LSRC survey had a duration of 3 months or less, 21 per cent had a duration of a year or more, and 2 per cent of 5 years or more. 10 concluded problems ($^{1}/_{2}$ per cent) continued for more than 10 years; the longest running of which – an employment problem concerning equal pay[387] – took 20 years and 8 months to conclude.[388] The average problem duration was around 8 months and 2 weeks.

Using information derived from screen interviews, we employed univariate analysis of covariance (ANCOVA) to test the influence of problem type, problem resolution strategy and the use of formal dispute resolution processes on problem duration. Technical details are set out at Appendix B.

Three of the four family problem types, along with problems relating to neighbours, were found to have been likely to last longer than other problem types.[389] So, as can be seen from Figure 4.3, relationship breakdown, divorce, domestic violence and neighbours problems all lasted, on average, for more than a year. Problems relating to children and immigration and nationality also lasted, on average, for more than a year, but because numbers were small, these were not statistically significant findings.

The analysis of covariance also indicated that problems in relation to which respondents sought advice were likely to have lasted longer than others, particularly if advice was sought from multiple sources. So, when respondents sought advice from multiple sources problems lasted 12 months, when they sought advice from one source problems lasted 10 months, and when they handled problems alone they lasted 6 months, on average. Interestingly, though, problems of different duration were associated with different types of adviser. When respondents sought advice from only a solicitor or a Citizens Advice Bureau, problems were no different in duration to those that were handled alone or in relation to which nothing was done. For other types of adviser, problem duration was significantly greater. That is not to say that

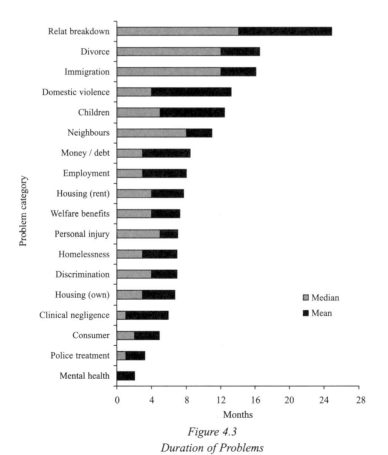

Figure 4.3
Duration of Problems

when respondents sought advice from only a solicitor the average duration of problems was 6 months; it was 11 months. However, much of the additional duration can be explained by the problem types that solicitors dealt with (e.g. divorce and relationship breakdown), and the common use they made of legal processes, which were also, unsurprisingly, found to be associated with problems that lasted longer (15 months on average). When respondents sought advice from only a Citizens Advice Bureau, problems on average lasted 7 months.

As with legal process, the use of an Ombudsman in resolving problems appeared to increase problem duration. Thus, when an Ombudsman was used, problems on average lasted 20 months. However, no increase in duration was observed in relation to mediation or conciliation. Nevertheless, because mediation and conciliation were most frequently used in relation to family problems, mediated or conciliated problems on average lasted 14 months.

Each of the problem types, problem resolution strategies and processes associated with problems of longer duration have been identified above as associated with relatively serious problems,[390] and so our findings relating to duration may be a reflection of a more fundamental link between problem duration and problem seriousness. We therefore used information derived from main interviews to investigate further the possible nature of such a link. As anticipated, when problems concerned money their duration correlated significantly with the sum involved.[391] Thus, whereas concluded problems that involved a sum of less than £1,000 had an average duration of 5 months, those that involved a sum of £10,000 had an average duration of 25 months. However, we found no significant difference between the average duration of problems respondents regarded as having been very important to sort out, and those they regarded as less important to sort out. Those who had taken no action to resolve problems, though, were not asked about how important they had been to resolve.[392]

UNINTENDED CONSEQUENCES

As was suggested above, the process of attempting to resolve justiciable problems can be stressful. Indeed, 59 per cent of respondents who made such an attempt described it as having been stressful. Furthermore, one-quarter of these respondents also said that their health had suffered as a result. Thus, not only can justiciable problems directly bring about ill-health, they can also indirectly bring about ill-health through the problem resolution process. Nevertheless, almost half of those respondents who said that acting to resolve problems had been stressful or had brought about ill-health also said that they were glad that they had 'stuck up' for themselves. This was, though, a smaller percentage than for respondents who had not found acting to resolve problems stressful or a cause of ill-health (47 per cent compared to 62 per cent).[393]

Respondents were less likely to report having become stressed or ill while attempting to resolve problems they did not regard as 'very important' to sort out.[394] Consequently, they were also less likely to report having become ill while attempting to resolve problems alone.[395] However, they were not significantly less likely to become stressed while attempting to resolve problems alone[396] This suggests that advisers may alleviate some of the stress of resolving problems by, for example, taking away some of the responsibility for progressing matters, removing the need to deal directly with other parties to disputes, providing emotional support, or, simply, by allowing those who experience problems to talk about them in an uncritical environment.[397]

Unsurprisingly, respondents were more likely to report that their health suffered through resolving problems that took longer to resolve. So, whereas ill-health was reported in relation to 14 per cent of problems that lasted for more than 2 years, it was reported in relation to just 7 per cent of problems that lasted for less than a year.[398] Also, respondents who failed to obtain their objectives in acting to resolve justiciable problems were more likely to report that their health suffered.[399] Lastly, respondents whose objectives in acting to resolve problems had been non-monetary were more likely to report that their health suffered.[400]

SUMMARY

There are many objectives that motivate people to act to resolve justiciable problems. Often, though, objectives have a monetary dimension. Thus, just over half of those respondents who took action to resolve a problem stated that they had a money or property related objective. Although monetary objectives often involved relatively small sums, this did not mean they were unimportant. Sums correlated with household income. They also varied by problem type, as did the nature of objectives in general.

Money or property related objectives were more likely among those who sought advice than those who handled their problems alone. This may indicate that people regard advice as more effective in securing such objectives. It may also, though, indicate that advisers introduce money and property dimensions to problems that were previously unrecognised, or that advisers tend to define problems in money or property terms. Although we found no significant difference between the likelihood of respondents who ultimately sought advice from local councils, employers or the police and the likelihood of those who handled their problems alone having had money or property objectives, those who ultimately sought advice from other types of adviser, especially insurance companies and advice agencies, were significantly more likely to have had such objectives.

Just over one-third of problems were on-going at the time of interview, although respondents were sometimes no longer trying to resolve them. Of those problems that had concluded, just under two-thirds were resolved by agreement between the parties. One in twenty were resolved by adjudication. For most of the remainder, it appeared that either no attempt had been made to resolve them, or an attempt had been abandoned. It is likely that on some occasions respondents will have abandoned trying to resolve problems because it became too difficult for them to continue their efforts. This may have sometimes led to injustice. Also, raising concerns about the ability of some people to enforce adjudications in their favour, two respondents who 'won' in court, subsequently gave up trying to resolve their problems and described them in interview as on-going.

Up to three-quarters of those who took action to deal with justiciable problems secured at least some of their objectives, and up to half secured their objectives in full. There was no difference in the rates at which objectives were met between problems resolved by adjudication or agreement. However, there was evidence that those who were represented at a court or tribunal hearing fared better than those who were unrepresented.

Overall, there was no significant difference in the rate at which objectives were met between those who obtained advice and those who did not. However, as indicated previously, the nature of those problems in relation to which respondents sought advice was very different to that of those problems respondents dealt with alone. It was not possible, therefore, to compare like with like. It is, though, self-evident that people are better placed to deal with problems if they have an understanding of their position and options for action, and good advice provides such an understanding. For those respondents who obtained advice, there was evidence that advice funded by legal aid was more frequently associated with the securing of some or all of respondents' objectives.

Demonstrating that the process of attempting to achieve a resolution of justiciable problems takes a toll on people, many respondents entered into agreements that they regarded as unfair; often because they would have found it too stressful to go on. This was in a context of one-fifth of problems continuing for a year or more, and the duration of problems appearing to reflect, at least in part, their seriousness.

More generally, over half of those respondents who attempted to resolve justiciable problems said that their attempt had been stressful. A significant minority of these respondents also said that their health had suffered as a result. Thus, it is clear that not only can justiciable problems directly bring about ill-health, but that they can also indirectly bring about ill-health through the problem resolution process.

Unsurprisingly, respondents were less likely to report having become stressed or ill while attempting to resolve problems they did not regard as 'very important' to sort out. Consequently, they were also less likely to report having become ill while attempting to resolve problems alone. However, they were not less likely to become stressed while attempting to resolve problems alone, suggesting that advisers may alleviate some of the stress of resolving problems. Also, respondents were more likely to report that their health suffered through trying to secure non-monetary objectives and through acting to resolve problems that took longer to resolve.

Importantly, almost half of those respondents who said that acting to resolve problems had been stressful or had brought about ill-health also said that they were glad that they had 'stuck up' for themselves – demonstrating the importance to individuals of acting to secure justice.

5

An Integrated Approach to Social Justice

This chapter summarises the principal findings detailed in the preceding three chapters and sets out their implications. It suggests that the nature of justiciable problems requires that they should be of general concern. It highlights the role of education and information in raising awareness of the civic context of justiciable problems and the methods that can be used to resolve them. It suggests that dedicated advice services should mirror more the needs and behaviour of those who wish to use them. It also underscores the importance of equipping those from whom people initially seek advice with the means to quickly and effectively refer them on when necessary, and the importance of accessible general advice services that act as gateways to formal advice and legal services. More broadly, it recognises the important role to be played by those who have routine professional contact with individuals vulnerable to justiciable problems in 'problem noticing' and signposting people to such gateways. The chapter then underlines the importance of development and co-ordination of advice and other services so that problems are not just dealt with in isolation, but also that their likelihood of occurring, or leading to further problems, is lessened through preventative action. It notes that our findings indicate how resources might be targeted to the end of problem prevention. Finally, it asks where investment should come from to develop the methods and services that will enable more people to benefit from early and effective advice, and suggests the key role of the government.

A GENERAL CONCERN

Our findings illustrate clearly that justiciable problems are ubiquitous. They affect many people and many aspects of people's lives. They are not problems that should concern only lawyers and those charged with civil law policy development. They are problems that should be of general concern; that relate to health, education, housing, welfare, commerce, citizenship, policing and communities. They are, in sum, problems that relate not narrowly to civil law, but broadly to social justice.

In all, more than one-third of LSRC survey respondents reported having experienced one or more justiciable problems during the three-and-a-half years survey reference period, and more than one-fifth reported having experienced multiple problems. Common problems, such as those relating to consumer transactions, were frequently reported by people from all walks of life. However, our findings demonstrate that differences in life circumstances entail differences in exposure to the 'defining circumstances' of problems and, consequently, differences in vulnerability to problems. As a result, the experience of problems was far from randomly distributed across the survey population. For example, consumer problems tended to affect people on higher incomes, problems relating to relationship breakdown and children tended to affect people at distinct stages of life, problems relating to discrimination tended to affect people with a long-term illness or disability, and problems relating to unfair treatment by the police tended to affect men.

Overall, those who reported long-standing ill-health or disability, lone parents, those living in the rented housing sector, those living in high density housing, those aged between 25 and 44, the unemployed, and those on very low incomes were found to be most likely to experience problems. Although there was also a tendency for those on very high incomes and those with academic qualifications to report problems at a higher than average rate, it appears, therefore, that people who are vulnerable to 'social exclusion' are also particularly vulnerable to justiciable problems.

However, reporting rates did not only reflect vulnerability. Justiciable problems can have a dramatic impact on people's lives and this, in turn, can be reflected in the profile of those who report them. Of particular concern, problems can sometimes constitute or lead to elements of social exclusion, and can, as the American Consortium on Legal Services and the Public have argued, undermine people's 'self-sufficiency'.[401] For example, our and others' findings indicate that problems relating to discrimination, personal injury and clinical negligence can bring about unemployment and a loss of income. Relationship breakdown can lead to downward mobility in the housing market, a loss of income and adversely affect children's education. Also, problems relating to domestic violence, relationship breakdown, personal injury, clinical negligence, poor housing, discrimination, employment and debt can bring about illness or disability.

Compounding this, vulnerability to justiciable problems is not static, but cumulative. Each time a person experiences a problem the likelihood of experiencing an additional problem increases; not just as a consequence of initial vulnerability, but also as a consequence of the increased vulnerability brought about by the impact of initial problems. Some 'trigger' problems, such as domestic violence and divorce, naturally bring about others, and these can be key elements of problem clusters, such as the four that we have identified in this book.

One implication of this is that, as well as socially excluded groups being particularly vulnerable to justiciable problems, some justiciable problems can reinforce and bring about social exclusion.

EDUCATION AND ENABLING PEOPLE TO ACT

Our findings confirm the diversity of people's responses to justiciable problems, and illustrate how people sometimes take no action at all to resolve apparently serious problems. In all, no action was taken to resolve almost one-fifth of problems reported through the LSRC survey, and the most common reason for this was a belief that nothing could be done. Our findings therefore indicate, as we have reported elsewhere, that such a belief may be responsible for no action being taken in respect of one million or more justiciable problems each year across England and Wales.[402] Coupled with our findings that indicate people's choices of advisers can be desperate and unpromising, it is clear that the continuing development of education and information strategies regarding rights, obligations, the basic principles of civil law, sources of advice, and methods for resolving justiciable problems has an important role to play in promoting social justice. Schemes of work for Citizenship within the National Curriculum now set out a basic framework for understanding rights and obligations.[403] Further development could see this extend beyond human rights, rights of protection against discrimination, consumer rights and employment rights, and provide more of an emphasis on sources of information and advice about rights, and methods of dispute resolution. Of course, developments within the National Curriculum will only translate to improvements in understanding if properly implemented,[404] and in the main they can only lead to improvements in the understanding of those who have not yet left school. More generally, therefore, the use and development of methods to raise levels of understanding among adults is also important. As Macdonald has indicated,[405] basic methods of increasing awareness, such as distributing information through pamphlets, videotapes and radio-spots 'can be very effective', and targeted distribution of information is also possible through services that routinely engage with the public, or are made available to the public at specific points in their lives. Macdonald provides the example of 'adding a legal dimension to pre-natal classes'. However, as Genn and Paterson have argued, such methods will need to overcome the often inaccurate impression regarding rights and processes that people receive 'through the haphazard and selective reports of journalists, whose primary interest is in selling newspapers, and via televised representations of legal proceedings in which the principal objective is entertainment.'[406] Also, the success of any methods used will rely, to a great extent, on the commitment of those who promote them and the resources that are made available to implement them. Importantly, the Legal Services Commission has greater scope and authority to promote general information and education than the Legal Aid Board it replaced,[407] and it now produces a broad range of general information pamphlets, hosts an information based website, and funds a range of education initiatives.[408] It does not, though, house a dedicated education department or post, or have a stated educational strategy, as does, for example, the New Zealand Legal Services Agency.[409]

However information and education is delivered, it is important that it stresses the many methods by which problems can be resolved, and states that legal process should generally be regarded as a rare and last resort. As Macdonald has cautioned, information and education must not 'co-opt citizens into thinking that they cannot obtain justice without the aid of lawyers, judges and official law.'[410] Such co-opting is, though, a possible consequence of information and education that sets out rights, obligations and processes in an overtly legal and/or technical framework.

Evidently, raising awareness of rights, responsibilities and options to enforce them is not all that is required to enable people to take effective action to resolve justiciable problems. As Genn and Paterson have also argued, drawing on Galanter's work of the 1970s,[411] individuals must have a broader 'capability' to act to resolve problems than simple understanding provides. They must, for example, be able to recognise problems, recognise when advice and assistance is necessary, and communicate effectively, whether in taking action on their own behalf, obtaining advice, or instructing others to act for them. Information and education are therefore necessary to enable people to take effective action to resolve problems, but not always sufficient. Those with language difficulties, poor verbal skills, or facing complex, intransigent or serious problems will often also require advice and assistance in order to act effectively. Also, as was noted in *Paths to Justice*, even 'the most self-reliant and confident people will, for certain types of problems, almost automatically obtain legal advice.'[412] Thus, as Giddings and Robertson have warned, information and education should not be regarded as cheap alternatives to advice and assistance.[413]

Furthermore, as indicated by our finding that almost one-quarter of respondents to the LSRC survey who took no action to deal with domestic violence had been too scared to act, people facing certain types of problem may require not just advice and representation, but also broader support if they are to be able to act effectively. This may require effective co-ordination of advice and non-advice services. Those facing domestic violence may, for example, require emergency housing or sheltering, perhaps arranged by a local council, and counselling, perhaps arranged through social or health services, if they are to be able to have confidence to act. Also, if there are children involved, co-ordination of advice with education services may be important if the impact of violence on their educational development is to be minimised.

Also, to maximise the ability of people to act to resolve the justiciable problems they face requires that laws and legal instruments be framed in the clearest language possible; although, as Moorhead and Pleasence have recently observed, the extent to which this is likely is unclear.[414]

BARRIERS TO ADVICE AND THE CO-ORDINATION OF ADVICE SERVICES

Our findings indicate that around one in seven people who seek advice to help resolve justiciable problems fail to obtain any. This is in part because the demand for particular advice services, and the manner in which they operate, can make it difficult for some people to access them. We found that respondents to the LSRC survey frequently encountered difficulties in getting through to advisers on the telephone. Confirming earlier findings, this seemed to be particularly so in relation to Citizens Advice Bureaux, which seem to routinely experience more demand than they have capacity, and it appears that difficulties were often compounded by the relatively sparse distribution of Citizens Advice Bureaux across the country – which results in their being often physically remote from people's home locations – and the hours during which their services tend to operate. Our findings suggest, for example, that people who work full-time face particular difficulty in accessing services that operate mainly during normal working hours. Consequently, people in full-time work are not only less likely than others to act to resolve problems, but also less likely to seek advice if they do act, and less likely to obtain advice.

While the resources that are currently available to advice services such as Citizens Advice Bureaux limit the extent to which they can develop their operations to mirror the behaviour of those who wish to use them, our findings demonstrate the importance of efforts to do so. This is especially so given that general advice providers are the most common gateway to advice and legal services. The benefits of 24-hour access to services, such as is provided by most insurance company legal help lines, and of remote points of access to information (either through physical locations or on the internet) are evident, and Citizens Advice Bureaux have in recent years developed their services to provide greater telephone access and a broader range of information delivery methods. The benefits of readily accessible physical locations at which services can be obtained, such as are provided by the extensive network of solicitor's firms across England and Wales, are also evident; although it is not apparent from our findings the *extent* to which readily accessible physical locations and the provision of direct face-to-face advice facilitate the obtaining of advice. While only rarely did respondents complain that they had been unable to obtain advice because an adviser had been too far away, this may have been in part because two in every five respondents who obtained advice had visited a solicitor at some stage, and solicitors' firms are, as just indicated, well distributed. However, it may also have been in part due to the broad availability of telephone, internet and other forms of remote advice delivery.

Face-to-face advice is no doubt important in relation to serious and sensitive problems, may be a preference for many people seeking help, suggests greater support and involvement on the part of advisers, and may enable advisers to more easily obtain the information they require in order to provide help. However, as people become more and more used to obtaining services via the telephone and internet, and as new technologies, such as remote video-linking, are perfected and become commonly used,[415] the central role of direct face-to-face advice may diminish considerably. It should not be forgotten, though, as Holdsworth has pointed out, that people who experience the multiple deprivation of social exclusion rarely have ready access to new information technologies.[416]

As well as it being important that advice services mirror the behaviour of those people who wish to use them, it is also important that they make efforts to exhibit cultural empathy towards such people. In addition, it is important that services can be provided in the languages of those who may wish to make use of them. As we have reported, a smaller proportion of black and minority ethnic respondents than other respondents obtained advice to deal with their problems, and findings relating to the provision of both legal and health services suggest that culturally rigid services and the unavailability of multiple language service provision or translation facilities can present significant barriers to the obtaining of advice.

Our findings also indicate that although physical barriers, such as those described above, commonly prevent people from obtaining advice, it is people's choices of adviser that most often undermine their efforts to do so. The most common reason reported by respondents to the LSRC survey for attempts to obtain advice having failed was that a chosen adviser was unable to provide any help. In many cases this was because respondents had simply sought advice from the wrong type of adviser. It is apparent that people seek advice from a wide range of types of adviser, and while choices of adviser are generally logical and apposite, they are sometimes, as noted in the last section, desperate and unpromising. In circumstances such as these it is vital that people are quickly and effectively referred on to the most appropriate adviser, and that advisers to whom people are referred are as accessible as possible. If people are not quickly and effectively referred on, they will often give up trying to resolve problems without attempting to obtain advice elsewhere – a matter of particular concern given the possibility we have raised that problem resolution strategies can become entrenched – or speculatively approach other advisers, who may or may not be able to help them. Although our findings suggest a general progression from generalist to specialist advisers, it is clear that confusion about where to obtain advice persists beyond just first advisers. It is also vital that people are quickly directed to the most appropriate adviser because of the evident phenomenon of referral fatigue, whereby the more times people are referred on to another advice service by an adviser, the less likely they become to act on a referral.

Of course, developing the means to facilitate quick and effective referrals is far from easy. As a matter of general principle, though, it seems that the effectiveness of referral systems depends upon the extent to which they are simple, active and work with the behaviours of both people with problems and service providers. In a referral system which is largely passive and in which clients are 'signposted' (i.e. one where the individual or organisation making referrals simply provides those they are referring with details of appropriate services), simplicity can be promoted through providing single, rather than multiple, options of appropriate services. As Pleasence, Maclean and Morley have noted, commenting on earlier work by Sherr, Moorhead and Paterson,[417] options can be something of a chimera when people have no knowledge or experience upon which to gauge their relative benefits.[418] From an adviser's perspective, simplicity can be achieved by making details of services readily accessible. This, for example, was a principal reason behind the production of the Community Legal Service Directory, although the success of the paper based Directory has so far been less effective in promoting and assisting referrals than had been hoped.[419]

In an active referral system (i.e. one where the individual or organisation making referrals makes arrangements for those they are referring to attend an appropriate service), integrated booking systems, such as the National Health Service electronic booking system that is due to be fully implemented by the end of 2005, provide greatest simplicity.[420] They also provide a means to audit referral systems, which in this context means track whether the referral was successful. The resources necessary to develop and implement a system such as the National Health Service electronic booking system could be prohibitive. However, the electronic storage and exchange of data does offer the potential for the development of low cost referral technology. For example, data on providers can be stored on CD-Rom and a web browser can be used to operate the interface which permits referral requests and records to be made and monitored.[421]

Ultimately, the success of a referral system depends on knowledge and trust. Those individuals approached by people with problems must in the first instance be able to recognise their many dimensions as well as have an understanding of what is the best gateway into, or route through, the plethora of advice and legal services available. For those outside of the recognised advice sector to whom people turn to obtain advice, the most appropriate referring action may be to provide the telephone number of the Community Legal Service Directory Line.[422] Where a dedicated advice service is the first organisation approached, the most appropriate action will most often be to direct people to specialist services that advisers already know about. Trust is also essential as the extent to which service providers think broadly about appropriate services will depend on their belief in the competence of other providers. There is evidence to suggest that barriers may persist in this regard; for example, the findings in this survey confirm findings from other studies that solicitors tend to refer within sector to other solicitors.[423] Similarly, clients themselves must have confidence that the organisation first approached is indeed acting to meet the need of the client and is not simply moving them on.

In illustrating the wide range of types of adviser from which respondents to the LSRC survey sought advice, and the great proportion of occasions on which advice is initially sought from those outside of the recognised advice sector (particularly from those who have routine professional contact with people vulnerable to justiciable problems), our findings suggest a role for such individuals that extends beyond mere referral when problems are brought to their attention. Our findings suggest that those who have routine professional contact with people vulnerable to justiciable problems could have a broader and potentially more important role in actively looking out for the signs of justiciable problems - problem noticing - and providing people who may have problems with basic literature about them and, if necessary, signposting them to appropriate advisers. Some professionals, such as those in the health sector, are uniquely placed to view aspects of people's lives that might raise the suspicion of their facing justiciable problems; although, evidently, the skills of problem noticing would need to be developed through training.

Clearly, the problems that professionals might look out for should relate to their field. The utility of the role would otherwise be diminished, especially as there would be resource implications if professionals were to be trained to spot problems and signpost those affected to appropriate advice. Nevertheless, the benefits of increasing the likelihood of problems being dealt with, or dealt with at a point before they have had the chance to escalate or bring about others, could contribute enormously to efforts to reduce their impact and extend the jurisdiction of social justice. In fact, there are already examples of training being provided to enable professionals to spot justiciable problems on the part of those they serve. At least a proportion of doctors in England and Wales have received training in identifying domestic violence,[424] and the British Medical Association has published advice on good practice in identifying and dealing with domestic violence.[425]

In the early 1990s, the Legal Action Group asserted that 'a comprehensive view of legal services must include all legal advice, assistance, and representation, ranging from preliminary advice with a legal component provided by agencies like Citizens Advice Bureaux to the specialised advocacy services of Queen's Council.'[426] We suggest that a comprehensive view of legal services must include even more than this. It must extend beyond the generalist gatekeepers to formal advice and legal services to all those types of individual or organisation to whom people routinely turn for advice, and even to those who might act simply as lookouts for problems. Clearly, though, this view gives rise to issues of responsibility, co-ordination and the control of the quality of such a broad range of legal services, and therefore presents considerable challenges to policymakers.

JOINED UP SOLUTIONS TO JOINED UP PROBLEMS[427]

Our findings demonstrate the importance of dealing with justiciable problems not in isolation, but in the context of their causes and consequences. We have explained how people's life circumstances can bring about justiciable problems, how justiciable problems can alter life circumstances, and how justiciable problems can therefore contribute to downward spirals in life quality, health, economic circumstances and self-sufficiency. We have revealed how some problems, such as domestic violence and divorce, are particularly likely to bring about further problems, sometimes directly – as, for example, when domestic violence leads to divorce – and sometimes indirectly – as, for example, when divorce leads to a drop in income, a need to find alternative accommodation, or a need to alter patterns of working to care for children, and consequently to problems with debt, welfare benefits, homelessness, housing, and employment. We have shown how professionals with routine contact with those vulnerable to justiciable problems can be ideally placed to identify justiciable problems. We have also set out the most apparent consequences of problems and links between them, and thus pointed out some of the additional considerations and areas of advice and assistance that those who provide advice should bear in mind and provide. We have thus indicated the broader roles that could be played by all those who have an interest in preventing and reducing the impact of justiciable problems.

As we have reported elsewhere, the relationship between justiciable problems and ill-health and disability requires that their identification, prevention, amelioration and resolution should be regarded as both public health and civil justice policy objectives.[428] To some extent, the coincidence of health and justice policy objectives is already being manifested. At a strategic level, some Community Legal Service Partnerships and Health Action Zones are working together to integrate aspects of service delivery that are mutually beneficial.[429] The setting up of Patient Advice and Liaison Services within National Health Service Trusts and Primary Care Trusts,[430] proposals for the creation of Independent Complaints Advocacy Services to assist those wishing to make complaints about NHS services,[431] the development of partnerships between health centres and advice agencies (enabling general and legal advice to be provided on-site in health centres),[432] and the training of health professionals in problem identification all provide examples of how this is possible. However, integration of health and justice policy and operations remains in its infancy; a reality confirmed by the rarity of allusions to the role that advice and legal services can play in promoting good health in health impact assessments. Also, the strategic development of Patient Advice and Liaison Services and proposals for Independent Complaints Advocacy Services is only loosely integrated with the development of the Community Legal Service and Community Legal Service Partnerships. The benefits of further integration and strategic co-ordination could be substantial.

Aside from integration of advice and health services, similar arguments can be made in relation to advice and social services (including the government's proposed multi-service children's centres),[433] Job Centre Plus, education services, and many other government services. Thus, a recent joint publication of the government and Law Centres Federation spoke of a commitment 'to see further links formed between legal and advice services and initiatives such as Job Centre Plus, Connexions, New Deal, New Deal for Communities, Care Direct, Sure Start, Crime and Disorder Partnerships, Education Action Zones and Health Action Zones.'[434] Our findings inidcate how and where such links might be developed.

More generally, we would hope that our findings will be used widely to inform the development of policy and initiatives aimed at reducing social exclusion. As Hills has argued, the causes and processes of social exclusion are complex and multi-dimensional, and the chances of developing effective policy to combat them are therefore greater the more that is understood about them.[435]

117

RESOURCING CHANGE, AND CO-ORDINATING AND TARGETING RESOURCES

In demonstrating that justiciable problems are a matter of general concern, impinge on the business of many governments departments, and play a significant role as a cause, and in the processes, of social exclusion, our findings suggest that investment to develop the methods and services that will enable more people to benefit from early and effective advice should come from across government. Advice about justiciable problems is already funded by a range of government departments and agencies, and resource intensive initiatives such as Patient Advice and Liaison Services, Independent Complaints Advocacy Services, Consumer Direct[436] and Consumer Support Networks[437] are evidence of a real interest and commitment to assisting people deal with justiciable problems across government. Evidence such as that presented in this book can only serve to heighten that interest and commitment. However, as with services (and 'solutions' more generally), public investment needs to be co-ordinated to reduce duplication of effort, to prevent initiatives being at odds and to best bring about government objectives.

As for where limited public resources should be targeted, if the objective is to promote social justice and combat social exclusion, then our findings provide much in the way of guidance. Investment in education and awareness could, for example, be targeted towards those population groups most likely not to act because they do not think anything can be done about their problems. Investment in support services could be targeted towards those people who are most likely not to act because they are scared to do so. Investment in advice services and problem noticing could be targeted towards those people most vulnerable to problems and those problems that are the most serious[438] and have greatest impact on people's lives. Again, investment in referral and quality assurance systems could be targeted towards those advisers who people naturally gravitate towards.

Of course, there is no reason for investment to emanate only from the public sector. In demonstrating the use of and potential demand for generalist gateways to advice and legal services, and the benefit that is gained from referrals from these gateways by advice services operating on a commercial basis, our findings also suggest that investment could come from the private sector. For example, the market for legal expenses insurance has developed relatively slowly in England and Wales since its introduction in the 1970s and seemingly has potential to expand to provide easy access to general advice to a greater number of people than at present.[439] Also, the solicitors' profession, which is the beneficiary of a substantial proportion of referrals to specialist legal services from generalist advisers, could potentially benefit greatly from contributing to the development of a comprehensive networked referral system; as could other advice providers operating on a commercial basis.

The development of the infrastructure of civil justice could, then, be resourced from both the private and public sector. However, the effective co-ordination and targeting of all resources is ultimately the responsibility of government. Thus, the key role for government over the years ahead will be a co-ordinating one. We hope that this book provides the empirical foundations for wide-ranging decision-making within civil justice policy, and beyond, to continue and develop this key role.

NOTES

[1] 'The bread and butter issues' described by the Consortium on Legal Services and the Public (1996) *Agenda for Access: The American People and Civil Justice*, Chicago: American Bar Association, p.vii.

[2] This is despite a more recent 'backlash against rights', characterised by internal review and complaints procedures. For a commentary on this and the rise of 'welfare rights', see T. Goriely (1998) 'Making the Welfare State Work', in F. Regan, A. Paterson, T. Goriely, and D. Fleming (eds.) *The Transformation of Legal Aid,* Oxford: Oxford University Press.

[3] H. Genn (1999) *Paths to Justice: What People Do and Think About Going to Law*, Oxford: Hart Publishing, p.12.

[4] R.H. Mnookin and L. Kornhauser (1979) Bargaining in the Shadow of the Law: The Case of Divorce, 88 *Yale Law Journal* 950.

[5] P. Lewis (1973) 'Unmet Legal Needs', in P. Morris, R. White and P. Lewis (eds.) *Social Needs and Legal Action*, Oxford: Martin Robertson.

[6] For an earlier discussion of this link see R. White (1976) *Report to the Lord Chancellor: The Unmet Need for Legal Services*, London: Lord Chancellor's Office.

[7] H. Genn (1999) above, n.3, p.32. See also, for example, American Bar Association (1994) *Legal Needs and Civil Justice: A Survey of Americans - Major Findings from the Comprehensive Legal Needs Study*, Chicago: American Bar Association, p.3.

[8] Social Exclusion Unit (2001) *Preventing Social Exclusion*, London: Cabinet Office, p.10.

[9] See below, chapter 3 and chapter 5, p.114.

[10] Lord Chancellor's Department (1998) *Modernising Justice,* London: HMSO (Cmd. 4155).

[11] Lord Chancellor's Department (1998) *Modernising Justice,* London: HMSO (Cmd. 4155), p.3.

[12] Legal Services Commission (2002) *Corporate Plan 2002/3-2003/4*, London: Legal Services Commission, p.9.

[13] Lord Chancellor's Department and Law Centres Federation (2001) *Legal and Advice Services: A Pathway out of Social Exclusion*, London: Lord Chancellor's Department, p.11.

[14] J. Stein (2001) *The Future of Social Justice in Britain: A New Mission for the Community Legal Service*, London: Centre for Analysis of Social Exclusion, London School of Economics, p.48.

[15] See, for example, B. Abel-Smith, M. Zander and R. Brooke (1973) *Legal Problems and the Citizen: A Study in Three London Boroughs*, London: Heinemann, and Royal Commission on Legal Services (1979) *Final Report*, London: HMSO (Cmd. 7648). For other jurisdictions see, for example, B. Curran (1977) *The Legal Needs of the Public*, Chicago: American Bar Foundation; M. Cass and R. Sackville (1975) *Legal Needs for the Poor*, Canberra: Australian Government Publishing Service; C. Messier (1975) *Les Mains de la Loi* (In the Hands of the Law), Montreal: Commission des Services Jurisdiques, K. Schuyt, K. Groenendijk and B. Sloot (1976) *De Weg naar Het Recht* (The Road to Justice), Deventer: Klewer. Also, for a more detailed commentary, see P. Pleasence, A. Buck, T. Goriely, J. Taylor, H. Perkins, H. Quirk (2001) *Local Legal Need*, London: Legal Services Research Centre.

[16] H Genn (1999), above, n.3; H. Genn and A. Paterson (2001) *Paths to Justice: What People Do and Think About Going to Law*, Oxford: Hart Publishing; American Bar Association (1994), above, n.7; G. Maxwell, C. Smith, P. Shepherd and A. Morris (1999) *Meeting Legal Service Needs: Research Report Prepared for the Legal Services Board*, Wellington: Legal Services Board. Also, see, National Consumer Council (1995) *Seeking Civil Justice: A Survey of People's Needs and Experiences*, London: National Consumer Council, and Scottish Consumer Council (1997) *Civil Disputes in Scotland,* Glasgow: Scottish Consumer Council, Report.

[17] H. Genn (1999), above, n.3, p.1.

[18] P. Pleasence, A. Buck, T. Goriely, J. Taylor, H. Perkins, H. Quirk (2001) *Local Legal Need*, London: Legal Services Research Centre, p.24; H. Genn (1999), above, n.3, p.25; American Bar Association (1994) *Report on the Legal Needs of the Low- and Moderate-Income Public: Findings of the Comprehensive Legal Needs Study*, Chicago: American Bar Association, p.43.

[19] P. Pleasence, A. Buck, N.J. Balmer and A. O'Grady (2002) *Summary Technical Report on the Legal Services Commission's Small Area Legal Need Models and the Lord Chancellor's Department's PSA Targets 3 and 6,* London: LSRC

[20] C. Clark and E. Corstvet (1938) The Lawyer and the Public: An A.A.L.S. Survey, 47 *Yale Law Journal*, p.1972. For a history, see P. Pleasence, A. Buck, T. Goriely, J. Taylor, H. Perkins, H. Quirk (2001) *Local Legal Need*, London: Legal Services Research Centre, pp.7-27.

[21] H. Genn (1999) *Paths to Justice: What People Do and Think About Going to Law*, Oxford: Hart Publishing, pp.12-14.

[22] No constituent problems were presented to respondents in respect of the consumer, homelessness, neighbours, divorce, personal injury and unfair treatment by the police categories. For these, it was deemed sufficient to refer to 'faulty good or services', 'being homeless or threatened with being homeless', 'noisy or anti-social neighbours', 'divorce', 'injuries or health problems … (caused) by an accident or … poor working conditions', and being 'unfairly treated by the police … (by) for example being assaulted by a police officer or being unreasonably arrested'.

[23] In full, constituent discrimination problems included difficulties relating to discrimination because of (a) race, (b) gender, (c) disability and (d) sexual orientation. Constituent employment problems included difficulties relating to (a) being sacked or made redundant, (b) being threatened with the sack, (c) getting pay or a pension to which entitled, (d) changes to terms and conditions, (e) other work rights, (f) unsatisfactory or dangerous working conditions, (g) unfair disciplinary procedures, and (h) harassment. Constituent owned housing problems included difficulties relating to (a) obtaining planning permission or consent, (b) buying or selling property (e.g. misleading surveys, problems with a lease), (c) communal repairs or maintenance, (d) repossession of the home or several mortgage payments being in arrears, (e) squatters, and (f) boundaries or rights of way or access to property. Constituent rented housing problems included difficulties relating to (a) unsafe living conditions, (b) otherwise unsuitable living conditions, (c) getting a deposit back, (d) renting out rooms to lodgers or sub-letting, (e) getting a landlord to make repairs, (f) getting a landlord to provide other services, (g) agreeing with a landlord on rent, council tax, housing benefit payments or other terms of a tenancy agreement, (h) getting a written tenancy agreement, (i) succession of tenancy, (j) harassment by a landlord, (k) eviction or being several rent payments in arrears, (l) boundaries or rights of way or access to property, and (m) flatmates (non-relatives) not paying the rent or behaving in an antisocial manner. Constituent money/debt problems included difficulties relating to (a) getting someone to pay money they owed, (b) insurance companies unfairly rejecting claims, (c) incorrect or disputed bills (excluding rent/mortgage payments), (d) incorrect or unfair tax demands, (e) incorrect information or advice that led to the purchase of financial products, (f) mismanagement of a pension fund, (g) unfair refusal of credit as a result of incorrect information, (h) disputed (repeated) penalty charges by banks or utilities, (i) unreasonable harassment by creditors, (j) division of the content of a will or property after the death of a family member, (k) severe difficulties managing money, (l) being threatened with legal action to recover money owed, and (m) being subject of a county court judgment. Constituent welfare benefits problems included difficulties relating to (a) legal entitlement to welfare benefits, and (b) the amount of welfare benefits. Constituent relationship breakdown problems included difficulties relating to (a) the division or money, pensions or property on divorce or separation, (b) obtaining maintenance for self, (c) agreeing to pay maintenance to a former partner (other than for children), (d) obtaining child support payments, (e) agreeing to pay child support payments, and (f) custody and access arrangements for children. Constituent domestic violence problems included (a) being violent or abusive to a partner, ex-partner or other family member, (b) suffering violence or abuse from a partner, ex-partner or other family member, (c) children suffering violence or abuse from a partner, ex-partner or other family member. Constituent children problems included difficulties relating to (a) fostering or adopting children, or becoming a legal guardian, (b) children being taken into care or being on the Child Protection Register, (c) abduction or threatened abduction of children, (d) children going to a school for which they are eligible, (e) children receiving an appropriate education (e.g. special needs), (f) children being unfairly excluded or suspended from school, and (g) children's safety at school or on school trips. Constituent clinical

negligence problems included suffering as a result of negligent or wrong (a) medical treatment, and (b) dental treatment. Constituent mental health problems included difficulties relating to (a) treatment or care received in hospital, (b) obtaining discharge from hospital or the restrictions or conditions of discharge, and (c) care after release from hospital. Constituent immigration problems included difficulties relating to (a) obtaining UK citizenship, (b) disputes over nationality, (c) obtaining authority to remain in the UK, (d) change of conditions under which it is possible to remain in the UK, (e) a partner or children entering the UK, and (f) asylum.

[24] This was because they were not defined as 'priority' problems by the Lord Chancellor's Department.

[25] The one problem was selected on an otherwise random weighted basis, to ensure the main section questions were asked of a reasonable number of all the main problem categories, and as many of the rarer categories as possible.

[26] All adults were screened in 2,971 households. Some adults were screened in 377 households.

[27] D. Down (2002) *Family Spending: A Report on the 2000-01 Family Expenditure Survey*, London: The Stationary Office.

[28] M. Rowland (2002) *Family Resources Survey: Annual Technical Report: 2000-01*, London: Office for National Statistics.

[29] A. Walker, J. Maher, M. Coulthard, E. Goddard, M. Thomas (2001) *Living in Britain: Results from the 2000-01 General Household Survey*, London: The Stationary Office.

[30] Three 'case study' areas (Cumbria (rural), Kirklees (urban/rural) and Birmingham (dense urban)) were oversampled to allow for comparative analysis between the three. We will report on this elsewhere. The general profile of LSRC survey respondents was similar to that of the general population. 33 per cent of households contained just one adult, 56 per cent contained two adults, and the remainder contained three or more. The average household size was 2.37, compared to the 2001 census average of 2.36. 25 per cent of respondents aged between 25 and 74 years old reported a long-term limiting illness or disability, compared to the 2001 census estimate of 24 per cent. Unweighted, LSRC survey respondents were 47 per cent male and 53 per cent female, compared to 48 per cent and 52 per cent respectively across the general population (2001 census). 8 per cent of them were aged between 18 and 24 years, 39 per cent between 25 and 44 years, 27 per cent between 45 and 59 years, and 26 per cent 60 years or older. This compared to 11 per cent, 38 per cent, 25 per cent and 27 per cent respectively across the general population (2001 census). 64 per cent of them were in households with a weekly income of less than £500, 27 per cent in households with a weekly income of between £500 and £999, and 9 per cent in households with a weekly income of £1,000 or more. This compared to 61 per cent, 28 per cent and 10 per cent respectively across the general population: Rowland M. (2002) *Family Resources Survey: Annual Technical Report: 2000-01*. London: Office for National Statistics.

[31] Bed and Breakfast Unit (2001) *Targets and Action for Reducing B&B – The Way Forward*, London: Department for Transport, Local Government and the Regions.

[32] Table S126 ('Type of communal establishment and sex by resident type and age'), available for download at http://www.nationalstatistics.gov.uk. The total number of people living in all forms of temporary accommodation is much higher than this. For example, the Office of the Deputy Prime Minister reports that at the end of March 2003 the total number of households accommodated in temporary accommodation by local authorities was 90,680: Table 623 ('Social housing: homeless households in temporary accommodation, by type of accommodation'), available for download at http://www.odpm.gov.uk.

[33] The census adult population estimate was 40,246,780.

[34] K. Swales (2001) *Measuring Legal Needs: Technical Report*, London: National Centre for Social Research.

[35] H. Genn (1999), above, n.3, p.13.

[36] H. Genn (1999), above, n.3, p.23 and p.271. This similarity holds despite the longer reference period of the *Paths to Justice* survey. Owing to the steep decline in recall of problems over time, the longer reference period is likely to have increased the *Paths to Justice* reporting rate by only a few per cent. See P. Pleasence, H. Genn, N.J. Balmer, A. Buck and A. O'Grady (2003) Causes of Action: First Findings of the LSRC Periodic Survey, 30(1) *Journal of Law and Society*, pp.11. Also, see Appendix C below.

[37] H. Genn and A. Paterson (2001), above, n.16, p.34 and p.275.

[38] American Bar Association (1994), above, n.7. The ABA sample was comprised of 1,782 low-income and 1,305 moderate-income households. The reported incidence rates were 47% and 52% respectively.

[39] G. Maxwell, C. Smith, P. Shepherd and A. Morris (1999) above, n.16.

[40] The United States survey included 67 problem categories, extending to concerns about the community/regional environment and problems connected with small businesses (American Bar Association (1994), above, n.15, Appendix B). The New Zealand survey included 27 problem categories, extending to crime, carer problems and disagreements with public bodies. It also provided an opportunity to report on problems or disagreements not included within the 27 categories (G. Maxwell, C. Smith, P. Shepherd and A. Morris (1999) above, n.16, p.30).

[41] H. Genn and A. Paterson (2001), above, n.16, p.251.

[42] P. Pleasence, H. Genn, N.J. Balmer, A. Buck and A. O'Grady (2003), above, n.36, p.18.

[43] H. Genn and A. Paterson (2001), above, n.16, p.41.

[44] The predictors are listed in descending order of influence, based on Wald statistics derived from a model incorporating age and academic qualifications as an interaction term. See Appendix B.

[45] 600 or 1395 (unweighted: 633 of 1495). Also, 54% (141/259) of respondents who were economically inactive as a result of 'sickness' reported problems.

[46] 147 of 223 (unweighted: 154 of 227). See, further, A. Buck, P. Pleasence, N.J. Balmer, A. O'Grady and H. Genn. The Experience of Justiciable Problems Among Lone Parents, forthcoming in *Journal of Social Policy and Administration*.

[47] This is a similar finding to that of G. Maxwell, C. Smith, P. Shepherd and A. Morris (1999) above, n.16, p.47.

[48] Age and gender were the only items of demographic information collected for all respondents in the *Paths to Justice* surveys. Nevertheless, our findings mirror in this regard those from the earlier surveys. See H. Genn (1999), above, n.3, p.28, and H. Genn and A. Paterson (2001), above, n.16, p.38. See also, American Bar Association (1994), above, n.7, National Consumer Council (1995), above, n.16, and Scottish Consumer Council (1997), above, n16, G. Maxwell, C. Smith, P. Shepherd and A. Morris (1999) above, n.16.

[49] 81 of 149 (unweighted: 89 of 161)

[50] This was almost significant within the model (p=0.078), but highly significant overall ($\chi^2{}_1 = 48.03$, p <0.001, thus indicating other aspects of viulnerability, such as employment status, provide a better explanation of variance.

[51] American Bar Association (1994), above, n.7.

[52] $\chi^2{}_1 = 9.5$, p = 0.002. 101 of 210 (unweighted: 123 of 263).

[53] G. Maxwell, C. Smith, P. Shepherd and A. Morris (1999) above, n.16, p.43.

[54] M. Noble, M. Lloyd, M. Sigala, G. Wright, M. Cox, C. Dibben, H. Perkins and N. Strudwick (2002) *Predictive Legal Needs Models Development Project,* unpublished report to the LSRC.

[55] H. Genn (1999), above, n.3, p.28. H. Genn and A. Paterson (2001), above, n.16, pp.37-38.

[56] The result was the same whether a binomial (white, other) or multinomial (white, black, Asian, mixed, other) variable was used in the analysis. Our result contrasts with that of the New Zealand survey, which found that Maori respondents reported problems more often than white respondents: G. Maxwell, C. Smith, P. Shepherd and A. Morris (1999) above, n.16, p.40. Again, this finding is possibly attributable to the broader range of problems surveyed.

[57] This compares to 6½ per cent of the population of England and Wales, as estimated by the 2001 Census.

[58] The mean age of temporary accommodation survey respondents was 30 years old, compared to 46 for LSRC survey respondents.

[59] Also, 18 per cent were unemployed, compared to 3 per cent of LSRC survey respondents.

[60] 32 per cent of temporary accommodation survey respondents had an income below £4,000, compared to 4 per cent of LSRC survey respondents.

[61] 165 of 197

[62] 164 of 197

[63] American Bar Association (1994), above, n.7, G. Maxwell, C. Smith, P. Shepherd and A. Morris (1999) above, n.16, H. Genn (1999), above, n.3. In *Paths to Justice Scotland* consumer problems were the second most frequently reported type of problem, and immigration problems the second least frequently reported: H. Genn and A. Paterson (2001), above, n.16.

[64] 340 of 5,611

[65] 204 of 5,611. Family breakdown problems include divorces and problems ancillary to the breakdown of any relationship. For more details see P. Pleasence, N.J. Balmer, A. Buck, A. O'Grady, M. Maclean and H. Genn (2003) Family Problems – What Happens and to Whom, 33 *Family Law*, p.497.

[66] See, for example, B.J. Reiser (1988) Predictive Inferencing in Autobiographical Memory Retrieval, in M.M. Gruneberg, P.E. Morris and R.N. Sykes (eds.) *Practical Aspects of Memory. Volume 1: Memory in Everyday Life*, New York: Wiley; B. Means and E. Loftus (1991) When Personal History Repeats Itself: Decomposing Memories for Recurring Events, 5 *Applied Cognitive Psychology*, p.297; A. Baddeley, V.J. Lewis and I. Nemo-Smith (1978) When Did You Last ...? In M.M. Gruneberg, P.E. Morris and R.N. Sykes (eds.) *Practical Aspects of Memory. Volume 1: Memory in Everyday Life*, New York: Wiley; U. Neisser (1986) Nested Structure in Autobiographical Memory, in D.C. Rubin (ed.) *Autobiographical Memory*, Cambridge: Cambridge University Press; D.C. Rubin and M. Kozin (1984) Vivid Memories, 16 Cognition, p.81; W.A. Wagenaar (1986) My Memory: A Study of Autobiographical Memory Over Six Years, 18 *Cognitive Psychology*, pp.225-252; P. Chapman and G. Underwood (2000) Forgetting Near-Accidents: The Roles of Severity, Culpability and Experience in the Poor Recall of Dangerous Driving Situations, 14(1) *Applied Cognitive Psychology*, p.31.

[67] See, for example, A.G. Turner (1982) What Subjects of Survey Research Believe About Confidentiality. In J.E. Sieber (ed.) *The Ethics of Social Research: Surveys and Experiments*, New York: Springer Verlag; C. Mirrlees-Black (1999) Domestic Violence: Findings From a New British Crime Survey Self-Completion Questionnaire. London: Home Office (Home Office Research Study 191); M. Ellsberg, A. Winkvist, L. Heise, R. Peña, S. Agurto (2001) Researching Domestic Violence Against Women: Methodological and Ethical Considerations, 32(1) *Studies In Family Planning*, pp.1-16.

[68] See, for example, Statistics New Zealand (1998) Young New Zealanders, Wellington: Statistics New Zealand.

[69] Office of the Deputy Prime Minister (2003) English House Condition Survey, London: HMSO

[70] T. Newburn (2002), Young People, Crime and Youth Justice, in M. Maguire, R. Morgan and R. Reiner (eds), *The Oxford Handbook of Criminology*, Third Edition. Oxford: Oxford University Press. Also, National Statistics (2003) Social Trends 33, London: The Stationary Office.

[71] Polgar, M. & Cabassa L. (2001) Continuity of Mental Health Care for Young Adults, 15(1) *Focal Point*, p.11.

[72] J. Dobson, K. Koser, G. Mclaughlan and J. Salt (2001) *International Migration and the United Kingdom: Recent Patterns and Trends*. London: Home Office, London: Home Office (RDS Occasional Paper No.75)

[73] At 42, 38 and 40 respectively.

[74] For more details relating to older people rough sleeping and experiencing homelessness, see M.Crane and A.M. Warnes (2000) Policy and Service Responses to Rough Sleeping Among Older People, in 29 *Journal of Social Policy*, p.645.

[75] L. Bird (1999) Fundamental Facts: All the Latest Facts and Figures on Mental Illness. London: The Mental Health Foundation.

[76] C. Mirrlees-Black (1999), above, n.67, p.68.

[77] C. Mirrlees-Black (1999), above, n.67, p.77.

[78] National Statistics (2001) Social Trends No. 31. London: The Stationary Office.

[79] M. Maguire, R. Morgan and R. Reiner (eds), *The Oxford Handbook of Criminology*, Third Edition. Oxford: Oxford University Press.

[80] $\chi^2_1 = 4.1$, $p < 0.05$.

[81] $\chi^2_1 = 7.6$, $p < 0.01$.

[82] $\chi^2_1 = 4.0$, $p < 0.05$.

[83] $\chi^2_1 = 6.8$, $p < 0.01$.

[84] See, for example, Welsh Assembly (2003) *The Housing and Socio-Economic Circumstances of Black and Minority Ethnic People Living in Wales*, Cardiff: Welsh Assembly (Housing Research Report HR 1/03), and G. Netto, R. Arshad, P. de Lima, F. A. Diniz, M. MacEwen, V. Patel and R. Syed (2001) *Audit of Research on Minority Ethnic Issues in Scotland from a 'Race' Perspective*, Edinburgh: Central Research Unit.

[85] D.J. Smith (1997) Ethnic Origins, Crime and Criminal Justice in England and Wales, in M. Tonry (ed.), *Ethnicity, Crime and Immigration: Comparative and Cross-National Perspectives*, Chicago: University of Chicago Press.

[86] We will report elsewhere on our findings using a 3 category multinomial variable: A. O'Grady, P. Pleasence, N. Balmer, A. Buck, H. Genn and B. Carter, *'Insitutional Racism' and Civil Justice: The Problems of applying a political concept in a research context,* forthcoming.

[87] J. Dobson, K. Koser, G. Mclaughlan and J. Salt (2001), above, n.72, p.42.

[88] C. Mirrlees-Black (1999), above, n.67, p.72.

124

[89] P. Pleasence, N.J. Balmer, A. Buck, A. O'Grady, M. Maclean and H. Genn (2003), above, n.65, p.500.

[90] R.M. Blackburn, A. Dale, and J. Jarman (1997) Ethnic Differences in Attainment in Education, Occupation and Lifestyle, in V. Karn (ed.) *Employment, Education and Housing among Ethnic Minorities in Britain*, London: HMSO. The suggested higher reporting rate of education problems by black respondents also concords with these patterns of educational attainment.

[91] See, for example, J. Bindel (1994) T*he Hidden Figure: Domestic Violence in North London*, report prepared for Islington Council, London, and Asian and Pacific Islander Institute on Domestic Violence (2002) *Fact Sheet: Domestic Violence in Asian and Pacific Islander Communities*, San Fransisco: Asian and Pacific Islander Institute on Domestic Violence, available for download at www.apiahf.org/apidvinstitute/PDF/Fact_Sheet.pdf

[92] Economic circumstances here include income, benefits status and economic activity.

[93] Respondents earning in excess of £50,000 reported no problems relating to homelessness.

[94] S. Gibbons and S. Machin (2003) Valuing English Primary Schools, in 53 *Journal of Urban Economics*, p.197.

[95] Home Office (2002), Criminal Statistics, England and Wales 2001. London: HMSO.

[96] See, for example, A. Dale (1986) Social Class and the Self-Employed, in 20 SIociology, pp.430-434, and B. Casey and S. Creigh (1988) Self-employment in Great Britain: Its definition in the Labour Force Survey, in tax and social security law, and in labour law, in 2 *Work, Employment and Society*, p.381.

[97] J.R. Jones, C.S. Huxtable and J.T. Hodgson (2001) *Self-Reported Work-Related Illness in 1998/99: Results from EUROSTAT Ill-Health Module in the 1999 Labour Force Summer Quarter*, London: Health and Safety Executive

[98] Unsurprisingly, there was, though, indication that respondents with mortgages were more likely to report problems with investment services.

[99] $\chi^2_4 = 339.85$, $p < 0.001$.

[100] Census 2001 estimate. Dataset KS20P available at www.neighbourhood.statistics.gov.uk. See, also, Office for National Statistics (2003) Social Trends, No.33, London: The Stationary Office.

[101] The number of lone parent families resulting from births to 'unattached mothers' is, though, increasing, a fact that will narrow this differential: J. Haskey (1998) One Parent Families and their Dependent Children in Great Britain, in 91 *Population Trends*, p.5.

[102] National Council for One Parent Families, Crisis, Health Action for Homeless People (2001) *A Secure Start for Young Families: the housing and support needs of young lone mothers*, London: NCOPF.

[103] See, for example, P. Wilcox (2000) Lone Motherhood: The Impact on Living Standards of Leaving a Violent Relationship, in 34(2) *Journal of Social Policy and Administration*, p.176, and C. Chambaz (2001) Lone Parent Families in Europe: A Variety of Economic and Social Circumstances, in 35(6) *Journal of Social Policy and Administration*, p.658.

[104] For the same reasons as stated above in relation to gender and employment, neighbours, personal injury and rented housing problems.

[105] This was identified using a simple χ^2 test: $\chi^2_3 = 13.91$, $p < 0.01$.

[106] J. Millar and T. Ridge (2001) *Families, Poverty, Work and Care – A Review of the Literature on Lone Parents and Low Income Couple Families with Children*, London: Department for Work and Pensions (Research Report No.153)

[107] The percentage of female lone parents in work increased from 44 per cent in 1997 to 50 per cent by 2001: National Council for One Parent Families (2001) *One Parent Families Today: The Facts*, London: National Council for One Parent Families.

[108] 86 per cent of lone parents in the LSRC survey were receiving one or more welfare benefits. See further, National Council for One Parent Families, Crisis, Health Action for Homeless People (2001), above, n.103, and National Council for One Parent Families (2001) *One Parent Families Today: The Facts*, London: NCOPF.

[109] $\chi^2_3 = 41.24$, $p < 0.001$.

[110] Men comprised 15 per cent of lone parents in the LSRC survey.

[111] $\chi^2_{24} = 41.37$, $p < 0.001$.

[112] $\chi^2_3 = 11.52$, $p < 0.01$.

[113] $\chi^2_{24} = 41.37$, $p < 0.001$.

[114] G. Allan, S. Hawker, G. Crow (2001) Family Diversity and Change in Britain and Western Europe, 22(7) *Journal of Family Issues*, p.819, at p.828. See also, for example, P.R. Amato (2000) The Consequences of Divorce for Adults and Children, 62 *Journal of Marriage and the Family*, p.1269.

[115] T. Tsushima and V. Gecas (2001) Role Taking and Socialisation in Single Parent Families, in 22(3) *Journal of Family Issues*, pp.267-288.

[116] See, for example, J. Millar and T. Ridge (2001) *Families, Poverty, Work and Care - A Review of the Literature on Lone parents and Low-income Couple Families with Children*, London: Department for Work and Pensions, Research Report No 153, and J. Popay and G. Jones (1990) Patterns of Health and Illness Amongst Lone Parents, 19(4) *Journal of Social Policy*, p.499.

[117] Lone parents were more likely than other respondents with resident children to report problems relating to children, reflecting the link between domestic violence and such problems. See, further, P. Pleasence, N.J. Balmer, A. Buck, A. O'Grady, M. Maclean and H. Genn (2003), above, n.65.

[118] M. Howard (1999) *Enabling Government: Joined up Policies for a National Disability Strategy*, London: Fabian Society.

[119] M. Howard, A. Garnham, G. Fimister, J. Veit-Wilson (2001) *Poverty: The Facts*, London: CPAB.

[120] B. Hughes (2002) Bauman's Strangers: Impairment and the invalidation of disabled people in modern and post-modern cultures, in 17 *Disability and Society*, p.571, at p.580.

[121] D. Easterlow, S.J. Smith, S. Mallinson (2000) Housing for Health: The Role of Owner Occupation, in 15 *Housing Studies*, p.367.

[122] British Medical Association (2003) *Housing and Health: Building for the Future*, London: British Medical Association, p.22.

[123] British Medical Association (1998) *Domestic Violence: A Health Care Issue?* London: British Medical Association, p.22.

[124] As a consequence, they reported mental health related justiciable problems five times more often than others.

[125] See, for example, British Medical Association (1998), above, n.122, and L. Walker (1979) *The Battered Woman*, New York: Harper and Row.

[126] When we looked only at rented housing problems relating to unsafe or unsatisfactory housing, long-standing ill-health or disability was not a significant predictor. However, unemployment as a result of ill-health was.

[127] See, for example, British Medical Association (2003), above n.122, and S. Hunt (1997) Housing Related Disorders, in J. Charlton and M. Murphy (eds.) *The Health of Adult Britain 1841-1994*, London: The Stationary Office.

[128] G.C. Gee (2002) A Multilevel Analysis of the Relationship Between Institutional and Individual Racial Discrimination and Health Status, in 92 *American Journal of Public Health*, p.615.

[129] At the very least in so far as they bring about unemployment. See, S.H. Wilson G.M. Walker (1993) Unemployment and Health, in 107 *Public Health*, p.153.

[130] See, for example, S. Edwards (2003) *In Too Deep: CAB Clients' Experience of Debt*, London: Citizens Advice Bureaux, and J. Sharpe and J. Bostock (2002) *Supporting People with Debt and Mental Health Problems: Research With Psychological Therapists in Northumberland,* Newcastle: Department of Psychological Services and Research, North Tyneside and Northumberland NHS Mental Health Trust.

[131] See, for example, P.R. Amato (2000), above, n.114, P.R. Amato and B. Keith (1991) Parental Divorce and the Well-Being of Children: A Meta-analysis, in 110 *Psychological Bulletin*, p.26, and G.R. Kitson and L.A. Morgan (1990) The Multiple Consequences of Divorce: A Decade Review, in 52 *Journal of Marriage and the Family*, p.913.

[132] S. Nettleton and R. Burrows (1998) Mortgage Debt, Insecure Home Ownership and Health: An Exploratory Analysis, in 20 *Sociology of Health and Illness*, p.731, and S. Nettleton and R. Burrows (2000) When a Capital Investment Becomes an Emotional Loss: The Health Consequences of the Experience of Mortgage Possession in England, in 15 *Housing Studies*, p.463.

[133] British Medical Association (2003), above n.122, p.59.

[134] $\chi^2{}_1 = 847.83$, $p < 0.001$.

[135] 52 per cent, compared to 6 per cent of respondents to the LSRC survey (8 per cent, unweighted).

[136] $\chi^2{}_1 = 106.13$, $p < 0.001$ (immigration); $\chi^2{}_1 = 32.34$, $p < 0.001$ (discrimination).

[137] $\chi^2{}_1 = 96.53$, $p < 0.001$.

[138] $\chi^2{}_1 = 23.37$, $p < 0.001$.

[139] For the definition of 'trivial' in this context, see H. Genn (1999), above, n.3, p.13. 3,817 non-trivial problems were reported in the 18 substantive justiciable problem categories.

[140] This is similar to the pattern of incidence of crime. See, for example, H. Genn (1988) Multiple Victimisation, in M. Maguire (ed.) *Victims of Crime: A New Deal?* Milton Keynes: Open University Press.

[141] See above, p.26.

[142] See above, p.22.

[143] See above, p.21.

[144] See, for example, M. Straus, R. Gelles and S. Steinmetz (1980) *Behind Closed Doors*, New York: Anchor.

[145] L.J. Weitzman and M. Maclean (eds.) (1992) *Economic Consequences of Divorce*, Oxford: Clarendon Press; G. Davis, S. Cretney and J. Collins (1994) *Simple Quarrels: Negotiations and Adjudications in Divorce*, Oxford: Clarendon Press; J. Eekelaar, M. Maclean and S. Beinart (2000) *Family Lawyers*, Oxford: Hart Publishing; P. Wilcox (2000) Lone Motherhood: The Impact on Living Standards of Leaving a Violent Relatioship, in 34 *Journal of Social Policy and Administration*, p.176; G. Davis, G. Bevan, S. Clisby, Z. Cumming, R. Dingwall, P. Fenn, S. Finch, R. Fitzgerald, S. Goldie, D. Greatbach, D. James and J. Pearce (2000) *Monitoring Publicly Funded Family Mediation*, London: Legal Services Commission; G. Allan and G. Crow (2001) *Families, Households and Society*, Basingstoke: Palgrave; Office of the Deputy Prime Minister (2002) *The Provision of Accommodation and Support for Households Experiencing Domestic Violence in England*, London: Office of the Deputy Prime Minister.

[146] D.N. Kyriacou, D. Anglin, E. Taliaferro, S. Stone, T. Tubb, J.A. Linden, R. Muelleman, E. Barton E and J.F. Kraus (1999) Risk Factors For Injury To Women From Domestic Violence, in 341(25) *New England Journal Of Medicine*, p.1892.

[147] S. Parker, L. Limbers, E. McKeon (2002) *Homelessness and Accommodation Models for People Living with Mental Health Problems*, Rozelle, New South Wales: Mental Health Coordinating Council.

[148] For a discussion of the link between mental illness and homelessness see, for example, G. Sullivan, A. Burnam and P. Koegel (2000) Pathways To Homelessness Among The Mentally Ill, in 35(10) *Social Psychiatry And Psychiatric Epidemiology*, p.444. See, also, Office of the Deputy Prime Minister (1996) *More than a Roof: A Report into Tackling Homelessness*, London: Office of the Deputy Prime Minister.

[149] H. Genn (1999), above, n.3, p.35.

[150] D. Harris, M. Maclean, H. Genn, S. Lloyd-Bostock, P. Fenn, P. Corfield and Y. Brittan (1984) *Compensation and Support for Illness and Injury*, Oxford: Clarendon Press.

[151] Law Commission (1994) *Personal Injury Compensation: How Much is Enough?* London: Law Commission (Report No. 225).

[152] *Ibid.*

[153] A nonparametric test for multiple independent samples. It produces a chi-squared test of whether more observations were greater than or less than or equal to the median for each problem type. We combine problems in the resulting contingency table to compare specific problems to all other problems combined.

[154] There was a clear difference in the triggering effect of the problems studied: $F(17) = 2.41$, $p < 0.01$. Marginal means = 1.1 before vs. 1.5 after (domestic violence)(not significant); 0.6 before vs.1.1 after (divorce) 0.9 before vs. 1.2 after (relationship breakdown). The difference in marginal means for domestic violence was not quite significant.

[155] For divorce, there were 26 problems less than or equal to the median compared to 10 greater than the median ($\chi^2_1 = 5.34$, $p < 0.05$, comparing divorce to all other problems). For relationship breakdown, there were 41 less than or equal to the median compared to 19 greater than the median ($\chi^2_1 = 5.75$, $p < 0.05$, comparing relationship breakdown to all other problems).

[156] 20 of 33.

[157] Thus, divorce was significantly more likely to be reported in first than last position: (20 v. 5) $\chi^2_1 = 8.82$, $p < 0.01$.

[158] This corresponds to 20 problems, compared to 9 reported as occurring last in such sequences: $\chi^2_1 = 3.97$, $p < 0.5$. However, in general, although domestic violence was more often observed towards the beginning than the end of sequences of problems, our findings in this regard were not statistically significant. There were 29 problems less than or equal to the median compared to 17 greater than the median: $\chi^2_1 = 1.82$, $p = 0.18$.

[159] 21 (of 60) relationship breakdown problems were reported as occurring first in sequences of four or more problems, compared to 6 reported as occurring last: $\chi^2_1 = 8.16$, $p < 0.01$.

[160] $\chi^2 = 6.25$, $p < 0.01$.

[161] $p = 0.026$ (exact test used, owing to small numbers: Mehta and Patel (1996) *SPSS Exact Tests 7.0 for Windows*. Chicago, IL: SPSS Inc.).

[162] $\chi^2 = 6.50$, $p < 0.01$ (domestic violence); $\chi^2 = 3.45$, $p < 0.05$ (divorce); $\chi^2 = 8.76$, $p < 0.01$ (relationship breakdown).

[163] p = 0.046 (rented housing); p = 0.011 (children) (exact test used, owing to small numbers: Mehta and Patel (1996), above, n.161).

[164] Marginal means = 0.62 before vs. 0.76 after.

[165] 16 v. 6, χ^2_1 = 4.34, p < 0.05.

[166] Marginal means = 1.03 before vs. 1.22 after (homelessness); Marginal means = 0.68 before vs. 1.00 after (mental health); Marginal means = = 0.27 before vs. 0.73 after (immigration). Also, in sequences of four or more problems, both mental health and immigration problems were more often first than last, but numbers were very small, so again the results were not statistically significant.

[167] Marginal means = 0.75 before vs. 0.53 after

[168] χ^2_1 = 14.94, p < 0.001, comparing consumer to other problems combined (64 problems less than or equal to the median, 98 greater). Consumer problems were also significantly more likely to have been reported as occurring in last than first place of sequences of four or more problems (68 v. 32): χ^2_1 = 17.3, p < 0.001.

[169] P. Pleasence, N.J. Balmer, A. Buck, A. O'Grady, M. Maclean and H. Genn (2003), above, n.65.

[170] See above, p.32 and p.34.

[171] χ^2_1 = 7.56, p < 0.01.

[172] If only education problems are looked at, the increased likelihood is only marginally less substantial: χ^2_1 = 50.23, p < 0.001.

[173] χ^2_1 = 64.19, p < 0.001.

[174] χ^2_1 = 135.53, p < 0.001.

[175] See above, p.21.

[176] 34 per cent (158 of 465).

[177] 8 per cent (3 of 36).

[178] See above, p.21.

[179] This represents over half of all respondents who reported multiple problems.

[180] W. Felstiner, R. Abel and A. Sarat (1981) The Emergence and Transformation of Disputes: Naming, Blaming, Claiming ..., 15 Law and Society Review, p.631. The five-part aetiology of how 'injurious experiences' (here taken as equivalent to 'justiciable problems') may become lawsuits involves the recognition of circumstances as "injurious" (naming); the identification of them as a grievance for which another is responsible (blaming); the confrontation of the wrongdoer with a complaint (claiming); and finally, if the response of the wrongdoer is unsatisfactory, the decision to pursue a remedy through the courts. Felstiner, Abel and Sarat described the five stages as 'subjective, unstable, reactive, complicated and incomplete,' and the model is very much a 'starting point' (H. Genn (1999), above, n.3) for an understanding of the decision making process.

[181] 'Acceptable behaviour to a young person can be difficult for an elderly neighbour to tolerate': Social Exclusion Unit (2000) National Strategy for Neighbourhood Renewal: Report of Policy Action Team 8: Anti-Social Behaviour, London: The Stationary Office, para. 1.1. Also, in this instance young people will themselves often constitute 'the problem'. See, further, T. Newburn (2002), above, n.70, and M. Rutter, H. Giller and A. Hagell (1998) Antisocial Behaviour by Young People, Cambridge: Cambridge University Press. Also, see above, p.15.

[182] See, for example, C. Mirrlees-Black (1999), above, n.67, and C. Kershaw, T. Budd, G. Kinshott, J. Mattinson, P. Mayhew and A. Myhill (2000) The 2000 British Crime Survey, London: Home Office (Home Office Statistical Bulletin 18/00), pp.36-7. Also, see above, n.17.

[183] Hughes Commission (1980) Report of the Royal Commission on Legal Services in Scotland, Edinburgh: HMSO (Cmd. 7846).

[184] H. Genn (1999), above, n.3, p.69.

[185] H. Genn (1999), above, n.3, p.70.

[186] H. Genn and A. Paterson (2001), above, n.16, p.87; H. Genn (1999), above, n.3, pp.69-70.

[187] H. Genn (1999), above, n.3, p.255.

[188] 11 per cent if only instances in which it was believed something could be done are included.

[189] 12 per cent if only instances in which it was believed something could be done are included. This was the only reason provided for which there was no overlap with the reason of it being believed that nothing could be done.

[190] Although this finding is in line with Felstiner, Abel and Sarat's idea that 'blame' must precede 'claim', evidently not everyone who claims against another person necessarily first directs blame towards them. They may simply see an opportunity for gain: R. Kidder (1981) The End of the Road? Problems in the Analysis of Disputes, 15 Law and Society Review, p.717. Also, people may come to blame someone only

as a result of embarking on resolving action: S. Lloyd Bostock (1991) Propensity to Sue in England and the United States of America: A Comment on Kritzer, 18 *Law and Society Review*, p.428. Also, problems may not originate from or involve other people, as, for example, in the case of those encountered in obtaining citizenship of a new country. Felstiner, Abel and Sarat's model of disputing behaviour has nothing to say about non-contentious issues.

[191] 9 per cent if only instances in which it was believed something could be done are included.

[192] 8 per cent if only instances in which it was believed something could be done are included.

[193] 3 per cent if only instances in which it was believed something could be done are included.

[194] 4 per cent if only instances in which it was believed something could be done are included.

[195] 6 per cent if only instances in which it was believed something could be done are included.

[196] 23 per cent of such respondents discussed their situation with a partner (44 per cent of those who discussed their situation with anyone). These figures are derived from information obtained from main interviews.

[197] W. Felstiner, R. Abel and A. Sarat (1981), above, n.180.

[198] H. Genn (1999), above, n.3, p.70.

[199] $\chi^2{}_{119} = 292.93$, p < 0.001, using a Monte Carlo test to account for sparseness in areas of the contingency table.

[200] Standardised residuals exceeding around two or three indicate a lack of fit of the null hypothesis (independence) in that cell: A. Agresti (2002) *Categorical Data Analysis, 2nd Edition*, Hoboken, NJ: Wiley, p.81.

[201] 9 of 14. This finding was, though, short of being statistically significant: Standard Pearson Residual = 1.6 (see above, n.200).

[202] 11 of 21. This finding was, though, short of being statistically significant: Standard Pearson Residual = 1.6 (see above, n.200).

[203] 20 of 88; Standard Pearson Residual = -2.1.

[204] 19 of 88; Standard Pearson Residual = 2.4.

[205] 0 of 19; Standard Pearson Residual = -1.6, suggesting this finding is not quite significant. There were five other problem types in relation to which no respondent failed to act on account of importance: owned housing, homelessness, welfare benefits, children and immigration. However, none of these findings were significant (see above, n.200).

[206] 32 of 88; Standard Pearson Residual = 6.9.

[207] 9 of 19; Standard Pearson Residual = 4.3. Homelessness was also more often regarded as involving no dispute by lumpers (2 of 2; Standard Pearson Residual = 3.6).

[208] 2 of 102; Standard Pearson Residual = 2.6.

[209] 4 of 120; Standard Pearson Residual = 2.1.

[210] 0 of 42; Standard Pearson Residual = 2.0. There were five other problem types in relation to which no respondent failed to act on account of their involving no dispute: owned housing, domestic violence, children, immigration and unfair treatment by the police. However, none of these findings were significant (see above, n.200).

[211] 5 of 19; Standard Pearson Residual = 2.5.

[212] 3 of 15; Standard Pearson Residual = 2.1.

[213] 0 of 34. This finding was, though, short of being statistically significant: Standard Pearson Residual = 1.5 (see above, n.200).

[214] 5 of 18; Standard Pearson Residual = 2.5.

[215] 18 of 102; Standard Pearson Residual = 3.5.

[216] 2 of 86. This finding was, though, short of being statistically significant: Standard Pearson Residual = -1.8. (see above, n.200).

[217] 14 of 102; Standard Pearson Residual = 3.1.

[218] 8 of 34; Standard Pearson Residual = 4.5.

[219] 1 of 120; Standard Pearson Residual = -2.2.

[220] 16 of 120; Standard Pearson Residual = 3.5.

[221] 10 of 86; Standard Pearson Residual = 2.1.

[222] 0 of 88; Standard Pearson Residual = -2.5. There were seven other problem types in relation to which no respondent failed to act on account of concerns about the time it might take to obtain a resolution: discrimination, owned housing, homelessness, welfare benefits, divorce, domestic violence, children and immigration. However, none of these findings were significant (see above, n.200).

[223] 2 of 11. This finding was, though, short of being statistically significant; Standard Pearson Residual = 1.8 (see above, n.200).

[224] 0 of 71. This finding was, though, short of being statistically significant: Standard Pearson Residual = -1.7 (see above, n.200).

[225] $\chi^2{}_8 = 256.69$, Monte Carlo p < 0.001; Standardised Pearson Residuals = 8.3. The adviser types used in this analysis were: Citizens Advice Bureau, solicitor, other advice agency, trade union or professional body, employer, local council, police, insurance company, and other.

[226] See, further, P. Pleasence, N.J. Balmer, H. Genn, A. Buck and A. O'Grady (2003) The Experience of Clinical Negligence Within the General Population, in 9(6) *Clinical Risk*, p.211. This finding is similar to that of *Paths to Justice*: H. Genn (1999), above, n.3, p.69.

[227] Legal standing in the former case, professional standing in the latter.

[228] As can be seen in Appendix B, our finding in relation to domestic violence was not quite statistically significant. However, inaction was disproportionately reported by those who experienced domestic violence, identified using a simple χ^2 test: $\chi^2{}_1 = 77.73$, p < 0.001.

[229] 35 per cent of occasions, when taken together.

[230] The inclusion in the LSRC survey of an additional category of problems relating to mental health, and separate categories for problems relating to clinical negligence, unfair treatment by the police and domestic violence, can be seen to explain, at least in part, why the proportion of respondents to the *Paths to Justice* survey who 'lumped' their problems was slightly lower than that reported here (16 per cent (H. Genn (1999), above, n.3, p.38 (this figure is derived from screen interview data, and is substantially higher than the 5 per cent figure derived from the *Paths to Justice* main interview data (p.68)))). The inclusion of problems relating to discrimination and the exclusion of the *Paths to Justice* category of problems relating to renting out property will also have had the same effect. The inclusion of the additional category of problems relating to homelessness will, though, have had a small contrary effect. In *Paths to Justice Scotland*, respondents faced with consumer and welfare benefits problems were reported to be less likely to act: H. Genn and A. Paterson (2001), above, n.16, p.87. However, their analysis seems to be based on a contrast with those who obtained advice, and is inconsistent with information they provide elsewhere in the text, that suggests a high rate of taking some form of action (p.51).

[231] Exp(B)=1.027, p = 0.018. H. Genn (1999), above, n.3, p.38; H. Genn and A. Paterson (2001), above, n.16, p.87.

[232] When the multinomial 'ethnicity' variable was used in the regression analysis, ethnicity was removed on the final step. However, the analysis indicated Asian respondents to be significantly less likely to act than others: Exp(B) = 0.548, p = 0.017. A simple chi-square test also indicated this to be a significant finding: $\chi^2{}_1 = 35.41$, p < 0.01.

[233] $\chi^2{}_8 = 13.74$, Monte Carlo p = 0.085

[234] $\chi^2{}_1 = 6.14$, p = 0.013

[235] They did so on 95 per cent of occasions.

[236] Figures relating to discussions with friends and family are derived from information obtained from main interviews. 36 per cent of friends and relatives recommended that action should be taken. Just 1 per cent of friends and relatives recommended against action being taken.

[237] 26 of 1178, compared to 217 of 1966: $\chi^2{}_1 = 80.64$, p < 0.001. In all, 8 per cent of all those who acted to deal with problems utilised a formal court or tribunal process (6 per cent of all problems). The difficulty people face in answering survey questions relating to formal processes is evident from the different responses provided to general screen section questions and more detailed main section questions. See, further, pp.74-75.

[238] See p.55, p.68, and Appendix C.

[239] As regards use of an Ombudsman, 19 of 1178, compared to 53 of 1966: $\chi^2{}_1 = 4.16$, p < 0.05. In all, 2 per cent of all those who acted to deal with problems utilised an Ombudsman (just under 2 per cent of all problems). As regards mediation, 9 of 1178, compared to 128 of 1966: $\chi^2{}_1 = 58.37$, p < 0.001. In all, 4 per cent of all those who acted to deal with problems utilised a mediation service (3 per cent of all problems). Again, as detailed in n. 237, clear disparities were evident between answers to screen and main section questions. See, further, pp.74-75.

[240] Respondents acting in relation to problems ancillary to relationship breakdown involving only money handled them alone less often than when they involved disputes concerning children (75 per cent, compared to 81 per cent). However, because of the small numbers involved, the difference was not statistically significant. See, further, P. Pleasence, N.J. Balmer, A. Buck, A. O'Grady and H. Genn (2003)

Family Problems: Who Does What and When: Further Findings from the LSRC Survey of Justiciable Problems, 33 *Family Law,* p.822.

[241] This evidence stems from a simple chi-square test: $\chi^2{}_1 = 8.25$, $p < 0.01$.

[242] $\chi^2{}_4 = 31.15$, $p < 0.001$; Standard Pearson Residual = 2.6.

[243] There was also some evidence that respondents who had not acted in relation to a past problem were less likely to act, but the results fell short of statistical significance. Overall, though, there seemed to be an association between previous strategies and whether action was taken to resolve a problem: $\chi^2{}_3 = 8.70$, $p < 0.05$. Standard Pearson Residuals suggested that the source of the association centred on respondents who had not acted in the past being more likely not to act (1.4). See above, though, n.200.

[244] $\chi^2{}_1 = 10.88$, $p < 0.01$.

[245] This was the case in respect of both binary logistic regression and a simple chi-square test: Exp(B) = 0.839, $p < 0.05$ (regression); $\chi^2{}_1 = 17.17$, $p < 0.001$ (chi-square).

[246] K.D. Bertakis, R. Azari, L.J. Helms, E.J. Callahan, J.A. Robbins (2000) Gender Differences In The Utilization Of Health Care Services, in 49(2) *Journal Of Family Practice*, p.147; A.V. Marcell, J.D. Klein, I. Fischer, M.J. Allan, P.K. Kokotailo (2002) Male Adolescent Use Of Health Care Services: Where Are The Boys? in 30(1) *Journal Of Adolescent Health*, p.35.

[247] 62.5 per cent and 62.4 per cent respectively: $\chi^2{}_1 = 0.002$, $p > 0.95$.

[248] See, for example, C.M. Ashton, P. Haidet, D.A. Paterniti, T.C. Collins, H.S. Gordon, K. O'Malley, L.A. Petersen, B.F. Sharf, M.E. Suarez-Almazor, N.P. Wray and R.L. Street (2003) Racial and Ethnic Disparities in the Use of Health Services - Bias, Preference, or Poor Communication? in 18(2) *Journal Of General Internal Medicine*, p.146, and K.A. Sproston, L.B. Pitson, and E. Walker (2001) The Use of Primary Care Services by the Chinese Population Living in England: Examining Inequalities, in 6(3-4) *Ethnicity & Health*, p.189.

[249] K.A. Sproston, L.B. Pitson, and E. Walker (2001), above, n.248.

[250] Q. Ngo-Metzger, M.P. Massagli, B.R. Clarridge, M. Manocchia, R.B. Davis, L.I. Iezzoni, R.S. Phillips (2003) Linguistic And Cultural Barriers To Care, in 18(1) *Journal Of General Internal Medicine*, p.44.

[251] S. Hughes (2002) *Addressing the Advice Needs of Black and Minority Ethnic Communities*, Brighton: Brighton and Hove Community Legal Service Partnership, pp.2-3. See, also, J. Hobson and P. Jones (2003) *Methods of Delivery: Telephone Advice Pilot: Evaluation Report*, London: Legal Services Commission, paragraph 1.21.

[252] 150 of 1038, compared to 313 of 420 problems: $\chi^2{}_1 = 25.03$, $p < 0.001$.

[253] We used ordinal logistic regression with the amount of money involved as our response variable and sought advice as against did not seek advice as a single dichotomous predictor: $Wald_1 = 32.6$, $p < 0.001$.

[254] $R^2 = 0.86$ and 0.82 respectively.

[255] 0.049 - 0.091 for those who sought advice, compared to 0.093 - 0.018 for those who did not.

[256] Again, including only problems where some action was taken: Spearman correlation coefficient = 0.720, $p < 0.01$. Interestingly, there was no significant correlation between rankings of problem type by the likelihood of advice being obtained and their stated importance: Spearman correlation coefficient = 0.383, $p = 0.130$.

[257] See, for example, H. Genn (1999), above, n.3, H. Genn and A. Paterson (2001), above, n.16, and G. Maxwell, C. Smith, P. Shepherd and A. Morris (1999), above, n.16. Also, for example, in the context of welfare benefits, Bryson noted in the early 1990s that people seek advice from many types of professional they come into contact with. He wrote that 'these informal advisors include staff in various branches of the health, social and probation services as well as others such as personnel officers and religious leaders': A. Bryson (1994) *Information and Advice about Benefits*, London: Policy Studies Institute, p.5.

[258] 291 of 1965. These figures are derived from screen interview data.

[259] $\chi^2{}_{17} = 84.01$, Monte Carlo $p < 0.001$; Standardised Pearson Residuals = 4.9, 4.0, 1.5 and 1.4 respectively. These figures are derived from screen interview data.

[260] 16 of 34 (47 per cent). The figures were 24 per cent for neighbours and 20 per cent for rented housing and welfare benefits. These figures are derived from screen interview data.

[261] Standardised Pearson Residuals = -2.7, -2.7 and -2.6 respectively; 4, 5 and 8 per cent respectively. These figures are derived from screen interview data.

[262] Information collected through main interviews indicated that 50 per cent, 47 per cent and 33 per cent respectively of respondents who obtained advice in relation to homelessness, welfare benefits and rented housing problems obtained advice from a local council, compared to 13 per cent in general. Information

was not collected for neighbours problems. Screen weighting was used as the analysis pertained to problem types. Information collected through screen interviews indicated that 68 per cent (23 of 34), 65 per cent (179 of 274), 54 per cent (45 of 84) and 53 per cent (57 of 107) respectively of respondents who tried to obtain information in relation to homelessness, neighbours, welfare benefits and rented housing problems tried to obtain information from a local council, compared to 32 per cent (597 of 1853) in general (29 per cent if neighbours problems are excluded).

[263] Local councils accounted for 18 per cent of all unsuccessful attempts to obtain advice.

[264] Information collected through the main interviews indicated that 96 per cent and 55 per cent respectively of respondents who experienced divorce and personal injury problems contacted a solicitor, compared to 39 per cent in general. Screen weighting was used as the analysis pertained to problem types. Information was not collected for neighbours problems. Information collected through screen interviews indicated that 92 per cent (87 of 95) and 46 per cent (53 of 115) respectively of respondents who divorce and personal injury problems tried to obtain information from a solicitor or other lawyer, compared to 34 per cent (639 of 1853) in general (39 per cent if neighbours problems are excluded).

[265] Solicitors accounted for 7 per cent of all unsuccessful attempts to obtain advice.

[266] 65 per cent of unsuccessful attempts and 47 per cent of all reasons provided.

[267] 37 per cent of unsuccessful attempts and 28 per cent of all reasons provided: $\chi^2_{49} = 121.01$, Monte Carlo $p < 0.001$ (overall); Standardised Pearson Residual $= -1.8$ (suggesting this fell just short of being statistically significant (see above, n.200)). A lesser proportion still was observed in relation to social workers.

[268] 77 per cent of unsuccessful attempts and 71 per cent of all reasons provided: Standardised Pearson Residuals $= 1.4$. Again, though, this fell short of being statistically significant (see above, n.200).

[269] 11 per cent of all reasons provided.

[270] See, for example, H. Genn (1999), above, n.3, p.76, H. Genn and A. Paterson (2001), above, n.16, p.94, and, from earlier, T. Goriely (1997) *Resolving Civil Disputes: Choosing Between Out of Court Schemes and Litigation*, London: Lord Chancellor's Department, and G. Petterson, P. Sissons and M. Wann (1995) *Users' Views of CAB Services,* London: NACAB. A 1998 National Association of Citizens Advice Bureaux report indicated that 80% of telephone calls were met with an engaged tone, although telephone systems have improved since then: National Association of Citizens Advice Bureaux (1998): *The CAB Service and Community Legal Services: A Paper for the Lord Chancellor*, London: NACAB.

[271] 51 per cent of unsuccessful attempts and 38 per cent of all reasons provided. Standardised Pearson Residual $= 5.7$. Citizens Advice Bureaux also accounted for 58 per cent of instances of this reason being given in relation to any source of advice.

[272] A survey of 146 Citizens Advice Bureaux in North London, the West Midlands and Yorkshire and Humberside indicated that only one-third (53) offered some sort of out-of-hours service. Furthermore, out-of-hours services were generally restricted to a few hours on one day per week, with advice offered by appointment only. The Citizens Advice Bureau in Scarborough, however, had a 24-hour telephone advice line, and some bureaux had internet advice facilities. Camden Citizens Advice Bureau operated an outreach service, where people who contact the bureau by telephone can arrange a face-to-face meeting in their own home. The survey was carried out using data obtained from the Community Legal Services Directory: Legal Services Commission (2003) *Community Legal Services Directory,* 5th edition, London: Legal Services Commission.

[273] 20 per cent of unsuccessful attempts and 14 per cent of all reasons provided. If compared against Citizens Advice Bureaux, $\chi^2_1 = 12.15$, $p < 0.001$ (unable to contact by any means); $\chi^2_7 = 14.89$, Monte Carlo $p = 0.01$, Standardised Pearson Residual $= -1.5$ (unable to get through by telephone) (see above, n.200). Also, there were fewer reports of respondents being unable to get through to an insurance company advice service than a Citizens Advice Bureau as a proportion of the total number of attempts to contact them (3 per cent and 7 per cent respectively), although the difference was not statistically significant: $\chi^2_1 = 1.23$, $p = 0.27$.

[274] 49 per cent.

[275] 5 per cent and 8 per cent of all reasons provided.

[276] 11 per cent and 14 per cent of occasions respectively (9 per cent and 8 per cent of reasons). Standardised Pearson Residuals $= 1.1$ (CAB) and 1.7 (local council), short of indicating statistical significance (see above, n.200). The 1998 National Association of Citizens Advice Bureaux report indicated that 13% of

people wait for more than an hour to be seen: National Association of Citizens Advice Bureaux (1998), above, p.268.

[277] 17 per cent and 24 per cent of occasions respectively (10 per cent and 19 per cent of reasons). Standardised Pearson Residuals = 0.9 (local council) and 1.9 (employer). Again, this is short of indicating statistical significance.

[278] 3 per cent of occasions and 2 per cent of all reasons provided.

[279] Consumers' Association (2000) *The Community Legal Service: Access for All?* London: Consumers' Association, p.37.

[280] M. Blacksell, K. Economides and C. Watkins (1991) *Justice Outside the City: Access to Legal Services in Rural Britain*, Harlow: Longman.

[281] Ibid.

[282] $\chi^2_8 = 69.62$, p < 0.001; Standardised Pearson Residuals = -3.2 (solicitor) and –1.5 (insurance company) (see above, n.200). Overall, respondents reported having not obtained advice from a solicitor or insurance company, following an attempt to do so or consideration of an attempt to do so on 99 and 13 occasions respectively. This compares to 337 and 50 occasions on which advice was obtained from solicitors or insurance companies. The overall ratio, for all advisers, was 1 consideration or unsuccessful attempt for every 4 successful attempts.

[283] Standardised Pearson Residual = 5.1. Overall, respondents reported having not obtained advice from a Citizens Advice Bureau, following an attempt to do so or consideration of an attempt to do so on 172 occasions. This compares to 201 occasions on which advice was obtained from Citizens Advice Bureaux.

[284] There are just 516 Citizens Advice Bureaux across England and Wales, compared to 9,862 solicitors' firms. Citizens Advice do, though, provide information through a further 2284 outreach services and information points, and the continuing development of these types of service will no doubt increase the effectiveness of Citizens Advice in reaching those populations that wish to make use of their services.

[285] See above, n.272.

[286] See above, n.270.

[287] $\chi^2_{17} = 135.78$, Monte Carlo p < 0.001; Standardised Pearson Residuals = -2.7 (rented housing), -2.3 (homelessness), -2.9 (money/debt), -2.3 (welfare benefits), -2.1 (children) and -2.0 (problems ancillary to relationship breakdown). Other problems in relation to which no respondents gave up trying to obtain a resolution following an unsuccessful attempt to obtain advice were: divorce (-1.1), domestic violence (-1.4), personal injury (-1.4), clinical negligence (-1.1), mental health (-0.6), immigration (-0.6) and unfair police treatment (-1.1). This analysis is based on screen interview data.

[288] 42 of 66 (neighbours), 26 of 33 (employment): Standardised Pearson Residuals = 4.5 (neighbours) and 4.7 (employment). 4 of 4 respondents also gave up trying to resolve discrimination problems after having been unable to obtain advice: Standardised Pearson Residual = 2.4.

[289] $\chi^{40} = 121.59$, Monte Carlo p < 0.001.

[290] $\chi^2_{24} = 63.76$, p < 0.001. See, for example, P. McCullagh (1980) Ordinal Regression Models, in 42(2) *Journal of the Royal Statistical Society. Series B (Methodological)*, p.109.

[291] 11 per cent of second advisers were friends or relatives, compared to 8 per cent of first advisers. This difference was, however, just short of being statistically significant: $\chi^2_2 = 2.95$, p = 0.086. Overall, 9 per cent of advisers were friends or relatives.

[292] $\chi^2_{152} = 806.12$, p < 0.001.

[293] The final adviser would be the first adviser if advice were obtained from only one adviser.

[294] $\chi^2_{152} = 650.28$, p < 0.001

[295] See, for example, M. Kilian (2003) Alternatives to Public Provision: The Role of Legal Expenses Insurance in Broadening Access to Justice: The German Experience, in 30(1) *Journal of Law and Society*, p.31.

[296] $\chi^2_1 = 28.89$, p < 0.001

[297] 54 per cent of all occasions on which proceedings were commenced after advice had been obtained.

[298] Solicitors dealt with 77 per cent of all reported divorces, and 95 per cent of divorces where the respondent obtained advice.

[299] Only very rarely are conveyances undertaken without the assistance of solicitors or licensed conveyancers.

[300] Including only the 18 substantive problem categories. Money/debt problems accounted for 14 per cent of instances, consumer problems 10 per cent, and employment problems 8 per cent. The remaining 24 per cent of instances were distributed among the remaining 11 problem categories.

[301] The figures were 12 per cent and 2 per cent respectively for screen interviews. However, the information collected from screen interviews was much less detailed, and it is not clear whether respondents always understood what they were being asked. The pattern of mediation use was similar though. After family problems, mediation was most often reported in relation to discrimination (9 per cent), employment (4 per cent), neighbours (2 per cent) and money/debt (2 per cent) problems.

[302] See, for example, G. Bevan, S. Clisby, Z. Cumming, G. Davis, R. Dingwall, P. Fenn, S. Finch, R. Fitzgerald, S. Goldie, D. Greatbatch, A. James and J. Pearce (2000) *Monitoring Publicly Funded Family Mediation: Report to the Legal Services Commission*, London: Legal Services Commission.

[303] H. Genn (1999), above, n.3, p.96.

[304] 0 per cent of those who obtained advice from employers had been referred from elsewhere. The percentages for the police, trade unions and professional bodies, local councils and insurance companies were 11, 13, 14 and 17 respectively.

[305] J. Eekelaar, M. Maclean and S. Beinart (2000) *Family Lawyers: The Divorce Work of Solicitors*, Oxford: Hart Publications. See, also, G. Davis, S. Cretney and J. Collins (1995) *Simple Quarrels*, Oxford: Oxford University Press, and G. Bevan, G. Davis and J. Pearce (1999) Piloting a Quasi-Market for Family Mediation Amongst Clients Eligible for Legal Aid, in 18 *Civil Justice Quarterly*, p.239.

[306] The problem of how to develop appropriate and effective referral strategies between different suppliers of legal information and advice is not new and was one of the central concerns in the development of the Community Legal Service and is clearly an area that would benefit from closer analysis: See discussion in H. Genn and A. Paterson, above, n.16, p.17, and associated references especially C. Miller Research (1999) *Referrals between Advice Agencies and Solicitors*, Edinburgh, CRU. See, also, for example, A. Bryson (1994), above, n.257.

[307] For further details on client satisfaction as an outcome measure for advice, see, for example, A. Sherr, R. Moorhead, and A. Paterson (1994) *Lawyers - The Quality Agenda, Volume 1: Assessing and Developing Competence and Quality in Legal Aid; The Report of the Birmingham Franchising Pilot*, London: HMSO; H. Sommerlad, (1999) English Perspectives on Quality: The Client-Led Model of Quality – A Third Way, 33(2) *University of British Columbia Law Review*, p.491; R. Moorhead, A. Sherr, L. Webley, S. Rogers, L. Sherr, A. Paterson and S. Domberger (2001) *Quality and Cost: Final Report on the Contracting of Civil, Non-Family Advice and Assistance Pilot*, London: TSO.

[308] $\chi^2_{48} = 104.56$, Monte Carlo p < 0.001.

[309] $\chi^2_1 = 3.04$, p < 0.081.

[310] $\chi^2_{48} = 104.56$, Monte Carlo p < 0.001; Standardised Pearson Residual = -2.2 (local council, quality of advice), 2.8 (CAB, not up to date), 2.5 (other advice agencies, quality of advice), 2.7 (trade unions, nothing could be done), 2.5 (insurance companies, nothing could be done), 4.0 (solicitors, expense).

[311] $\chi^2_1 = 5.62$, p < 0.05.

[312] 54 per cent. It should be noted, though, that numbers were small (n=11)

[313] Hence, the percentages in this section do not add up to 100 per cent.

[314] It seems likely, though, that legal aid funded advice has been underreported through the LSRC survey, although the survey period extends back to before the period of substantial growth of legal aid funding of advice services.

[315] M. Kilian (2003), above, n.295.

[316] See, for example, P. Pleasence (1998) *Personal Injury Litigation in Practice*, London: LABRU.

[317] Advice both funded and provided by unions was described as being provided in person on half of all occasions, although numbers are small (8 of 16). It was described less so in relation to insurance companies (2 of 8).

[318] Access to Justice Act 1999

[319] Courts and Legal Services Act 1990; Conditional Fee Agreements Regulations 1995. For a discussion of the introduction of conditional fees and a commentary on conditional fee practice, see S. Yarrow and P. Abrams (1999) *Nothing to Lose? Clients' Experiences of Using Conditional Fees*, London: University of Westminster; R. Moorhead (2000) Conditional Fee Agreements, Legal Aid and Access to Justice, in 33 *University of British Columbia Law Review*, p.471; and S. Yarrow (2000) *Just Rewards? The Outcome of Conditional Fee Cases*, London: University of Westminster.

[320] 6 and 2.

[321] Many trade unions now provide general legal help lines as one of the benefits of membership.

[322] 97 per cent (33 of 34) (divorce); 83 per cent (15 of 18) (owned housing).

[323] In terms of money, $\chi^2_{16} = 36.30$, p < 0.01. Standardised Pearson Residuals = -3.3 (less than £1,000),

2.0 (£1,000-9999), 2.5 (£10,000 plus). In terms of memory, we fitted simple exponential decay functions, using non-linear regression, to the number of problems starting in each of fourteen time periods that together made up the LSRC survey reference period as a proportion of the highest number of problems starting in any time period (see Appendix C for details). We found little evidence of memory decay in relation to problems dealt with by solicitors. The decay coefficient was 0.04, with the lower 95 per cent confidence band equal to 0 (upper = 0.077), and the R^2 value was 0.272. For Citizens Advice Bureaux, the decay coefficient was also 0.04, with the 95 per cent confidence interval straddling 0 (-0.005 to 0.088), and the R^2 value was 0.230. In contrast, however, the decay co-efficient for 'other' advisers was 0.11, the lower 95 per cent confidence band was 0.04 (upper = 0.182), and the R^2 value was 0.582. Interestingly, Citizens Advice Bureaux seemed less likely to deal with problems involving larger sums of money: Standardised Pearson Residuals = 1.6 (less than £1,000), -1.7 (£1,000-9999), -0.2 (£10,000 plus) (see above, n.200).

[324] See page 56 above and Appendix C.

[325] $\chi^2_2 = 8.33$, p < 0.05. Standardised Pearson Residuals = -1.8 (less than £1,000), 0.7 (£1,000-9999), 1.9 (£10,000 plus) (legal aid). $\chi^2_6 = 30.17$, p < 0.001, Standardised Pearson Residuals = -2.0 (less than £1,000), 1.2 (£1,000-9999), 1.6 (£10,000 plus) (private funding (all)). $\chi^2_6 = 30.17$, p < 0.001, Standardised Pearson Residuals = -2.0 (less than £1,000), 0.4 (£1,000-9999), 2.8 (£10,000 plus) (private funding (part)) (see above, n.200).

[326] We found little evidence of memory decay in relation to problems in relation to which legal aid or privately funded advice was obtained. The decay coefficients were 0.03 and 0.01 respectively, and in each case the 95 per cent confidence interval straddled 0 (-0.041 to 0.106; -0.082 to 0.0562). Also, the R^2 values were just 0.076 and 0.011. In contrast, there was evidence of considerable decay in respect of problems in relation to which 'free' advice was obtained, and slight decay in respect of problems in relation to which otherwise funded advice had been obtained. The decay coefficients were 0.09 and 0.07 respectively, and in the former case the lower 95 per cent confidence band was 0.0563 (above the higher 95 per cent confidence band of private funding) and the R^2 value was 0.820. In the case of otherwise funded advice, the lower 95 per cent confidence band was only marginally above 0 (0.005), and the R^2 value was 0.333.

[327] $\chi^2_1 = 6.67$, p < 0.05.

[328] See, further, above p.10 and pp. 27-29.

[329] $\chi^2_{48} = 12.05$, p < 0.001.

[330] Spearman correlation coefficient = 0.626, p < 0.01.

[331] $\chi^2_8 = 28.80$, p < 0.001. Standardised Pearson Residual = 3.2.

[332] $\chi^2_8 = 52.86$, p < 0.001. Standardised Pearson Residual = 5.3.

[333] $\chi^2_8 = 28.80$, p < 0.001. Standardised Pearson Residual = 2.4.

[334] $\chi^2_8 = 52.86$, p < 0.001. Standardised Pearson Residual = 0.7 (see above, n.200).

[335] $\chi^2_8 = 28.80$, p < 0.001. Standardised Pearson Residual = -1.6 (see above, n.200).

[336] $\chi^2_8 = 52.86$, p < 0.001. Standardised Pearson Residual = -0.8 (see above, n.200).

[337] Spearman correlation coefficient = 0.523, p < 0.05.

[338] $\chi^2_8 = 88.60$, p < 0.001. Standardised Pearson Residual = 7.6.

[339] $\chi^2_8 = 83.77$, p < 0.001. Standardised Pearson Residual = 7.0.

[340] $\chi^2_8 = 88.60$, p < 0.001. Standardised Pearson Residuals = -2.6 (employer), -2.3 (trade union).

[341] $\chi^2_8 = 83.77$, p < 0.001. Standardised Pearson Residuals = -2.3 (employer), -0.5 (trade union) (see above, n.200).

[342] $\chi^2_8 = 88.60$, p < 0.001. Standardised Pearson Residual = -1.8. The same was also true of advice agencies other than Citizens Advice Bureaux (Standardised Pearson Residuals = -1.8), though this was probably due to a significant difference in the number of consumer problems (see above, n.200). Thus, the difference in use of such advice agencies was not apparent once problem type was controlled for.

[343] $\chi^2_8 = 83.77$, p < 0.001. Standardised Pearson Residual = -3.8.

[344] See, for example, National Consumer Council (1995), above, n.16, Scottish Consumer Council (1997), above, n.16; M. Rosenthal, L. Mulcahy, S. Lloyd-Bostock (eds.) (1999) *Medical Mishaps: Pieces of the Puzzle*, Buckingham: Open University Press; Genn (1999), above, n.3; H. Genn and A. Paterson (2001), above, n.16.

[345] *Paths to Justice* reported that 51 per cent of respondents' main objectives were money or property related, and the corresponding figure reported in *Paths to Justice Scotland* was 50 per cent: Genn (1999), above, n.3, p.180, H. Genn and A. Paterson (2001), above, n.16, p.182.

[346] See, for example, Genn (1999), above, n.3, p.83.

[347] $\chi^2_{28} = 272.48$, p < 0.001. Standardised Pearson Residuals = -5.3 (consumer), -2.1 (personal injury),

-2.6 (money/debt), 11.3 (welfare benefits).

[348] Standardised Pearson Residuals = 2.6 (divorce), 3.0 (relationship breakdown), 2.3 (domestic violence), 3.1 (children).

[349] Claimant respondents did not always have a particular amount in mind (15 per cent). These respondents have been excluded from this analysis.

[350] $\chi^2_{28} = 102.43$, p < 0.001.

[351] Standardised Pearson Residuals = 1.8 (consumer, < £1000), -2.8 (personal injury, < £1000), 3.6 (divorce, > £5000), 4.1 (relationship breakdown, > £5,000).

[352] Spearman correlation coefficient = 0.173, p < 0.01.

[353] $\chi^2_{95} = 582.47$, p < 0.001. Standardised Pearson Residuals = 7.5 (rented housing, property only), 5.9 (consumer, property only), 6.5 (consumer, money and property).

[354] $\chi^2_{19} = 286.37$, p < 0.001. Standardised Pearson Residuals = -5.8 (children), 2.1 (domestic violence), -1.9 (divorce), -2.3 (discrimination), -2.4 (unfair police treatment), -1.8 (immigration). Our findings in relation to immigration were not statistically significant, but the indication was that immigration problems did not relate to money or property, and the nature of the problems supports this.

[355] Standardised Pearson Residual = -4.0 (clinical negligence).

[356] P. Pleasence, N.J. Balmer, H. Genn, A. Buck and A. O'Grady (2003) The Experience of Clinical Negligence Within the General Population, in 9(6) *Clinical Risk*, p.211. See also, for example, Chief Medical Officer (2003) *Making Amends: A Consultation Paper Setting Out Proposals for Reforming the Approach to Clinical Negligence in the NHS,* London: Department of Health; S. Lloyd-Bostock and L. Mulcahy (1994), above, n.344; H. Genn and S. Lloyd-Bostock (1995) *Medical Negligence Research Project: The Operation of the Tort System in Medical Negligence Cases,* London: HMSO; M. Rosenthal, L. Mulcahy, S. Lloyd-Bostock (eds.) (1999), above, n.344; and L. Mulcahy, M. Selwood and A. Netten (2000) *Mediating Medical Negligence Claims: An Option for the Future?* Norwich: The Stationary Office.

[357] $\chi^2_{112} = 534.07$, p < 0.001.

[358] Standardised Pearson Residuals = 5.5 (money/debt), 6.2 (unfair police treatment).

[359] Standardised Pearson Residuals = 7.0 (employment), 4.3 (discrimination), 2.3 (personal injury), 2.2 (immigration).

[360] Standardised Pearson Residuals = 4.3 (personal injury), 1.9 (clinical negligence). See above, n.200.

[361] Where a binomial 'strategy' variable was used (handled alone, sought advice), Wald$_1$ = 17.51, Exp(B) = 0.543, p < 0.001. Details of the model where a multinomial variable was used is set out in Appendix B. This difference was not observable overall: $\chi^2_1 = 0.734$, p = 0.392.

[362] $\chi^2_1 = 8.17$, p < 0.01.

[363] 1 per cent of these agreements were arrived at following a mediation session being attended.

[364] This figure most likely under-represents the percentage of problems resolved by adjudication. Respondents do not appear to have always understood questions relating to formal legal processes, and did not always recognise the use of formal processes within the dispute resolution process.

[365] The proportion of problems in relation to which respondents took no resolving action was lower in main interviews than screen interviews.

[366] 23 per cent of problems that respondents did not attempt to resolve remained on-going at the time of interview. A further 6 per cent concluded with a court judgment.

[367] This finding was not, though, statistically significant: $\chi^2_1 = 1.90$, p = 0.169. However, additional support is also provided by the fact that those who sought advice had abandoned fewer attempts to resolve on-going problems than those who handled their problems alone: $\chi^2_1 = 5.63$, p < 0.05.

[368] $\chi^2_{48} = 274.70$, p < 0.001.

[369] Standardised Pearson Residuals = 8.5 (divorce), 1.9 (relationship breakdown) and 1.6 (domestic violence). Though see above, n.200.

[370] H. Genn (1999), above, n.3, p.155. Standardised Pearson Residual = 2.1. Interestingly, welfare benefits problems were least likely to be resolved by agreement: Standardised Pearson Residual = -2.1. They tended to be either adjudicated or abandoned (Standardised Pearson Residual = 2.4).

[371] Employment problems were reported to be more likely to conclude in adjudication in *Paths to Justice*: H. Genn (1999), above, n.3, p.155.

[372] $\chi^2_2 = 12.00$, p < 0.01. Standardised Pearson Residual = -2.4.

[373] Respondents who did not state their objectives were not asked if their objectives were met.

[374] Where an objective was stated: $\chi^2_4 = 187.29$, p < 0.001. Standardised Pearson Residual = 10.8. Where no objective was stated and respondent apparently gave up: $\chi^2_4 = 442.12$, p < 0.001. Standardised Pearson Residual = 12.0.

[375] $\chi^2{}_2 = 0.639$, p = 0.726.

[376] $\chi^2{}_1 = 2.868$, p = 0.090.

[377] See, for example, H. Genn and Y. Genn (1989) *The Effectiveness of Representation at Tribunals*, London: Lord Chancellor's Department.

[378] $\chi^2{}_1 = 48.67$, p < 0.001.

[379] $\chi^2{}_1 = 22.95$, p < 0.001.

[380] H. Genn (1999), above, n.3, p.213.

[381] Respondents were free to provide multiple reasons, so these percentages cannot be added together.

[382] This was the case whichever method of determining whether objectives were met was used: $\chi^2{}_1 = 4.04$, p < 0.05 (whether objectives met stated); $\chi^2{}_1 = 5.04$, p < 0.05 (if those respondents who did not say whether their objectives had been met and who reported that their problems concluded without agreement or adjudication were assumed to be unsuccessful in securing their objectives).

[383] Only 25 respondents reported receiving legal aid and stated whether their objectives had been met in respect of a problem that had concluded.

[384] $\chi^2{}_2 = 18.60$, p < 0.001. Standard Pearson Residual = 3.2. This was still significant if those respondents who did not say whether their objectives had been met and who reported that their problems concluded without agreement or adjudication were assumed to be unsuccessful in securing their objectives: $\chi^2{}_2 = 21.39$, p < 0.001.

[385] $\chi^2{}_2 = 26.20$, p < 0.001. Standardised Pearson Residual = -3.6. However, if those respondents who did not say whether their objectives had been met and who reported that their problems concluded without agreement or adjudication were assumed to be unsuccessful in securing their objectives, then this was no longer significant.

[386] Some justiciable problems may continue beyond the death of the person initially involved. The estate or relatives of a deceased person may continue to pursue 'justice' in relation to, for example, an accident or industrial disease.

[387] The respondent was partially successful in her claim against her employer, and was awarded a sum of money by an employment tribunal, at which she was represented by her trade union.

[388] As would be expected, at the time of interview on-going problems had already lasted for an average of 7 months longer than concluded problems (15 months compared to 8 months). 42 per cent of on-going problems had already lasted for a year or more, and 3 per cent for 5 years or more. 16 on-going problems (1 per cent) had already lasted for more than 10 years.

[389] Only concluded problems were included in this analysis. When all problems were included, employment, money/debt, personal injury and immigration problems were also significant: t = 2.413, p < 0.05 (employment), t = 2.374, p < 0.05 (money/debt), t = 2.122, p < 0.05 (personal injury), t = 2.235, p < 0.05 (immigration). This is in part a reflection of the fact that money/debt, personal injury and immigration problems were more likely to be on-going: Wald = 4.158, Exp(B) = 0.461, p < 0.05 (employment), Wald = 9.727, Exp(B) = 0.289, p < 0.01 (personal injury), Wald = 4.617, Exp(B) = 0.257, p < 0.05 (immigration). Also, the distribution of durations of employment problems was highly skewed (kurtosis = 84.64).

[390] See above, p.57, p.80, n.326 and Appendix C.

[391] Pearson correlation coefficient = 0.260, p < 0.001.

[392] t = 0.522, p = 0.602.

[393] $\chi^2{}_1 = 30.32$, p < 0.001.

[394] $\chi^2{}_6 = 179.73$, p < 0.001. Standard Pearson Residuals = -2.4 (stress), -2.9 (ill-health). They were also less likely to have regarded the resolution process in beneficial terms (-2.4).

[395] $\chi^2{}_6 = 121.10$, p < 0.001. Standard Pearson Residuals = -4.2

[396] Standard Pearson Residual = -1.3

[397] See, for example, G. Davis, S. Cretney and J. Collins (1995) *Simple Quarrels*, Oxford: Oxford University Press, and J. Eekelaar, M. Maclean and S. Beinart (2000) *Family Lawyers: The Divorce Work of Solicitors*, Oxford: Hart.

[398] $\chi^2{}_{12} = 32.91$, p < 0.01. Standard Pearson Residuals = 2.5.

[399] $\chi^2{}_1 = 5.81$, p < 0.05.

[400] $\chi^2{}_6 = 28.83$, p < 0.001. Standard Pearson Residuals = 2.2.

[401] Consortium on Legal Services and the Public (1996), above, n.1, p.ix.

[402] P. Pleasence, H. Genn, N.J. Balmer, A. Buck and A. O'Grady (2003), above n.35, p.26.

[403] See Unit 7 of Key Stages 1 and 2, Unit 3 of Key Stage 3, and Units 3, 9 and 10 of Key Stage 4.

[404] See, for example, Office for Standards in Education (2003) *National Curriculum Citizenship: Planning and Implementation 2002/03: An Inspection Report of 25 Schools*, available for download at www.ofsted.gov.uk/publications.

[405] R.A. Macdonald (2003) *Foundation Paper: Access to Justice in 2003 – Scope, Scale and Ambitions*, paper prepared for the Law Society of Upper Canada.

[406] H. Genn and A. Paterson (2001), above, n.16, p.261.

[407] See, s.4 of the Legal Aid Act 1988 and s.4 of the Access to Justice Act 1999.

[408] See, for example, www.legalservices.gov.uk/misl/news/press/pib_budget_projects.pdf.

[409] Legal Services Agency (2002) *Annual Report 2001-2*,Wellington: Legal Services Agency. The Legal Services Commission is, though, developing an integrated information strategy which encompasses educational elements.

[410] R.A. Macdonald (2003), above, n.409.

[411] M. Galanter (1974) Why the 'Haves' Come Out Ahead, in 9 *Law and Society Review*, p.95.

[412] H. Genn (1999), above, n.3, p.253.

[413] J. Giddings and M. Robertson (2003) Large Scale map or the A-Z? The Place of Self-Help Services in Legal Aid, in 30(1) *Journal of Law and Society*, p.102.

[414] R. Moorhead and P. Pleasence (2003) Access to Justice after Universalism: Introduction, in 30(1) *Journal of Law and Society*, p.1.

[415] See, for example, the use of remote advice kiosks in the East Ridings. Details available at www.eastriding.gov.uk/council/citizenlink.html. For an overseas example see the video link operated by Legal Aid Queensland. Details available at www.legalaid.qld.gov.au/services.

[416] M. Holdsworth (1999) *Social Exclusion: Is Advice a Solution?* London: Advice Services Alliance.

[417] A. Sherr, R. Moorhead and A. Paterson (1993) *Franchising Legal Aid: Final Report*, London: Legal Aid Board, p.23.

[418] P. Pleasence, S. Maclean and A. Morley (1996) *Profiling Civil Litigation: The Case for Research*, London: LABRU.

[419] See for example, R. Moorhead and A. Sherr (2003) *An Anatomy of Access: Evaluating Entry and Initial Advice and Signposting Using Model Clients*, London: Legal Services Commission, who found little evidence that the Directory was being used by Specialist Quality Mark holders to signpost clients which the advice provider was unable to assist.

[420] See, for example, Department of Health (2003) *NHS Plan Booking Systems: Electronic Booking Systems: Scoping paper for the Strategic Outline Case for Information Systems for Health Community-Wide Booking*, London: Department of Health.

[421] The South East Regional Partnership and Planning team of the Legal Services Commission have developed such a system which was recently launched. At the moment it still requires the referral request to be made by phone (for active referral) but the system designed could be altered to allow the referral request to be carried out completely electronically, which is the plan

[422] This is a local rate call centre number, 0845 608 1122, which will identify suitable providers.

[423] See, for example, R. Moorhead and A. Sherr (2003), above, n.419.

[424] P. Abbott and E. Williamson (1997) *Women, Health and Domestic Violence*. Paper presented at the BSA Medical Conference, 1997, reported in British Medical Association (1998) *Domestic Violence: A Health Care Issue?* London: British Medical Association.

[425] British Medical Association (1998), above, n.424.

[426] Legal Action Group (1992) *A Strategy for Justice*, London: Legal Action Group.

[427] The phrase 'joined up solutions to joined up problems' was used to describe the purpose of the Social Exclusion Unit. See the 10 Downing Street press release of 25th September 2000, downloadable from http://www.number-10.gov.uk/output/page2857.asp.

[428] P. Pleasence, N.J. Balmer, A. Buck, A. O'Grady and H. Genn, Civil Law Problems and Morbidity, forthcoming in *Journal of Epidemiology and Community Health*.

[429] Legal Services Commission (2001) Joining Up With the Health Sector, in *CLSP News*.

[430] See, for example, Department of Health (2002) *Supporting the Implementation of Patient Advice and Liaison Services*, London: Department of Health.

[431] Department of Health (2003) *NHS Complaints: Making Things Right*, London: Department of Health, p.12. These Independent Complaints Advocacy Services would be commissioned or provided by Primary Care Trust Patient Care Forums, and delivered according to standards identified and disseminated by a new Commission for Healthcare Audit and Inspection.

138

[432] See, for example, Legal Services Commission (2001), above, n.430, S. Abbot and L. Hobby (2003) Who Uses Welfare Benefits Advice Services in Primary Care? in 11(2) *Health and Social Care in the Community*, pp.168-174.

[433] See the speech of Rt. Hon. Tony Blair, Prime Minster, of 8th September 2003 setting out the government's aim 'to create 800 new children's centres, one in every disadvantaged neighbourhood. Some will be part of schools. Others will be newly built centres. These will bring together early years education, parenting and family support, and health - high quality services located together in one place.' The speech is downloadable from http://www.number10.gov.uk/output/Page4426.asp.

[434] Lord Chancellor's Department and Law Centres Federation (2001), above, n.13.

[435] J. Hills (2002), 'Does a Focus on 'Social Exclusion' Change the Policy Response', In J. Hills, J. Le Grand and D. Piachaud (eds.), *Understanding Social Exclusion*, Oxford University Press, Oxford.

[436] Details are available at http://www.dti.gov.uk/ccp/topics1/facts/consumerdirect.htm.

[437] http://www.csnsupport.org.uk.

[438] See, further, Appendix C.

[439] See, for example, M. Kilian (2003), above, n.295.

Appendix A

Overview

Chapter 1 explains that the problems to which the principles of civil law apply are not abstract legal problems, but in most part problems of everyday life. It observes that legal process does not always provide the best, a good, or even a sensible means through which to resolve such problems, as many alternative means of resolution exist. However, it asserts that the existence of a defining framework of civil law applicable to many problems of everyday social life and social well-being, and the possibilities for utilising legal services and process to reach solutions to such 'justiciable' problems when necessary, mean that the infrastructure of civil justice today plays an important role in realising social justice. It also plays an important role in tackling social exclusion. The chapter then introduces the first Legal Services Research Centre (LSRC) national periodic survey of justiciable problems, along with a parallel survey of people living in temporary accommodation. These surveys have allowed a comprehensive and unique analysis to be undertaken of the experience and impact of 18 categories of 'justiciable' problem (discrimination, consumer, employment, neighbours, owned housing, rented housing, homelessness, money/debt, welfare benefits, divorce, relationship breakdown, domestic violence, children, personal injury, clinical negligence, mental health, immigration and unfair police treatment), the difficulties people face in resolving them, and the degree to which advice, legal services and formal processes facilitate problem prevention and resolution.

Chapter 2 sets out the pattern of experience of justiciable problems across England and Wales, by describing the 37 per cent of LSRC survey respondents who reported having experienced one or more problems in the three-and-a-half years survey reference period. It provides a detailed analysis of how differences in life circumstances entail differences in vulnerability to problems, and why different rates of problem incidence are therefore associated with differently constituted population groups, both in general terms and within individual problem categories. As part of this, it describes the vulnerability of certain population groups to problems that can be constituent elements of social exclusion, and the particular vulnerability of socially excluded groups to the experience of justiciable problems. It then explains how some types of problem are experienced commonly in combination, and how certain justiciable problems are more likely to lead to others, or to other social, economic and health problems. In doing this, it reveals how, by reinforcing the disadvantage of those who are vulnerable to justiciable problems, the experience of problems has an additive effect – meaning that each time a person experiences a problem they become increasingly likely to experience additional problems. Moreover, it demonstrates how people who experience multiple problems become disproportionately more likely to experience some of the problems that play a direct role in social exclusion. Lastly, it details how some problems tend to occur together or in sequence in defined problem 'clusters'. Four distinct clusters are identified, that we have characterised as family, homelessness, health and welfare, and economic clusters.

Chapter 3 sets out the ways in which people deal with justiciable problems. It highlights the sense of powerlessness and helplessness often experienced by those who face them, and confirms there is a general lack of knowledge about obligations, rights and procedures on the part of the general public. It reports that no action was taken to resolve 19 per cent of problems reported through the LSRC survey, and explains that inaction is particularly common in relation to some serious problem types (such as mental health and domestic violence), and also more likely among some disadvantaged population groups (such as minority ethnic people). It also reports that inaction owing to fear is common in relation to some problem types (such as neighbours and domestic violence). When action is taken to resolve problems, formal advice is sought on 62 per cent of occasions, although it is actually obtained on fewer occasions (53 per cent). In describing the problems in relation to which people most often seek advice, it demonstrates that advice is more likely to be sought in relation to more serious problems, but explains how decisions on whether or not to obtain advice influence the way later problems are resolved. The chapter then details the many sources from which people attempt to obtain advice (from solicitors to social workers, trade unions to politicians, and the police to the media), the difficulties they experience in doing so, and the nature of the advice and additional help received by those who are successful in doing so. Through this, it illustrates how people's choices of advisers, although often logical and apposite, can also be desperate and unpromising and, also, how people's choices can be undermined by the provision of services in manners that do not fit with people's lives. In addition, it exposes the phenomenon of referral fatigue, whereby the more times people are referred on to another advice service by an adviser, the less likely they become to act on a referral. The chapter also demonstrates the relative infrequency of court, tribunal and alternative dispute resolution processes being used as part of the process of resolving problems. Lastly, it details the people and organisations that pay for advice. It confirms that most advice is provided free at the point of delivery and, where advice is paid for, it is commonly paid for by legal aid, trade unions, legal expenses insurance and private individuals. It also observes that legal aid appears to be targeted towards more serious problems, but this is in large part because it is focused on a relatively narrow range of problem types, and advice services.

Chapter 4 sets out the range of objectives that motivate people to act to resolve justiciable problems (such as obtaining an apology for a wrongdoing, obtaining or retaining money, obtaining or retaining a job, improving working conditions or securing access to children). It illustrates the different objectives associated with different problem types, problem resolution strategies, advisers and population groups. As part of this, it describes how objectives vary along with the consequences of problems, and confirms that certain problems are more likely to lead to others. It then details the ways in which problems conclude, and the extent to which people obtain their objectives. It points to evidence that those who are represented before courts and tribunals fare better than those who are not, and also that objectives are more often met in relation to the most important problems. It also explains that, because the problems in relation to which people obtain advice are fundamentally different from those they resolve on their own, it is not possible to compare the outcomes of these two sets of problems. Nevertheless, it suggests that it is self-evident that advice is beneficial to the problem resolution process. It also observes that those who obtain advice that is funded by legal aid appear to fare better than others who obtain advice. The chapter then explains how the duration of problems varies by problem and adviser type, and also, seemingly, by seriousness. Lastly, it shows that although people can greatly benefit from taking action to resolve justiciable problems, the resolution process can be stressful and even bring about ill-health.

Chapter 5 draws together the findings detailed in earlier chapters and sets out their implications. It suggests that the nature of justiciable problems requires that they should be of general concern, and that their prevention and resolution should be seen as a central part of efforts to tackle social exclusion. It highlights the role of education and information in raising awareness of the civic context of justiciable problems and the methods that can be used to resolve them, and consequently stresses the importance of framing laws and legal instruments in the clearest language possible. It underlines the importance of development and co-ordination of advice and other services so that problems are not just dealt with in isolation once they have arisen, but also that their likelihood of occurring or leading to further problems is lessened through preventative action. It notes that our findings indicate how resources might be targeted towards problem prevention. It also underlines the importance of co-ordination of services to provide support for those who would otherwise be unable to escape problems for fear of the consequences of trying to do so. The chapter then suggests that dedicated advice services should mirror more the needs and behaviour of those who wish to use them. Noting the phenomenon of referral fatigue, the chapter highlights the importance of equipping those from whom people initially seek advice with the means to quickly and effectively refer them on to the most appropriate adviser, and the importance of accessible general advice services that act as formal gateways to the great array of advice and legal services. More broadly, it recognises the important role to be played by those who have routine professional contact with individuals vulnerable to justiciable problems in 'problem noticing' and signposting people to such gateways. It then discusses where investment should come from to develop the methods and services that will enable more people to benefit from early and effective advice. Given that advice on the resolution of justiciable problems is already provided under the remit of a range of government departments and local authorities, and that a range of government departments and local authorities can benefit greatly from the timely resolution of justiciable problems, it suggests that public investment should come from across government. It also suggests that public sector investment could be complemented by private sector investment. The development of initial advice and referral services will, for example, inevitably generate demand for commercial advice services. The chapter warns, though, that investment, as well as development of the broad infrastructure of civil justice, must be properly co-ordinated and targeted to maximise the public benefit they deliver, and suggests that this is a key challenge for government.

Appendix B

Complex Statistical Analysis

In this Appendix we set out the methods and results of the complex statistical analyses reported in the main text.

BINARY LOGISTIC REGRESSION [1]

Binary logistic regression is used to examine associations of binary response variables with one or more predictors which can be categorical, dichotomous, continuous or a mix of these. Logistic regression estimates the probabilities (or more correctly the odds ratios) associated with the binary options and how these probabilities vary due to differences in the predictor/independent variables. We used binary logistic regression to examine possible predictors of justiciable problems overall, and individual problem types. We entered a range of continuous and discrete social and demographic predictors (detailed in the following output tables) and used both block entry of variables and backward elimination methods (based on the likelihood ratio statistic) where eliminations were based on the change in the residual sum-of-squared as a consequence of removal. In some cases, an age by academic qualifications interaction term was also included. Age and academic qualifications are related, with younger respondents more likely to have academic qualifications. An interaction term was included to allow differences with age to vary for those with and those without academic qualifications. Binary logistic regression was also used to determine social and demographic factors likely to influence membership of problem clusters identified by hierarchical cluster analysis (see below).

---

[1] See further, for example, B.S. Everitt and G. Dunn (2001) *Applied Multivariate Analysis*, 2nd Edition, London; Arnold, and B. G. Tabachnick and L. S. Fidell (2000) *Using Multivariate Statistics*, Needham Heights, MA: Allyn and Bacon.

ANALYSIS OF COVARIANCE [2]

Analysis of variance is used to partition variance that can be attributed to one cause from variance attributable to another. Comparing variances using F-tests allows a determination of differences between several means. The response variable should be quantitative, and factors categorical. The response variable should be a random sample from the normal distribution, though analysis is fairly robust to departures from normality. Analysis of covariance is an extension of analysis of variance, whereby predictor variables are assessed after response variable scores have been adjusted for differences associated with quantitative covariates. In the present context, covariates are typically respondent's age (linear and quadratic terms) and equivalised income. In general, it is assumed that covariates are unaffected by factors and have a linear relationship with the response variable. We used analysis of covariance to examine factors influencing total number of problems reported by respondents, using a range of social and demographic predictors. This allowed us to assess whether certain groups reported a greater number of problems. Analysis of covariance was also used to determine predictors of factor membership (see exploratory factor analysis below). Having extracted factors we saved factor scores, showing how each individual related to each factor. Since the extracted factors were not related, we conducted analysis of covariance for each factor using these continuous factor scores as response variables and again using the same range of social and demographic predictors.

LINEAR REGRESSION [3]

Linear Regression estimates the coefficients of a linear equation, involving one or more independent variables, that best predict the value of a dependent variable. Linear regression was used to examine the changing profile of problem types as the number of problems increased (i.e. which problems became more or less prevalent). In this

---

[2] See, for example, B. G. Tabachnick and L. S. Fidell (2000), above, n.1.

[3] See, for example, J. H. Zar (1998) *Biostatistical Analysis*. Upper Saddle River, NJ: Prentice Hall.

context, we used linear regression to fit linear equations to observed and expected data for each problem type. Each linear equation yielded a gradient and an intercept term. We were specifically interested in assessing whether the gradient for observed and expected data was different (i.e. did certain problem types become more prevalent than would be expected as the total number of problems reported increased). To compare gradients, we used simple student's t-tests to determine whether observed and expected gradients were significantly different from each other for each problem type. Calculating the expected proportion of respondents reporting one or more of each problem (with n problems overall) depended upon the prevalence of each problem type. We derived expected proportions of respondents with each problem type as the total number of problems increased, while accounting for differences in overall prevalence.

REPEATED MEASURES GENERAL LINEAR MODEL [4]

Repeated measures general linear models allow an analysis of data (providing an analysis of variance) where the same measurement is made more than once for each unit. Again the response variable should be quantitative and normally distributed, though as before, analysis is fairly robust to departures from normality. In this case our repeated response variable was the number of problems reported by respondents, with this measurement made twice (before and after) for each unit or respondent. We used a repeated measures general linear model to assess whether each problem type was likely to trigger further problems, specifying one within-problem factor, before/after and one between-problem factor, type of problem. So for each instance of each problem type we calculated a count of further problems reported both before and after that problem and assessed whether the after count exceeded the before count. We used estimated marginal means (i.e. the predicted mean values based on the models) before and after experiencing a problem to assess the triggering effect of each problem type.

---

[4] See, for example, B. G. Tabachnick and L. S. Fidell (2000), above, n.1.

146

HIERARCHICAL CLUSTER ANALYSIS [5]

Cluster analysis is commonly used to classify observations or variables into homogenous subgroups or clusters. Agglomerative hierarchical cluster analysis attempts to identify relatively homogeneous groups of variables (in this case problem types), using an algorithm that starts with each problem type as a separate cluster and combines clusters until only one is left. In this instance we aimed to organise respondents' experience of each problem type (twenty-one columns of binary data) into coherent subgroups of problem clusters, identifying which problems were likely to be experienced together. Analysis was carried out on a similarity matrix of our discrete problem types, using Jaccard scores as a measure of similarity. These scores are commonly used as a similarity measure for binary data where co-absences (zero-zero) are of little interest. In this case, co-absences were ignored as individuals who had experienced both problems clearly had something in common, while this was not necessarily the case for those who had experienced neither problem. Average between groups linkage was used as the clustering method as a relatively robust intermediate between complete and single linkage. Cluster analysis results were summarised in a dendrogram, which illustrates the divisions made at each step of the analysis. Binary logistic regression was used to examine social and demographic predictors of cluster membership (see above).

EXPLORATORY FACTOR ANALYSIS [6]

Exploratory factor analysis is used to investigate relationships between variables, and identify underlying latent variables, or factors, that explain relationships (patterns of correlation). We used factor analysis to investigate overlap between problem types with the aim of identifying underlying dimensions in the data. While hierarchical cluster analysis simply aimed to identify clusters of variables, factor analysis was used to attempt to identify underlying latent variables or dimensions, and relate these back to various social and demographic characteristics of respondents. Analysis was carried out on counts of each of the twenty-one problem types reported by each respondent. Since data are assumed to be bivariate normal for each pair of variables

[5] See, for example, B. S. Everitt, S. Landau and M. Leese (2001) *Cluster Analysis*, Fourth Edition, New York: Arnold.
[6] See, for example, B. G. Tabachnick and L. S. Fidell (2000), above, n.1.

(problem types), they were subjected to a transformation for Poisson type data to make the counts more acceptably normally distributed. Since no prior assumptions were made about manifest variables, we used exploratory rather than confirmatory factor analysis. The number of factors (using principal component extraction) to be extracted was chosen following examination of a scree plot. The scree plot displayed ordered eigenvalues of a correlation matrix. Critically, an 'elbow' in the plot indicated how many factors should be extracted. Varimax (orthogonal) rotation was applied to aid factor interpretation by maximising variable loading on a single factor (whilst minimising loadings on all other factors). Similarities between pattern (allowing correlations) and structure (equivalent to Varimax solution) matrices, as well as low correlations between factors suggested factors were independent and orthogonal rotation was appropriate. Having identified five factors, we saved factor scores relating to each of the extracted factors, and used analysis of covariance (described above) to relate each factor to social and demographic predictors.

OUTPUT TABLES

Table B1: Any Problem Type

		B	S.E.	Wald	df	p	Exp(B)
House type	Flat			27.358	3	.000	
	Detached	-.544	.130	17.511	1	.000	.580
	Semi	-.579	.118	24.284	1	.000	.560
	Terrace	-.368	.117	9.855	1	.002	.692
Family type	Single no children			36.363	3	.000	
	Couple children	-.114	.104	1.201	1	.273	.892
	Couple no children	-.243	.092	6.957	1	.008	.784
	Lone parent	.811	.179	20.442	1	.000	2.249
Tenure type	Own			35.531	4	.000	
	Mortgage	.373	.098	14.496	1	.000	1.452
	Rent public	.525	.120	19.090	1	.000	1.690
	Rent private	.521	.137	14.382	1	.000	1.683
	Rent free	-.155	.184	.714	1	.398	.856
Economic activity	Full-time employed			14.842	8	.062	
	Part-time employed	-.072	.099	.521	1	.470	.931
	Self-employed	.043	.117	.138	1	.710	1.044
	Unemployed/scheme	.553	.196	7.915	1	.005	1.738
	Education	.409	.268	2.332	1	.127	1.505
	Sick	.298	.171	3.024	1	.082	1.347
	Home/care	.091	.120	.565	1	.452	1.095
	Retired	.273	.157	2.998	1	.083	1.313
	Other/unknown	.069	.563	.015	1	.902	1.072
Long-term illness/disability		.711	.082	75.793	1	.000	2.036

	B	S.E.	Wald	df	p	Exp(B)
Academic qualifications	-.643	.265	5.906	1	.015	.526
Benefits status	-.168	.095	3.101	1	.078	.846
Age	.053	.013	16.227	1	.000	1.055
Age2	-.001	.000	20.965	1	.000	.999
Income	.025	.008	8.716	1	.003	1.025
Interaction term	-.001	.005	.016	1	.901	.999
Constant	-1.237	.322	14.779	1	.000	.290

Variables removed from the equation: availability of private transport, gender, ethnicity. ($R^2 = .120$)

Table B2: Any Discrimination Problem

		B	S.E.	Wald	df	p	Exp(B)
Ethnicity	White			45.259	4	.000	
	Asian	2.234	.373	35.934	1	.000	9.341
	Black	-1.345	1.651	.664	1	.415	.261
	Mixed	2.232	.744	8.998	1	.003	9.318
	Other	1.639	.820	3.996	1	.046	5.149
House type	Flat			9.861	3	.020	
	Detached	-1.489	.505	8.702	1	.003	.226
	Semi	-1.068	.410	6.775	1	.009	.344
	Terrace	-.762	.403	3.570	1	.059	.467
Family type	Single no children			8.705	3	.033	
	Couple children	.724	.436	2.759	1	.097	2.063
	Couple no children	1.030	.399	6.651	1	.010	2.800
	Lone parent	1.382	.591	5.464	1	.019	3.983
Tenure type	Own			11.704	4	.020	
	Mortgage	.647	.442	2.145	1	.143	1.910
	Rent public	.105	.518	.041	1	.840	1.111
	Rent private	.122	.596	.042	1	.838	1.130
	Rent free	1.773	.619	8.200	1	.004	5.886
Economic activity	Full-time employed			24.352	8	.002	
	Part-time employed	.504	.361	1.951	1	.162	1.655
	Self-employed	.540	.396	1.856	1	.173	1.715
	Unemployed/scheme	.009	.773	.000	1	.991	1.009
	Education	-.783	1.545	.257	1	.612	.457
	Sick	1.606	.398	16.308	1	.000	4.981
	Home/care	-.515	.586	.771	1	.380	.598
	Retired	-.217	.853	.065	1	.799	.805
	Other/unknown	2.015	1.147	3.087	1	.079	7.504
Long-term illness/disability		1.485	.287	26.731	1	.000	4.414
Academic qualifications		-1.490	1.375	1.175	1	.278	.225
Age		.173	.078	4.880	1	.027	1.189
Age2		-.002	.001	4.629	1	.031	.998
Interaction Term		.015	.028	.272	1	.602	1.015
Constant		-8.729	1.620	29.015	1	.000	.000

Variables removed from the equation: availability of private transport, benefits status, gender, equivalised income. ($R^2 = .203$)

Table B3: Any Consumer Problem

		B	S.E.	Wald	df	p	Exp(B)
House type	Flat			7.703	3	.053	
	Detached	-.158	.170	.859	1	.354	.854
	Semi	-.371	.158	5.471	1	.019	.690
	Terrace	-.299	.158	3.585	1	.058	.742
Tenure type	Own			24.230	4	.000	
	Mortgage	.159	.133	1.422	1	.233	1.172
	Rent public	-.311	.183	2.888	1	.089	.733
	Rent private	-.187	.194	.922	1	.337	.830
	Rent free	-1.072	.310	11.953	1	.001	.342
Economic activity	Full-time employed			14.469	8	.070	
	Part-time employed	-.231	.144	2.592	1	.107	.794
	Self-employed	.243	.147	2.737	1	.098	1.276
	Unemployed/scheme	.233	.267	.761	1	.383	1.262
	Education	.791	.350	5.097	1	.024	2.205
	Sick	.191	.235	.661	1	.416	1.210
	Home/care	.057	.164	.121	1	.728	1.059
	Retired	.323	.225	2.049	1	.152	1.381
	Other/unknown	-.274	.841	.106	1	.744	.760
Long-term illness/disability		.435	.110	15.739	1	.000	1.545
Academic qualifications		-.930	.469	3.944	1	.047	.394
Benefits status		-.380	.122	9.726	1	.002	.684
Age		.036	.020	3.234	1	.072	1.037
Age^2		-.001	.000	5.712	1	.017	.999
Income		.035	.010	11.461	1	.001	1.036
Interaction term		-.002	.009	.066	1	.798	.998
Constant		-1.952	.467	17.446	1	.000	.142

Variables removed from the equation: family type, availability of private transport, gender, ethnicity. ($R^2 = .088$)

Table B4: Any Employment Problem

		B	S.E.	Wald	df	P	Exp(B)
Family type	Single no children			5.933	3	.115	
	Couple children	-.271	.181	2.239	1	.135	.763
	Couple no children	-.329	.173	3.614	1	.057	.720
	Lone parent	-.754	.417	3.266	1	.071	.471
Tenure type	Own			12.095	4	.017	
	Mortgage	.546	.230	5.632	1	.018	1.726
	Rent public	.719	.280	6.610	1	.010	2.052
	Rent private	.904	.277	10.630	1	.001	2.470
	Rent free	.463	.348	1.773	1	.183	1.589
Economic activity	Full-time employed			56.072	8	.000	
	Part-time employed	-.038	.171	.050	1	.823	.962
	Self-employed	-1.221	.319	14.695	1	.000	.295
	Unemployed/scheme	.608	.297	4.188	1	.041	1.837
	Education	-.790	.571	1.917	1	.166	.454
	Sick	-.581	.335	3.010	1	.083	.559
	Home/care	-1.124	.330	11.629	1	.001	.325
	Retired	-2.031	.424	22.903	1	.000	.131

150

		B	S.E.	Wald	df	p	Exp(B)
	Other/unknown	.219	.871	.063	1	.801	1.245
Long-term illness/disability		.882	.146	36.470	1	.000	2.416
Academic qualifications		-1.036	.686	2.281	1	.131	.355
Benefits status		.364	.203	3.217	1	.073	1.439
Age		-.007	.006	1.239	1	.266	.993
Income		.028	.015	3.389	1	.066	1.028
Interaction term		.008	.014	.371	1	.542	1.009
Constant		-2.989	.435	47.144	1	.000	.050

Variables removed from the equation: house type, availability of private transport, age, age squared, gender, ethnicity. (R^2 = .113)

Table B5: Any Neighbours Problem

		B	S.E.	Wald	df	p	Exp(B)
Ethnicity	White			6.192	4	.185	
	Asian	.027	.292	.009	1	.925	1.028
	Black	-1.045	.492	4.514	1	.034	.352
	Mixed	-2.503	1.952	1.645	1	.200	.082
	Other	-.138	.628	.048	1	.826	.871
House type	Flat			63.434	3	.000	
	Detached	-1.228	.186	43.788	1	.000	.293
	Semi	-1.179	.163	52.418	1	.000	.308
	Terrace	-.688	.158	18.958	1	.000	.502
Family type	Single no children			14.220	3	.003	
	Couple children	.474	.164	8.339	1	.004	1.606
	Couple no children	.243	.144	2.865	1	.091	1.276
	Lone parent	.805	.236	11.654	1	.001	2.237
Economic activity	Full-time employed			21.050	8	.007	
	Part-time employed	.093	.162	.332	1	.565	1.098
	Self-employed	-.102	.203	.254	1	.614	.903
	Unemployed/scheme	.297	.290	1.050	1	.305	1.346
	Education	-1.358	.958	2.011	1	.156	.257
	Sick	.444	.224	3.915	1	.048	1.559
	Home/care	.620	.164	14.269	1	.000	1.858
	Retired	.054	.249	.046	1	.830	1.055
	Other/unknown	.315	.900	.122	1	.726	1.370
Long-term illness/disability		.402	.125	10.299	1	.001	1.494
Academic qualifications		-.425	.429	.981	1	.322	.654
Age		.067	.021	9.876	1	.002	1.069
Age2		-.001	.000	7.897	1	.005	.999
Interaction term		.004	.008	.304	1	.582	1.004
Constant		-3.389	.456	55.321	1	.000	.034

Variables removed from the equation: tenure type, availability of private transport, benefits status, gender, equivalised income. (R2 = .058)

Table B6: Any Owned Housing Problem

		B	S.E.	Wald	df	p	Exp(B)
House type	Flat			12.162	3	.007	
	Detached	-.631	.332	3.624	1	.057	.532

		B	S.E.	Wald	df	p	Exp(B)
	Semi	-1.075	.327	10.798	1	.001	.341
	Terrace	-.875	.326	7.206	1	.007	.417
Family type	Single no children			8.614	3	.035	
	Couple children	.622	.374	2.766	1	.096	1.863
	Couple no children	.643	.326	3.882	1	.049	1.901
	Lone parent	1.454	.529	7.538	1	.006	4.278
Tenure type	Own			20.903	4	.000	
	Mortgage	.566	.290	3.824	1	.051	1.762
	Rent public	-2.072	.683	9.216	1	.002	.126
	Rent private	-.046	.446	.010	1	.918	.955
	Rent free	-.766	.879	.760	1	.383	.465
Long-term illness/disability		.557	.222	6.307	1	.012	1.745
Academic qualifications		-2.499	1.236	4.085	1	.043	.082
Benefits status		-.504	.300	2.812	1	.094	.604
Age		-.004	.009	.144	1	.705	.996
Income		.068	.023	9.018	1	.003	1.071
Interaction term		.033	.020	2.734	1	.098	1.034
Constant		-3.740	.708	27.932	1	.000	.024

Variables removed from the equation: economic activity, availability of private transport, age squared, gender, ethnicity. (R^2 = .094)

Table B7: Any Owned Housing Problem (Tenure Removed)

		B	S.E.	Wald	df	p	Exp(B)
House type	Flat			7.786	3	.051	
	Detached	-.362	.321	1.276	1	.259	.696
	Semi	-.783	.313	6.238	1	.013	.457
	Terrace	-.630	.316	3.978	1	.046	.532
Family type	Single no children			9.426	3	.024	
	Couple children	.812	.329	6.084	1	.014	2.252
	Couple no children	.680	.284	5.740	1	.017	1.975
	Lone parent	1.370	.506	7.340	1	.007	3.937
Long-term illness/disability		.523	.220	5.657	1	.017	1.687
Academic qualifications		-2.607	1.217	4.590	1	.032	.074
Age		-.006	.008	.665	1	.415	.994
Income		.105	.021	25.719	1	.000	1.111
Interaction term		.034	.020	2.887	1	.089	1.034
Constant		-4.488	.527	72.635	1	.000	.011

Variables removed from the equation: economic activity, availability of private transport, benefits status, age squared, gender, ethnicity. (R^2 = .066)

Table B8: Any Rented Housing Problem

		B	S.E.	Wald	df	p	Exp(B)
House type	Flat			8.160	3	.043	
	Detached	-.544	.334	2.642	1	.104	.581
	Semi	-.572	.217	6.939	1	.008	.564
	Terrace	-.511	.207	6.074	1	.014	.600
Family type	Single no children			12.065	3	.007	
	Couple children	-.265	.238	1.240	1	.266	.767

		B	S.E.	Wald	df	p	Exp(B)
	Couple no children	.159	.214	.554	1	.457	1.173
	Lone parent	.627	.275	5.205	1	.023	1.872
Tenure type	Own			105.251	4	.000	
	Mortgage	.897	.655	1.877	1	.171	2.453
	Rent public	3.160	.649	23.691	1	.000	23.576
	Rent private	3.261	.650	25.184	1	.000	26.076
	Rent free	2.532	.701	13.043	1	.000	12.573
Long-term illness/disability		.500	.189	7.034	1	.008	1.649
Academic qualifications		-1.004	.533	3.545	1	.060	.366
Benefits status		-.669	.206	10.593	1	.001	.512
Age		-.041	.009	23.507	1	.000	.959
Income		.056	.020	7.468	1	.006	1.058
Gender		-.249	.161	2.390	1	.122	.779
Interaction term		.014	.012	1.384	1	.239	1.014
Constant		-3.233	.777	17.333	1	.000	.039

Variables removed from the equation: economic activity, availability of private transport, age squared, ethnicity. ($R^2 = .262$)

Table B9: Any Rented Housing Problem (Tenure Removed)

		B	S.E.	Wald	df	p	Exp(B)
House type	Flat			26.428	3	.000	
	Detached	-1.279	.313	16.676	1	.000	.278
	Semi	-.964	.210	21.075	1	.000	.381
	Terrace	-.698	.201	12.076	1	.001	.498
Family type	Single no children			16.741	3	.001	
	Couple children	-.402	.213	3.546	1	.060	.669
	Couple no children	-.001	.203	.000	1	.995	.999
	Lone parent	.681	.241	8.002	1	.005	1.976
Long-term illness/disability		.548	.180	9.320	1	.002	1.730
Transport avail.		-.408	.182	5.034	1	.025	.665
Benefits status		-.815	.190	18.459	1	.000	.443
Age		-.051	.006	83.110	1	.000	.950
Constant		.369	.282	1.704	1	.192	1.446

Variables removed from the equation: economic activity, academic qualifications, age squared, gender, ethnicity, equivalised income. ($R^2 = .178$)

Table B10: Any Rented Housing Problem
(Unsafe/Unsatisfactory Condition Only) (Tenure Removed)

		B	S.E.	Wald	df	p	Exp(B)
Ethnicity	White			8.914	4	.063	
	Asian	1.313	.526	6.229	1	.013	3.716
	Black	1.009	.573	3.104	1	.078	2.743
	Mixed	.815	.890	.838	1	.360	2.259
	Other	-16.724	5568.2	.000	1	.998	.000
House type	Flat			9.915	3	.019	
	Detached	-1.456	.742	3.850	1	.050	.233
	Semi	-1.135	.387	8.598	1	.003	.321
	Terrace	-.676	.347	3.798	1	.051	.509
Family type	Single no children			25.219	3	.000	

	Couple children	1.093	.517	4.471	1	.034	2.984
	Couple no children	1.613	.510	10.013	1	.002	5.017
	Lone parent	2.434	.528	21.273	1	.000	11.404
Economic activity	Full-time employed			11.771	8	.162	
	Part-time employed	-1.046	.665	2.472	1	.116	.351
	Self-employed	-1.941	1.735	1.250	1	.263	.144
	Unemployed/scheme	-.031	.540	.003	1	.955	.970
	Education	-.321	.847	.144	1	.704	.725
	Sick	.910	.547	2.771	1	.096	2.484
	Home/care	-.095	.475	.040	1	.842	.909
	Retired	2.051	1.074	3.643	1	.056	7.773
	Other/unknown	-1.123	2.422	.215	1	.643	.325
Transport avail.		-1.290	.334	14.898	1	.000	.275
Academic qualifications		-.898	.415	4.692	1	.030	.407
Age		-.055	.248	.049	1	.825	.947
Age^2		.000	.006	.000	1	.990	1.000
Income		-.086	.050	2.952	1	.086	.917
Interaction term		.000	.000	.009	1	.924	1.000
Constant		-1.009	3.031	.111	1	.739	.365

Variables removed from the equation: long-term illness/disability, benefits status, age, gender. ($R^2 = .319$)

Table B11: Any Homelessness Problem

		B	S.E.	Wald	df	p	Exp(B)
House type	Flat			6.449	3	.092	
	Detached	-15.62	1061.9	.000	1	.988	.000
	Semi	-1.168	.496	5.540	1	.019	.311
	Terrace	-.870	.437	3.967	1	.046	.419
Transport avail.		-.939	.421	4.978	1	.026	.391
Academic qualifications		-3.375	1.940	3.026	1	.082	.034
Benefits status		-1.708	.502	11.559	1	.001	.181
Age		-.045	.018	6.054	1	.014	.956
Income		-.152	.064	5.568	1	.018	.859
Interaction term		.028	.038	.537	1	.464	1.028
Constant		.163	.625	.068	1	.794	1.177

Variables removed from the equation: family type, tenure type, economic activity, long-term illness/disability, age squared, gender, ethnicity. ($R^2 = .312$)

Table B12: Any Money/Debt Problem

		B	S.E.	Wald	df	p	Exp(B)
Tenure type	Own			17.270	4	.002	
	Mortgage	.279	.171	2.648	1	.104	1.321
	Rent public	.352	.202	3.054	1	.081	1.422
	Rent private	.659	.215	9.380	1	.002	1.934
	Rent free	-.399	.330	1.459	1	.227	.671
Economic activity	Full-time employed			25.708	8	.001	
	Part-time employed	-.554	.179	9.617	1	.002	.575
	Self-employed	.168	.172	.950	1	.330	1.183
	Unemployed/scheme	-.378	.311	1.484	1	.223	.685
	Education	-1.056	.598	3.116	1	.078	.348

Sick	-.465	.258	3.241	1	.072	.628
Home/care	-.321	.192	2.782	1	.095	.726
Retired	.570	.269	4.485	1	.034	1.768
Other/unknown	-.238	.796	.089	1	.765	.788
Long-term illness/disability	.847	.122	47.988	1	.000	2.332
Academic qualifications	-.238	.481	.245	1	.620	.788
Benefits status	-.473	.136	12.031	1	.001	.623
Age	.054	.024	5.295	1	.021	1.056
Age^2	-.001	.000	9.356	1	.002	.999
Interaction term	-.015	.009	2.395	1	.122	.986
Constant	-2.851	.529	29.074	1	.000	.058

Variables removed from the equation: housing type, family type, availability of private transport, gender, ethnicity, equivalised income. ($R^2 = .082$)

Table B13: Any Money/Debt Problem (Money Owed To Respondent Only)

		B	S.E.	Wald	df	P	Exp(B)
Economic activity	Full-time employed			19.520	8	.012	
	Part-time employed	-1.044	.472	4.886	1	.027	.352
	Self-employed	.854	.296	8.308	1	.004	2.348
	Unemployed/scheme	-3.112	2.980	1.091	1	.296	.045
	Education	.366	.790	.215	1	.643	1.442
	Sick	.494	.429	1.326	1	.250	1.639
	Home/care	-.034	.383	.008	1	.930	.967
	Retired	.776	.463	2.812	1	.094	2.172
	Other/unknown	-17.142	9820.9	.000	1	.999	.000
Long-term illness/disability		.688	.240	8.236	1	.004	1.989
Academic qualifications		.548	1.015	.292	1	.589	1.730
Age		.084	.044	3.664	1	.056	1.087
Age^2		-.001	.000	3.898	1	.048	.999
Gender		-.481	.217	4.927	1	.026	.618
Interaction term		-.033	.019	2.843	1	.092	.968
Constant		-5.436	.960	32.096	1	.000	.004

Variables removed from the equation: house type, family type, tenure type, availability of private transport, benefits status, ethnicity, equivalised income. ($R^2 = .065$)

Table B14: Any Money/Debt Problem
(Respondent Owes Money / Severe Money Difficulties Only)

		B	S.E.	Wald	df	p	Exp(B)
Ethnicity	White			5.065	4	.281	
	Asian	-2.855	1.516	3.545	1	.060	.058
	Black	-.794	.891	.794	1	.373	.452
	Mixed	.731	.888	.677	1	.410	2.078
	Other	-16.788	6068.7	.000	1	.998	.000
House type	Flat			9.797	3	.020	
	Detached	.762	.433	3.091	1	.079	2.142
	Semi	.028	.376	.006	1	.940	1.029
	Terrace	.624	.355	3.088	1	.079	1.866
Tenure type	Own			10.574	4	.032	

		B	S.E.	Wald	df	p	Exp(B)
	Mortgage	.670	.506	1.754	1	.185	1.953
	Rent public	.922	.532	3.001	1	.083	2.514
	Rent private	1.490	.544	7.498	1	.006	4.438
	Rent free	.983	.630	2.433	1	.119	2.673
Economic activity	Full-time employed			16.993	8	.030	
	Part-time employed	-.708	.351	4.060	1	.044	.493
	Self-employed	-.062	.388	.025	1	.873	.940
	Unemployed/scheme	-.731	.471	2.410	1	.121	.481
	Education	-2.240	1.270	3.111	1	.078	.106
	Sick	-1.215	.441	7.595	1	.006	.297
	Home/care	-.468	.343	1.863	1	.172	.627
	Retired	.288	.748	.148	1	.700	1.334
	Other/unknown	1.363	.933	2.135	1	.144	3.908
Long-term illness/disability		1.411	.223	39.891	1	.000	4.101
Academic qualifications		-.485	.919	.279	1	.598	.615
Benefits status		-1.429	.255	31.488	1	.000	.240
Age		.113	.058	3.752	1	.053	1.120
Age^2		-.002	.001	6.305	1	.012	.998
Income		-.051	.029	3.014	1	.083	.951
Interaction term		-.003	.022	.021	1	.884	.997
Constant		-4.850	1.251	15.041	1	.000	.008

Variables removed from the equation: family type, availability of private transport, gender. (R^2 = .190)

Table B15: Any Money/Debt Problem (Problems With Financial Services Only)

		B	S.E.	Wald	df	p	Exp(B)
Tenure type	Own			10.005	4	.040	
	Mortgage	.548	.303	3.284	1	.070	1.730
	Rent public	.517	.381	1.840	1	.175	1.676
	Rent private	.997	.379	6.929	1	.008	2.709
	Rent free	-3.287	2.304	2.035	1	.154	.037
Economic activity	Full-time employed			16.446	8	.036	
	Part-time employed	-1.047	.368	8.082	1	.004	.351
	Self-employed	-.246	.306	.647	1	.421	.782
	Unemployed/scheme	-1.488	1.010	2.172	1	.141	.226
	Education	.363	.779	.217	1	.641	1.437
	Sick	-1.291	.601	4.610	1	.032	.275
	Home/care	-.520	.359	2.096	1	.148	.594
	Retired	-.838	.429	3.809	1	.051	.433
	Other/unknown	-1.433	2.319	.382	1	.537	.239
Long-term illness/disability		.901	.204	19.503	1	.000	2.463
Academic qualifications		.950	.878	1.171	1	.279	2.587
Age		.003	.009	.136	1	.712	1.003
Income		.047	.020	5.535	1	.019	1.048
Interaction term		-.032	.018	3.319	1	.068	.969
Constant		-4.355	.562	60.144	1	.000	.013

Variables removed from the equation: house type, family type, availability of private transport, benefits status, age, age squared, gender, ethnicity. (R^2 = .083)

Table B16: Any Benefits Problem

		B	S.E.	Wald	df	p	Exp(B)
Tenure type	Own			10.956	4	.027	
	Mortgage	-.414	.323	1.642	1	.200	.661
	Rent public	.048	.308	.024	1	.876	1.049
	Rent private	.575	.354	2.637	1	.104	1.778
	Rent free	-.349	.529	.435	1	.510	.706
Long-term illness/disability		.849	.205	17.143	1	.000	2.338
Benefits status		-1.086	.235	21.342	1	.000	.337
Age		.080	.034	5.631	1	.018	1.083
Age^2		-.001	.000	8.266	1	.004	.999
Income		-.084	.029	8.115	1	.004	.920
Constant		-4.064	.821	24.512	1	.000	.017

Variables removed from the equation: house type, family type, economic activity, availability of private transport, academic qualifications, gender, ethnicity. ($R^2 = .128$)

Table B17: Any Benefits Problem (Benefit Status Removed)

		B	S.E.	Wald	df	p	Exp(B)
Tenure type	Own			18.890	4	.001	
	Mortgage	-.263	.328	.642	1	.423	.769
	Rent public	.507	.301	2.833	1	.092	1.660
	Rent private	.879	.359	6.009	1	.014	2.408
	Rent free	-.391	.547	.511	1	.475	.677
Economic activity	Full-time employed			12.492	8	.131	
	Part-time employed	.637	.330	3.728	1	.054	1.891
	Self-employed	.642	.402	2.559	1	.110	1.901
	Unemployed/scheme	1.172	.402	8.504	1	.004	3.228
	Education	.163	.828	.039	1	.844	1.177
	Sick	.787	.376	4.370	1	.037	2.196
	Home/care	.365	.368	.979	1	.322	1.440
	Retired	1.039	.488	4.533	1	.033	2.827
	Other/unknown	-1.194	2.960	.163	1	.687	.303
Long-term illness/disability		.879	.225	15.307	1	.000	2.409
Age		.084	.039	4.636	1	.031	1.087
Age^2		-.001	.000	6.700	1	.010	.999
Income		-.103	.032	10.649	1	.001	.902
Constant		-5.191	.932	31.032	1	.000	.006

Variables removed from the equation: house type, family type, availability of private transport, academic qualifications, gender, ethnicity. ($R^2 = .107$)

Table B18: Any Divorce Problem (2 Ethnicity Categories)

		B	S.E.	Wald	df	p	Exp(B)
House type	Flat			14.414	3	.002	
	Detached	-.860	.383	5.031	1	.025	.423
	Semi	-1.040	.314	10.996	1	.001	.353
	Terrace	-.287	.281	1.042	1	.307	.751
Family type	Single no children			109.778	3	.000	
	Couple children	-1.692	.303	31.204	1	.000	.184
	Couple no children	-1.768	.289	37.521	1	.000	.171

	Lone parent	1.122	.279	16.178	1	.000	3.070
Tenure type	Own			8.435	4	.077	
	Mortgage	.318	.378	.707	1	.400	1.374
	Rent public	-.097	.416	.055	1	.815	.907
	Rent private	.774	.427	3.285	1	.070	2.169
	Rent free	-17.000	2174.58	.000	1	.994	.000
Age		.292	.057	26.442	1	.000	1.340
Age^2		-.003	.001	26.187	1	.000	.997
Ethnicity		1.047	.530	3.900	1	.048	2.848
Constant		-9.339	1.336	48.875	1	.000	.000

Variables removed from the equation: economic activity, long-term illness/disability, availability of private transport, academic qualifications, benefits status, gender, equivalised income. (R^2 = .208)

Table B19: Any Divorce Problem (5 Ethnicity Categories)

		B	S.E.	Wald	df	p	Exp(B)
Ethnicity	White			2.645	4	.619	
	Asian	-.893	.815	1.200	1	.273	.410
	Black	-.847	.693	1.494	1	.222	.429
	Mixed	-17.803	6869.2	.000	1	.998	.000
	Other	-17.277	5532.1	.000	1	.998	.000
House type	Flat			15.400	3	.002	
	Detached	-.925	.379	5.955	1	.015	.396
	Semi	-1.002	.308	10.563	1	.001	.367
	Terrace	-.250	.277	.818	1	.366	.779
Family type	Single no children			111.468	3	.000	
	Couple children	-1.704	.294	33.589	1	.000	.182
	Couple no children	-1.742	.276	39.800	1	.000	.175
	Lone parent	1.067	.275	15.052	1	.000	2.907
Tenure type	Own			7.811	4	.099	
	Mortgage	.313	.361	.753	1	.386	1.368
	Rent public	-.115	.399	.083	1	.773	.892
	Rent private	.708	.413	2.940	1	.086	2.029
	Rent free	-16.975	2070.2	.000	1	.993	.000
Age		.298	.056	28.594	1	.000	1.347
Age^2		-.003	.001	28.592	1	.000	.997
Constant		-8.383	1.205	48.412	1	.000	.000

Variables removed from the equation: economic activity, long-term illness/disability, availability of private transport, academic qualifications, benefits status, gender, equivalised income (R^2 = .206)

Table B20: Any Post-Relationship Problem (2 Ethnicity Categories)

		B	S.E.	Wald	df	P	Exp(B)
House type	Flat			10.252	3	.017	
	Detached	-.825	.433	3.627	1	.057	.438
	Semi	-.524	.343	2.332	1	.127	.592
	Terrace	.045	.327	.019	1	.890	1.046
Family type	Single no children			110.328	3	.000	
	Couple children	-.665	.323	4.250	1	.039	.514
	Couple no children	-.863	.333	6.743	1	.009	.422
	Lone parent	2.113	.330	41.100	1	.000	8.271
Tenure type	Own			11.975	4	.018	
	Mortgage	.952	.568	2.811	1	.094	2.590
	Rent public	.860	.607	2.004	1	.157	2.362

		B	S.E.	Wald	df	P	Exp(B)
	Rent private	1.683	.608	7.659	1	.006	5.382
	Rent free	1.018	.744	1.869	1	.172	2.767
Economic activity	Full-time employed			13.185	8	.106	
	Part-time employed	.135	.293	.212	1	.645	1.144
	Self-employed	.210	.385	.299	1	.584	1.234
	Unemployed/scheme	.484	.438	1.222	1	.269	1.623
	Education	-17.401	3966.2	.000	1	.996	.000
	Sick	-.753	.545	1.914	1	.167	.471
	Home/care	.825	.302	7.439	1	.006	2.281
	Retired	.022	1.142	.000	1	.985	1.022
	Other/unknown	1.246	.983	1.606	1	.205	3.477
Long-term illness/disability		1.129	.238	22.429	1	.000	3.094
Transport avail.		.658	.298	4.886	1	.027	1.931
Academic qualifications		.903	1.154	.613	1	.434	2.468
Age		.277	.080	12.030	1	.001	1.320
Age^2		-.004	.001	11.516	1	.001	.997
Ethnicity		-.043	.030	2.058	1	.151	.958
Interaction term		.897	.475	3.570	1	.059	2.452
Constant		-10.908	1.690	41.681	1	.000	.000

Variables removed from the equation: benefits status, equivalised income. (R^2 = .255)

Table B21: Any Post-Relationship Problem (5 Ethnicity Categories)

		B	S.E.	Wald	df	P	Exp(B)
Ethnicity	White			3.209	4	.523	
	Asian	-1.301	.877	2.203	1	.138	.272
	Black	-.454	.592	.586	1	.444	.635
	Mixed	-1.933	2.801	.476	1	.490	.145
	Other	-16.801	5769.4	.000	1	.998	.000
House type	Flat			10.239	3	.017	
	Detached	-.828	.433	3.649	1	.056	.437
	Semi	-.531	.343	2.394	1	.122	.588
	Terrace	.039	.327	.014	1	.905	1.040
Family type	Single no children			107.593	3	.000	
	Couple children	-.652	.324	4.044	1	.044	.521
	Couple no children	-.862	.333	6.717	1	.010	.422
	Lone parent	2.097	.330	40.357	1	.000	8.143
Tenure type	Own			11.943	4	.018	
	Mortgage	.946	.568	2.776	1	.096	2.576
	Rent public	.841	.608	1.911	1	.167	2.319
	Rent private	1.671	.609	7.544	1	.006	5.320
	Rent free	1.003	.745	1.813	1	.178	2.727
Economic activity	Full-time employed			13.202	8	.105	
	Part-time employed	.127	.293	.187	1	.666	1.135
	Self-employed	.225	.384	.343	1	.558	1.252
	Unemployed/scheme	.469	.437	1.151	1	.283	1.599
	Education	-17.379	3936.8	.000	1	.996	.000
	Sick	-.747	.544	1.884	1	.170	.474
	Home/care	.823	.303	7.395	1	.007	2.277
	Retired	.002	1.142	.000	1	.998	1.002
	Other/unknown	1.281	.990	1.675	1	.196	3.601

Long-term illness/disability		1.127	.239	22.265	1	.000	3.086
Transport avail.		.629	.299	4.442	1	.035	1.876
Academic qualifications		.892	1.157	.594	1	.441	2.440
Age		.275	.080	11.869	1	.001	1.317
Age²		-.003	.001	11.367	1	.001	.997
Interaction term		-.043	.030	2.017	1	.156	.958
Constant		-9.934	1.598	38.673	1	.000	.000

Variables removed from the equation: benefits status, equivalised income. (R^2 = .256)

Table B22: Any Post-Relationship Problem (Obtaining Maintenance Only)

		B	S.E.	Wald	df	p	Exp(B)
Family type	Single no children			37.459	3	.000	
	Couple children	-.299	.474	.399	1	.528	.741
	Couple no children	-1.961	.741	7.006	1	.008	.141
	Lone parent	1.777	.466	14.553	1	.000	5.912
Long-term illness/disability		681	.341	3.983	1	.046	1.976
Transport avail.		.937	.383	5.998	1	.014	2.552
Benefits status		-.709	.383	3.433	1	.064	.492
Age		.246	.108	5.164	1	.023	1.279
Age²		-.003	.001	5.636	1	.018	.997
Gender		-2.704	.698	14.996	1	.000	.067
Constant		-8.324	1.910	18.992	1	.000	.000

Variables removed from the equation: house type, tenure type, economic activity, academic qualifications, ethnicity, equivalised income. (R^2 = .312)

Table B23: Any Post-Relationship Problem (Care And Control Only)

		B	S.E.	Wald	df	p	Exp(B)
Family type	Single no children			56.715	3	.000	
	Couple children	-.975	.573	2.890	1	.089	.377
	Couple no children	-.510	.514	.986	1	.321	.601
	Lone parent	2.134	.442	23.256	1	.000	8.448
Tenure type	Own			6.753	4	.150	
	Mortgage	.040	.766	.003	1	.958	1.041
	Rent public	.627	.774	.657	1	.418	1.872
	Rent private	.944	.803	1.382	1	.240	2.571
	Rent free	-2.858	2.347	1.483	1	.223	.057
Long-term illness/disability		.664	.365	3.311	1	.069	1.943
Age²		-.001	.000	10.352	1	.001	.999
Ethnicity		1.428	1.010	1.999	1	.157	4.170
Constant		-5.508	1.320	17.425	1	.000	.004

Variables removed from the equation: house type, economic activity, availability of private transport, academic qualifications, benefits status, age, equivalised income. (R^2 = .251)

Table B24: Any Post-Relationship Problem (Disputes Over Assets Only)

		B	S.E.	Wald	df	p	Exp(B)
Family type	Single no children			87.753	3	.000	
	Couple children	-.993	.589	2.835	1	.092	.371
	Couple no children	-.974	.586	2.767	1	.096	.377
	Lone parent	2.997	.547	29.977	1	.000	20.019
Tenure type	Own			10.931	4	.027	
	Mortgage	1.262	.973	1.682	1	.195	3.533
	Rent public	-2.677	1.853	2.088	1	.149	.069
	Rent private	1.963	1.043	3.542	1	.060	7.121
	Rent free	1.558	1.173	1.766	1	.184	4.751
Economic activity	Full-time employed			16.045	8	.042	
	Part-time employed	.346	.454	.581	1	.446	1.413
	Self-employed	-2.006	1.795	1.249	1	.264	.135
	Unemployed/scheme	.998	.732	1.860	1	.173	2.712
	Education	-16.600	3771.6	.000	1	.996	.000
	Sick	-1.280	1.236	1.074	1	.300	.278
	Home/care	.997	.522	3.656	1	.056	2.711
	Retired	-13.451	987.25	.000	1	.989	.000
	Other/unknown	3.199	1.018	9.876	1	.002	24.515
Long-term illness/disability		1.477	.409	13.057	1	.000	4.381
Transport avail.		1.834	.716	6.551	1	.010	6.256
Academic qualifications		-11.118	18.459	.363	1	.547	.000
Age		.206	.151	1.875	1	.171	1.229
Age^2		-.003	.002	1.705	1	.192	.997
Interaction term		.131	.402	.107	1	.744	1.140
Constant		-11.656	3.001	15.091	1	.000	.000

Variables removed from the equation: house type, benefits status, gender, ethnicity, equivalised income. ($R^2 = .350$)

Table B25: Victim Of Domestic Violence (2 Ethnicity Categories)

		B	S.E.	Wald	df	p	Exp(B)
House type	Flat			13.000	3	.005	
	Detached	-1.740	.618	7.933	1	.005	.176
	Semi	-1.033	.359	8.300	1	.004	.356
	Terrace	-1.055	.373	7.989	1	.005	.348
Family type	Single no children			68.431	3	.000	
	Couple children	-.814	.441	3.408	1	.065	.443
	Couple no children	-1.203	.465	6.684	1	.010	.300
	Lone parent	1.790	.375	22.765	1	.000	5.989
Long-term illness/disability		1.216	.297	16.764	1	.000	3.374
Age		.147	.071	4.223	1	.040	1.158
Age^2		-.002	.001	6.212	1	.013	.998
Gender		-.782	.340	5.295	1	.021	.457
Ethnicity		1.261	.786	2.572	1	.109	3.530
Constant		-6.465	1.535	17.743	1	.000	.002

Variables removed from the equation: tenure type, economic activity, availability of private transport, academic qualifications, benefits status. ($R^2 = .256$)

Table B26: Victim Of Domestic Violence (5 Ethnicity Categories)

		B	S.E.	Wald	df	p	Exp(B)
Ethnicity	White			1.019	4	.907	
	Asian	-2.234	2.214	1.019	1	.313	.107
	Black	-.008	.652	.000	1	.990	.992
	Mixed	-17.589	6593.7	.000	1	.998	.000
	Other	-16.154	5718.2	.000	1	.998	.000
House type	Flat			12.884	3	.005	
	Detached	-1.751	.616	8.071	1	.004	.174
	Semi	-1.044	.358	8.492	1	.004	.352
	Terrace	-.993	.367	7.340	1	.007	.370
Family type	Single no children			74.078	3	.000	
	Couple children	-.773	.442	3.056	1	.080	.462
	Couple no children	-1.189	.465	6.534	1	.011	.305
	Lone parent	1.894	.373	25.784	1	.000	6.644
Long-term illness/disability		1.194	.296	16.292	1	.000	3.301
Age		.146	.072	4.145	1	.042	1.157
Age^2		-.002	.001	6.165	1	.013	.998
Gender		-.643	.329	3.811	1	.051	.526
Constant		-5.296	1.320	16.104	1	.000	.005

Variables removed from the equation: tenure type, economic activity, availability of private transport, academic qualifications, benefits status. (R^2 = .263)

Table B27: Any Children Problem

		B	S.E.	Wald	df	p	Exp(B)
House type	Flat			10.528	3	.015	
	Detached	1.176	.593	3.937	1	.047	3.240
	Semi	.536	.569	.887	1	.346	1.709
	Terrace	1.125	.561	4.016	1	.045	3.081
Family type	Single no children			19.790	3	.000	
	Couple children	.762	.386	3.893	1	.048	2.143
	Couple no children	-.017	.464	.001	1	.970	.983
	Lone parent	1.567	.428	13.393	1	.000	4.790
Long-term illness/disability		.473	.249	3.603	1	.058	1.604
Academic qualifications		1.238	1.489	.692	1	.406	3.449
Age		.538	.106	25.625	1	.000	1.713
Age^2		-.007	.001	24.509	1	.000	.993
Income		-.126	.031	16.127	1	.000	.882
Interaction term		-.049	.038	1.607	1	.205	.952
Constant		-14.198	2.034	48.743	1	.000	.000

Variables removed from the equation: tenure type, economic activity, availability of private transport, benefits status, gender, ethnicity. (R^2 = .190)

Table B28: Any Children Problem (Education Only)

		B	S.E.	Wald	df	p	Exp(B)
Ethnicity	White			1.403	4	.844	
	Asian	-.578	.714	.657	1	.418	.561
	Black	.470	.562	.699	1	.403	1.600

		B	S.E.	Wald	df	p	Exp(B)
	Mixed	-17.482	6979.6	.000	1	.998	.000
	Other	-16.660	5786.3	.000	1	.998	.000
House type	Flat			7.662	3	.054	
	Detached	.868	.608	2.035	1	.154	2.382
	Semi	.391	.577	.460	1	.498	1.478
	Terrace	.978	.568	2.967	1	.085	2.660
Family type	Single no children			7.658	3	.054	
	Couple children	.586	.393	2.225	1	.136	1.796
	Couple no children	.050	.467	.012	1	.914	1.052
	Lone parent	1.065	.454	5.502	1	.019	2.902
Long-term illness/disability		.613	.256	5.729	1	.017	1.846
Academic qualifications		.955	1.807	.279	1	.597	2.598
Age		.693	.130	28.615	1	.000	2.000
Age^2		-.009	.002	27.518	1	.000	.991
Income		-.139	.033	17.539	1	.000	.870
Interaction term		-.044	.046	.900	1	.343	.957
Constant		-16.842	2.487	45.862	1	.000	.000

Variables removed from the equation: tenure type, economic activity, availability of private transport, benefits status, gender, ethnicity, equivalised income. ($R^2 = .192$)

Table B29: Any Personal Injury Problem

		B	S.E.	Wald	df	p	Exp(B)
House type	Flat			8.586	3	.035	
	Detached	-.763	.299	6.516	1	.011	.466
	Semi	-.450	.244	3.394	1	.065	.638
	Terrace	-.198	.238	.690	1	.406	.820
Family type	Single no children			8.596	3	.035	
	Couple children	-.437	.240	3.302	1	.069	.646
	Couple no children	.148	.193	.584	1	.445	1.159
	Lone parent	-.250	.457	.298	1	.585	.779
Tenure type	Own			16.562	4	.002	
	Mortgage	.892	.278	10.305	1	.001	2.441
	Rent public	.813	.305	7.095	1	.008	2.254
	Rent private	1.189	.330	13.019	1	.000	3.285
	Rent free	1.323	.368	12.948	1	.000	3.754
Economic activity	Full-time employed			28.453	8	.000	
	Part-time employed	-.564	.260	4.702	1	.030	.569
	Self-employed	-1.301	.427	9.308	1	.002	.272
	Unemployed/scheme	-.466	.443	1.104	1	.293	.628
	Education	.012	.491	.001	1	.981	1.012
	Sick	-.498	.306	2.639	1	.104	.608
	Home/care	-1.197	.412	8.464	1	.004	.302
	Retired	-.952	.263	13.113	1	.000	.386
	Other/unknown	-1.865	2.678	.485	1	.486	.155
Long-term illness/disability		1.054	.171	38.076	1	.000	2.870
Constant		-3.522	.366	92.586	1	.000	.030

Variables removed from the equation: availability of private transport, academic qualifications, benefits status, age, age squared, gender, ethnicity, equivalised income. ($R^2 = .081$)

Table B30: Any Clinical Negligence Problem

		B	S.E.	Wald	df	p	Exp(B)
Economic activity	Full-time employed			22.301	8	.004	
	Part-time employed	.807	.348	5.365	1	.021	2.241
	Self-employed	.910	.385	5.574	1	.018	2.484
	Unemployed/scheme	.407	.845	.232	1	.630	1.502
	Education	1.459	.778	3.519	1	.061	4.303
	Sick	.946	.418	5.114	1	.024	2.574
	Home/care	.527	.428	1.515	1	.218	1.694
	Retired	-.442	.395	1.249	1	.264	.643
	Other/unknown	-16.354	10549.1	.000	1	.999	.000
Long-term illness/disability		1.606	.244	43.132	1	.000	4.981
Income		.065	.024	7.144	1	.008	1.067
Gender		-.579	.252	5.286	1	.021	.561
Constant		-5.305	.394	181.583	1	.000	.005

Variables removed from the equation: house type, family type, tenure type, availability of private transport, academic qualifications, benefits status, age, age squared, ethnicity. (R^2 = .092)

Table B31: Any Mental Health Problem

		B	S.E.	Wald	df	p	Exp(B)
Family type	Single no children			8.946	3	.030	
	Couple children	2.118	.804	6.947	1	.008	8.317
	Couple no children	1.395	.687	4.120	1	.042	4.033
	Lone parent	2.887	1.100	6.889	1	.009	17.948
Tenure type	Own			11.631	4	.020	
	Mortgage	1.063	.748	2.021	1	.155	2.894
	Rent public	.691	.833	.687	1	.407	1.995
	Rent private	1.531	.938	2.662	1	.103	4.623
	Rent free	2.962	.930	10.138	1	.001	19.334
Economic activity	Full-time employed			10.658	8	.222	
	Part-time employed	-15.163	1501.7	.000	1	.992	.000
	Self-employed	1.547	.629	6.052	1	.014	4.696
	Unemployed/scheme	-1.408	3.040	.215	1	.643	.245
	Education	-15.433	4467.7	.000	1	.997	.000
	Sick	2.040	.826	6.094	1	.014	7.690
	Home/care	.313	.898	.122	1	.727	1.368
	Retired	2.039	1.051	3.764	1	.052	7.679
	Other/unknown	-14.872	10384	.000	1	.999	.000
Long-term illness/disability		1.521	.493	9.513	1	.002	4.577
Age		-.154	.068	5.096	1	.024	.857
Age^2		.001	.001	4.052	1	.044	1.001
Income		.133	.059	5.096	1	.024	1.142
Constant		-6.659	1.834	13.182	1	.000	.001

Variables removed from the equation: availability of private transport, benefits status, age, age squared, gender, ethnicity. (R^2 = .165)

Table B32: Any Immigration Problem

		B	S.E.	Wald	df	p	Exp(B)
Ethnicity	White			54.828	4	.000	
	Asian	-.398	2.252	.031	1	.860	.671
	Black	3.760	.667	31.764	1	.000	42.954
	Mixed	-14.896	7002.1	.000	1	.998	.000
	Other	4.854	.732	44.020	1	.000	128.308
House type	Flat			5.829	3	.120	
	Detached	-1.482	1.016	2.125	1	.145	.227
	Semi	-2.469	1.135	4.734	1	.030	.085
	Terrace	-.419	.618	.459	1	.498	.658
Family type	Single no children			4.478	3	.214	
	Couple children	.601	.798	.568	1	.451	1.824
	Couple no children	1.511	.751	4.043	1	.044	4.531
	Lone parent	-16.323	2336.1	.000	1	.994	.000
Benefits status		-1.867	.654	8.151	1	.004	.155
Age^2		-.001	.000	4.173	1	.041	.999
Constant		-4.383	.878	24.890	1	.000	.012

Variables removed from the equation: tenure type, economic activity, long-term illness/disability, availability of private transport, academic qualifications, age, gender, equivalised income. ($R^2 = .392$)

Table B33: Any Unfair Police Treatment Problem

	B	S.E.	Wald	df	p	Exp(B)
Long-term illness/disability	.675	.374	3.250	1	.071	1.964
Benefits status	-1.112	.349	10.181	1	.001	.329
Age	-.050	.012	16.337	1	.000	.951
Gender	1.388	.393	12.458	1	.000	4.007
Ethnicity	2.077	1.630	1.623	1	.203	7.980
Constant	-5.266	1.694	9.663	1	.002	.005

Variables removed from the equation: housing type, family type, tenure type, economic activity, availability of private transport, academic qualifications, age squared, equivalised income. ($R^2 = .112$)

Table B34: Total Number Of Problems Experienced (Ancova)

Parameter		B	St. Error	t	Sig.
House Type	Detached	-.587	.092	-6.352	.000
Cf. Flat	Semi-detached	-.607	.084	-7.252	.000
	Terrace	-.473	.084	-5.659	.000
Family Type	Couple: Children	.034	.075	.451	.652
Cf. Single	Couple: No Children	.026	.065	.401	.689
	Lone Parent	1.243	.127	9.814	.000
Tenure Type	Mortgage	.105	.066	1.577	.115
Cf. Own	Rent Public	.038	.084	.459	.646
	Rent Private	.228	.097	2.358	.018
	Rent Free	-.038	.123	-.312	.755
Economic Activity	Part-Time Employed	-.073	.074	-.991	.322
Cf. Full-Time Employed	Self-Employed	.065	.083	.785	.432
	Unemployed	.352	.139	2.536	.011
	Education	-.167	.187	-.892	.372

	Sick	.139	.123	1.126	.260
	Home/Care	.128	.089	1.441	.150
	Retired	.054	.107	.509	.611
	Unknown	.331	.384	.863	.388
Long-Standing Illness/Disability	Yes	.479	.057	8.458	.000
Transport Available	Yes	-.012	.069	-.169	.865
Academic Qualifications	None	-.341	.059	-5.806	.000
Benefits Status (None)	None	-.195	.068	-2.880	.004
Age		.012	.008	1.484	.138
Age Squared		.000	.000	-2.664	.008
Income		.010	.006	1.612	.107
Gender	Male	.052	.047	1.115	.265
Ethnicity	White	.139	.094	1.477	.140
Intercept		.995	.233	4.280	.000

$(R^2 = .100)$

Table B35: Prevalence In Sequences Of Increasing Magnitude (Cascades)

Problem Type	T-value	Observed significantly steeper	Expected significantly steeper
Domestic Violence	+20.95	●	
Homelessness	+6.50	●	
Post-Relationship	+5.79	●	
Police Treatment	+3.23		
Discrimination	+1.97		
Children	+0.36		
Mental Health	+0.14		
Money / Debt	-0.35		
Divorce	-1.86		
Housing (Renting)	-1.91		
Housing (Owning)	-2.15		
Consumer	-3.70		
Employment	-4.14		●
Immigration	-4.84		●
Neighbours	-5.18		●
Welfare Benefits	-9.00		●
Clinical Negligence	-10.33		●
Personal Injury	-12.29		●

Table 36: Component Matrix Of Variable Loadings Following Orthogonal Rotation (Clustering)

Problem Type	Component/factor				
	1	2	3	4	5
Relationship breakdown	.709				
Divorce	.680				
Domestic violence	.544				
Children	.356				
Homelessness		.677			
Police treatment		.500			
Housing (renting)		.454			
Legal action against Respondent		.428			
Mental health			.607		
Immigration			.528		

Clinical negligence	.478	
Welfare benefits	.372	
Respondent thought of legal action		
Resp. threatened with legal action	.568	
Money/debt	.539	
Housing (owning)	.418	
Employment		-.554
Personal injury		-.501
Consumer	.395	.477
Neighbours		.466
Discrimination		

Table B37: Multiple Problems In Family Cluster

		B	S.E.	Wald	df	p	Exp(B)
House type	Flat			12.204	3	.007	
	Detached	-.450	.536	.703	1	.402	.638
	Semi	-.741	.424	3.055	1	.080	.477
	Terrace	.295	.380	.602	1	.438	1.343
Family type	Single no children			115.817	3	.000	
	Couple children	-.976	.404	5.829	1	.016	.377
	Couple no children	-1.130	.435	6.738	1	.009	.323
	Lone parent	2.319	.357	42.206	1	.000	10.166
Tenure type	Own			12.866	4	.012	
	Mortgage	.155	.621	.063	1	.802	1.168
	Rent public	-.250	.658	.145	1	.703	.778
	Rent private	.977	.652	2.245	1	.134	2.657
	Rent free	-.283	.957	.088	1	.767	.753
Long-term illness/disability		.902	.291	9.611	1	.002	2.464
Age		.424	.110	14.982	1	.000	1.529
Age^2		-.006	.001	15.565	1	.000	.994
Constant		-11.304	2.055	30.268	1	.000	.000

Variables removed from the equation: economic activity availability of private transport, benefits status, gender, ethnicity, equivalised income. ($R^2 = .290$)

Table B38: Multiple Problems In Homelessness Cluster

		B	S.E.	Wald	df	p	Exp(B)
Tenure type	Own			9.173	4	.057	
	Mortgage	-.203	1.174	.030	1	.863	.816
	Rent public	1.300	1.060	1.506	1	.220	3.670
	Rent private	1.115	1.091	1.045	1	.307	3.050
	Rent free	-.639	1.337	.228	1	.633	.528
Transport avail.		-.672	.387	3.011	1	.083	.511
Long-term illness/disability		.673	.378	3.175	1	.075	1.961
Academic qualifications		-3.832	1.780	4.632	1	.031	.022
Benefits status		-1.237	.490	6.369	1	.012	.290
Age		-.067	.021	10.661	1	.001	.935
Income		-.116	.070	2.729	1	.099	.891
Interaction term		.044	.036	1.484	1	.223	1.045
Constant		-1.231	1.312	.880	1	.348	.292

Variables removed from the equation: house type, family type, economic activity availability of private transport, age squared, gender, ethnicity ($R^2 = .301$)

Table B39: Multiple Problems In Health And Welfare Cluster

		B	S.E.	Wald	df	p	Exp(B)
Ethnicity	White			16.155	4	.003	
	Asian	-.918	2.258	.165	1	.684	.399
	Black	2.140	.722	8.789	1	.003	8.500
	Mixed	-15.616	6666	.000	1	.998	.000
	Other	2.925	.994	8.654	1	.003	18.628
Family type	Single no children			12.374	3	.006	
	Couple children	-1.104	1.072	1.060	1	.303	.331
	Couple no children	1.637	.650	6.352	1	.012	5.141
	Lone parent	-.142	.993	.020	1	.887	.868
Tenure type	Own			12.988	4	.011	
	Mortgage	2.031	2.190	.860	1	.354	7.620
	Rent public	2.110	2.230	.895	1	.344	8.252
	Rent private	3.923	2.202	3.174	1	.075	50.537
	Rent free	3.635	2.315	2.466	1	.116	37.910
Long-term illness/disability		1.408	.542	6.745	1	.009	4.086
Benefits status		-1.850	.622	8.847	1	.003	.157
Age		.283	.140	4.126	1	.042	1.328
Age^2		-.004	.002	4.705	1	.030	.996
Constant		-13.034	3.512	13.772	1	.000	.000

Variables removed from the equation: house type, economic activity, availability of private transport, academic qualifications, gender, equivalised income. (R^2 = .279)

Table B40: Economic Cluster

		B	S.E.	Wald	df	p	Exp(B)
House Type	Flat			20.853	3	.000	
	Detached	-.530	.186	8.147	1	.004	.588
	Semi	-.726	.164	19.558	1	.000	.484
	Terrace	-.398	.160	6.231	1	.013	.672
Family type	Single no children			8.189	3	.042	
	Couple children	-.123	.154	.641	1	.423	.884
	Couple no children	-.042	.138	.091	1	.763	.959
	Lone parent	.486	.230	4.454	1	.035	1.626
Tenure type	Own			22.618	4	.000	
	Mortgage	.411	.180	5.186	1	.023	1.508
	Rent public	.626	.212	8.673	1	.003	1.870
	Rent private	.906	.216	17.547	1	.000	2.475
	Rent free	.175	.299	.342	1	.559	1.191
Long-term illness/disability		.921	.114	65.685	1	.000	2.513
Academic qualifications		-.710	.491	2.093	1	.148	.492
Age		.042	.022	3.538	1	.060	1.042
Age^2		-.001	.000	8.391	1	.004	.999
Income		.030	.012	6.110	1	.013	1.030
Gender		.232	.097	5.762	1	.016	1.262
Interaction term		-.003	.010	.076	1	.783	.997
Constant		-2.812	.486	33.531	1	.000	.060

Variables removed from the equation: economic activity, availability of private transport, benefits status, gender, ethnicity. (R^2 = .112)

Table B41: Family Cluster (ANCOVA)

Parameter		B	St. Error	t	Sig.
House Type	Detached	-.183	.084	-2.191	.029
Cf. Flat	Semi-detached	-.192	.072	-2.664	.008
	Terrace	-.075	.070	-1.066	.287
Family Type	Couple: Children	-.169	.069	-2.450	.014
Cf. Single	Couple: No Children	-.219	.061	-3.602	.000
	Lone Parent	.962	.100	9.603	.000
Tenure Type	Mortgage	.063	.070	.907	.364
Cf. Own	Rent Public	.083	.085	.978	.328
	Rent Private	.230	.092	2.496	.013
	Rent Free	.902	.352	2.558	.011
Economic Activity	Part-Time Employed	.123	.071	1.730	.084
Cf. Full-Time Employed	Self-Employed	.084	.078	1.088	.277
	Unemployed	-.263	.113	-2.323	.020
	Education	-.308	.169	-1.826	.068
	Sick	-.002	.100	-.018	.986
	Home/Care	.167	.082	2.038	.042
	Retired	.048	.111	.433	.665
	Unknown	.902	.352	2.558	.011
Long-Standing	Yes	-.001	.051	-.029	.977
Transport Available	Yes	.060	.065	.930	.353
Illness/Disability					
Academic Qualifications	None	-.013	.060	-.210	.834
Benefits Status (None)	None	-.075	.063	-1.207	.228
Age		.026	.009	2.912	.004
Age Squared		.000	.000	-2.897	.004
Income		-.009	.005	-1.678	.094
Gender	Male	-.010	.044	-.233	.815
Ethnicity	White	.171	.088	1.938	.053
Intercept		-.525	.229	-2.293	.022

($R^2 = .163$)

Table B42: Homelessness Cluster (ANCOVA)

Parameter		B	St. Error	t	Sig.
House Type	Detached	-.165	.094	-1.764	.078
Cf. Flat	Semi-detached	-.106	.081	-1.308	.191
	Terrace	-.139	.079	-1.764	.078
Family Type	Couple: Children	.158	.077	2.043	.041
Cf. Single	Couple: No Children	.099	.068	1.449	.147
	Lone Parent	.208	.112	1.849	.065
Tenure Type	Mortgage	-.172	.078	-2.204	.028
Cf. Own	Rent Public	.123	.095	1.302	.193
	Rent Private	.086	.103	.830	.407
	Rent Free	.080	.144	.555	.579
Economic Activity	Part-Time Employed	-.175	.080	-2.190	.029
Cf. Full-Time Employed	Self-Employed	.169	.087	1.945	.052
	Unemployed	.202	.127	1.598	.110
	Education	-.177	.189	-.937	.349
	Sick	-.105	.113	-.929	.353
	Home/Care	-.056	.092	-.613	.540

		B	St. Error	t	Sig.
	Retired	-.030	.124	-.239	.811
	Unknown	-.193	.395	-.487	.626
Long-Standing Illness/Disability	Yes	.070	.057	1.225	.221
Transport Available	Yes	-.163	.073	-2.245	.025
Academic Qualifications	None	-.174	.068	-2.574	.010
Benefits Status (None)	None	-.286	.070	-4.081	.000
Age		-.018	.010	-1.793	.073
Age Squared		.000	.000	.726	.468
Income		-.011	.006	-1.868	.062
Gender	Male	.094	.050	1.896	.058
Ethnicity	White	.046	.099	.464	.643
Intercept		1.028	.257	4.006	.000

($R^2 = .123$)

Table B43: Health And Welfare Cluster (ANCOVA)

Parameter		B	St. Error	t	Sig.
House Type	Detached	-.091	.091	-.992	.321
Cf. Flat	Semi-detached	-.079	.079	-1.009	.313
	Terrace	-.088	.077	-1.140	.254
Family Type	Couple: Children	.073	.075	.963	.336
Cf. Single	Couple: No Children	.181	.066	2.727	.006
	Lone Parent	-.002	.110	-.015	.988
Tenure Type	Mortgage	-.045	.076	-.595	.552
Cf. Own	Rent Public	-.115	.092	-1.240	.215
	Rent Private	.048	.101	.471	.637
	Rent Free	.147	.140	1.046	.296
Economic Activity	Part-Time Employed	.147	.078	1.882	.060
Cf. Full-Time Employed	Self-Employed	.125	.085	1.473	.141
	Unemployed	.185	.124	1.499	.134
	Education	.042	.185	.229	.819
	Sick	.259	.110	2.361	.018
	Home/Care	.184	.089	2.053	.040
	Retired	.194	.121	1.596	.111
	Unknown	-.349	.385	-.905	.366
Long-Standing Illness/Disability	Yes	.221	.056	3.943	.000
Transport Available	Yes	-.030	.071	-.428	.669
Academic Qualifications	None	.011	.066	.163	.870
Benefits Status (None)	None	-.169	.068	-2.476	.013
Age		-.012	.010	-1.218	.224
Age Squared		.000	.000	.812	.417
Income		.008	.006	1.347	.178
Gender	Male	-.015	.048	-.310	.757
Ethnicity	White	-.446	.097	-4.612	.000
Intercept		.683	.250	2.732	.006

($R^2 = .047$)

Table B44: Strategy: Took Any Action

		B	S.E.	Wald	df	p	Exp(B)
Problem type	Discrimination			204.660	17	.000	

		B	S.E.	Wald	df	p	Exp(B)
	Consumer	.672	.296	5.144	1	.023	1.958
	Employment	.326	.311	1.098	1	.295	1.385
	Neighbours	.168	.301	.311	1	.577	1.183
	Owned housing	1.462	.442	10.911	1	.001	4.313
	Rented housing	.481	.334	2.080	1	.149	1.618
	Homelessness	2.066	.894	5.337	1	.021	7.891
	Money/debt	.528	.304	3.025	1	.082	1.696
	Welfare benefits	.958	.402	5.677	1	.017	2.606
	Divorce	.603	.391	2.386	1	.122	1.828
	Relationship breakdown	1.339	.442	9.168	1	.002	3.814
	Domestic violence	-.592	.361	2.688	1	.101	.553
	Children	1.274	.454	7.858	1	.005	3.575
	Personal injury	-.724	.312	5.389	1	.020	.485
	Clinical negligence	-1.310	.350	13.981	1	.000	.270
	Mental health	-1.453	.511	8.097	1	.004	.234
	Immigration	3.611	2.545	2.014	1	.156	37.003
	Unfair police Treatment	-.835	.427	3.827	1	.050	.434
Tenure type	Own			29.787	4	.000	
	Mortgage	.074	.166	.201	1	.654	1.077
	Rent public	-.277	.178	2.401	1	.121	.758
	Rent private	-.354	.197	3.217	1	.073	.702
	Rent free	-.873	.237	13.618	1	.000	.418
Economic activity	Full-time employed			15.611	8	.048	
	Part-time employed	-.144	.161	.806	1	.369	.866
	Self-employed	-.354	.170	4.349	1	.037	.702
	Unemployed/scheme	.376	.256	2.156	1	.142	1.456
	Education	.660	.448	2.177	1	.140	1.935
	Sick	.331	.201	2.708	1	.100	1.392
	Home/care	.046	.174	.070	1	.791	1.047
	Retired	-.093	.180	.269	1	.604	.911
	Other/unknown	3.534	2.800	1.593	1	.207	34.250
Gender		-.211	.102	4.240	1	.039	.810
Ethnicity		.454	.183	6.192	1	.013	1.575
Constant		.964	.355	7.364	1	.007	2.623

Variables removed from the equation: transport availability, long-term illness/disability, academic qualifications, benefits status, age, age squared, equivalised income. ($R^2 = .125$)

Table B45: Strategy: Tried To Obtain Advice (Excluding Those Who Took No Action)

		B	S.E.	Wald	df	p	Exp(B)
Problem type	Discrimination			274.696	17	.000	
	Consumer	-.875	.297	8.664	1	.003	.417
	Employment	.527	.318	2.746	1	.098	1.693
	Neighbours	.147	.310	.224	1	.636	1.158
	Owned housing	.911	.363	6.309	1	.012	2.487
	Rented housing	-.395	.331	1.424	1	.233	.674
	Homelessness	2.006	.786	6.513	1	.011	7.434
	Money/debt	-.660	.304	4.708	1	.030	.517
	Welfare benefits	.299	.363	.680	1	.410	1.349
	Divorce	2.775	.657	17.847	1	.000	16.044
	Relationship breakdown	1.370	.409	11.212	1	.001	3.935
	Domestic violence	1.263	.506	6.229	1	.013	3.534

	Children	.485	.376	1.659	1	.198	1.624
	Personal injury	1.074	.376	8.176	1	.004	2.927
	Clinical negligence	-.434	.424	1.049	1	.306	.648
	Mental health	-1.619	.805	4.044	1	.044	.198
	Immigration	1.336	.801	2.781	1	.095	3.802
	Unfair police Treatment	.277	.565	.241	1	.624	1.319
Tenure type	Own			11.639	4	.020	
	Mortgage	.224	.146	2.348	1	.125	1.252
	Rent public	.493	.171	8.286	1	.004	1.638
	Rent private	.449	.185	5.859	1	.015	1.567
	Rent free	.023	.263	.008	1	.929	1.024
Economic activity	Full-time employed			32.351	8	.000	
	Part-time employed	.229	.142	2.603	1	.107	1.257
	Self-employed	.828	.177	21.821	1	.000	2.289
	Unemployed/scheme	.409	.225	3.310	1	.069	1.505
	Education	-.036	.363	.010	1	.920	.964
	Sick	.407	.186	4.789	1	.029	1.502
	Home/care	.318	.155	4.213	1	.040	1.374
	Retired	.562	.175	10.319	1	.001	1.755
	Other/unknown	.384	.586	.429	1	.512	1.467
Academic qualifications		.245	.139	3.118	1	.077	1.277
Previous strategy	No previous problem			24.303	3	.000	
	Did nothing	.173	.221	.612	1	.434	1.188
	Handled alone	-.644	.136	22.438	1	.000	.525
	Obtained advice	-.136	.101	1.819	1	.177	.873
Constant		.170	.323	.278	1	.598	1.186

Variables removed from the equation: housing type, family type, transport availability, long-term illness/disability, benefits status, age, age squared, gender, ethnicity, equivalised income ($R^2 = .210$)

B46 Relative Likelihood Of Different Types Of Adviser Being Used Earlier Or Later In Sequences Of Advisers

		Estimate	Std. Error	Wald	Sig.	95% Confidence Interval	
						Lower B	Upper B
Threshold	1	-.537	.137	15.435	.000	-.804	-.269
	2	1.569	.149	110.188	.000	1.276	1.862
	3	3.053	.203	225.114	.000	2.654	3.452
	4	4.196	.305	189.443	.000	3.598	4.793
Adviser (Cf. Solicitor)	CAB	-1.624	.228	50.546	.000	-2.072	-1.177
	Other	.732	.191	14.714	.000	.358	1.106
	Other advice agency	-.255	.267	.917	.338	-.778	.267
	Union or prof. body	-.502	.281	3.196	.074	-1.053	.048
	Employer	-.637	.321	3.938	.047	-1.265	-.008
	Local council	-.207	.266	.603	.438	-.728	.315
	Police	.116	.304	.145	.704	-.480	.711
	Insurance co.	-.036	.344	.011	.917	-.710	.639

Link function: Logit. $R^2 = 0.145$

Table B47: Money Or Property Objective

		B	S.E.	Wald	df	p	Exp(B)
Family type	Single no children			11.383	3	.010	
	Couple children	-.182	.194	.881	1	.348	.834
	Couple no children	.027	.194	.019	1	.890	1.027
	Lone parent	-.913	.290	9.894	1	.002	.401
Benefits Status	None	-.376	.184	4.175	1	.041	.687
Strategy	Handled Alone			51.935	10	.000	
	Tried/Failed Obtain Advice	-.132	.202	.428	1	.513	.876
	CAB (last)	1.124	.332	11.474	1	.001	3.078
	Solicitor (last)	.782	.221	12.495	1	.000	2.187
	Other Advice Agency (last)	1.484	.359	17.056	1	.000	4.413
	Trade Union (last)	.771	.350	4.858	1	.028	2.162
	Employer (last)	.370	.413	.799	1	.371	1.447
	Local Council (last)	-.216	.406	.282	1	.596	.806
	Police (last)	.749	.614	1.489	1	.222	2.115
	Insurance Company (last)	1.349	.528	6.528	1	.011	3.854
	Other (last)	.724	.201	12.952	1	.000	2.062
Problem type	Employment			148.357	16	.000	
	Discrimination	-1.310	.500	6.868	1	.009	.270
	Consumer	.971	.210	21.346	1	.000	2.641
	Owned Housing	-.272	.352	.598	1	.439	.762
	Rented Housing	.681	.319	4.548	1	.033	1.976
	Homelessness	-.463	.925	.251	1	.617	.629
	Money/Debt	.781	.231	11.401	1	.001	2.183
	Welfare Benefits	2.399	.443	29.376	1	.000	11.016
	Divorce	-.854	.394	4.700	1	.030	.426
	Relationship Breakdown	.462	.329	1.969	1	.161	1.587
	Domestic Violence	-1.641	.666	6.067	1	.014	.194
	Children	-2.409	.542	19.774	1	.000	.090
	Personal Injury	.900	.325	7.674	1	.006	2.459
	Clinical Negligence	-2.776	.883	9.898	1	.002	.062
	Mental Health	-1.633	1.275	1.641	1	.200	.195
	Immigration	-21.108	20513	.000	1	.999	.000
	Unfair Police Treatment	-2.272	1.201	3.580	1	.058	.103
Claimant	Yes	1.231	.234	27.788	1	.000	3.424
Constant		-1.601	.343	21.741	1	.000	.202

Variables removed: tenure type, economic activity, transport available, long-term illness/disability, academic qualifications, age, age squared, equivalised income, gender, ethnicity. (Main interview data used, n=1347) ($R^2 = 0.301$)

Table B48: Problem Duration (ANCOVA)

Parameter		B	St. Error	t	Sig.
Problem Type	Discrimination	.226	.309	.732	.464
(Cf. Police Treatment)	Consumer	.115	.239	.483	.629
	Employment	.309	.250	1.235	.217
	Neighbours	.562	.248	2.267	.024

	Owned Housing	.119	.272	.439	.661
	Rented Housing	.326	.258	1.266	.206
	Homelessness	.130	.335	.389	.697
	Money / Debt	.402	.244	1.647	.100
	Welfare Benefits	.241	.282	.855	.392
	Divorce	1.176	.278	4.239	.000
	Relationship B'down	2.045	.298	6.853	.000
	Domestic Violence	.696	.286	2.437	.015
	Children	.490	.281	1.743	.082
	Personal Injury	.244	.273	.893	.372
	Medical Negligence	.202	.288	.703	.482
	Mental Health	.018	.377	.048	.962
	Immigration	.978	.535	1.828	.068
Strategy	Handled Alone	.045	.091	.492	.623
(Cf. Did nothing)	Sought Advice (Sol only)	-.016	.128	-.129	.898
	Sought Advice (CAB only)	.101	.137	.735	.463
	Sought Advice (TU only)	.581	.195	2.977	.003
	Sought Advice (Coun. only)	.332	.126	2.641	.008
	Sought Advice (Other only)	.431	.115	3.737	.000
	Sought Multiple Advice	.408	.115	3.559	.000
Court/Tribunal	None	-.251	.121	-2.070	.039
Mediation/Conciliation	None	.128	.157	.820	.412
Ombudsman	None	-.881	.232	-3.799	.000
Intercept		1.140	.369	3.092	.002

$(R^2 = .106)$

Appendix C

Autobiographical Memory and the Seriousness of Problems

It is well proven that memory decays with time,[1] though the form of the equations used to model this decay continue to change over time. Increasingly complex models are now being developed,[2] building upon the simple exponential models first proposed.[3] Recently, psychophysical methodology has been used to model decay,[4] and some authors have suggested a power law model may perform better than exponential models,[5] particularly with respect to modelling autobiographical memory.[6,7] In many cases, though, different functions lead to very similar results.[8]

As expected, respondents to the LSRC survey reported fewer problems in earlier time periods within the overall survey reference period. Because of this,

---

[1] See, for example, D.C. Rubin and A.E. Wenzel (1996) One Hundred Years of Forgetting: A Quantitative Description of Retention, 103(4) *Psychological Review,* p.734.

[2] See, for example, D.C. Rubin, S. Hinton and A.E. Wenzel (1999) The Precise Time Course of Retention, 25(5) J*ournal of Experimental Psychology – Learning, Memory and Cognition,* p.1161, and P.R. Killeen (2001) Writing and Overwriting of Short-Term Memory, 8(1) *Psychonomic Bulletin and Review,* p.18.

[3] See, for example, S. Sudman and N.M. Bradburn (1973) Effects of Time and Memory Factors on Response in Surveys, 68(344) *Journal of the American Statistical Society,* p.805, and D.C. Rubin (1982) On the Retention Function for Autobiographical Memory, 21(1) *Journal of Learning and Verbal Behavior,* p.21.

[4] K.G. White (2002) Psychophysics of Remembering: The Discrimination Hypothesis, 11(4) *Current Directions in Psychological Science,* p.141.

[5] S.W. Elliott and J.R. Anderson (1995) Effect of Memory Decay on Predictions from Changing Categories, 21(4) *Journal of Experimental Psychology – Learning, Memory and Cognition,* p.815.

[6] D.C. Rubin (1982) On the Retention Function for Autobiographical Memory, 21 *Journal of Verbal Learning and Verbal Behavior,* p.21.

[7] D.C. Rubin and A.E. Wenzel (1996), above, n.1.

[8] D.C. Rubin and A.E. Wenzel (1996), above, n.1.

important to our understanding of respondents' experiences of justiciable problems are the potential causes of memory decay relating to them. A number of factors may have influenced the rate of decay, such as experimental/survey protocols, the frequency or similarity of aspects of problems under study, the characteristics of respondents and, most importantly in the current context, the importance or salience of respondents' experiences.[9] Of these factors, frequency, similarity and respondents' characteristics (in particular age) are likely to have had relatively little influence. Multiple problems of the same type were quite rare. Also, while some differences in experience were observed with age, no problem types or strategies appeared to be particularly common among older age groups where rates of decay may increase. On the other hand, importance or saliency is likely to have varied considerably by problem type. Thus, we have been able to compare and rank the importance and saliency of different problem types (as aspects of respondents' experience of them) by comparing memory decay between them. Of course, this gives only a general indication of importance and saliency between defined groups of problems. Importance and saliency are likely to vary considerably within such groups. The fact that problems of one type are generally more important or salient than another does not mean that all problems of one type are more important or salient than all problems of another. Also, our findings must be understood in the context of there being manifold reasons for the omission of experiences relevant to surveys.

The methodology we adopted to compare relative rates of memory decay between defined groups of problems was simple. First, we split our survey reference period into fourteen equal time periods (equivalent to a quarter of a year). For each aspect of respondents' experiences of interest, such as problem category and problem resolution strategy, we then calculated counts of problems that started in each of these fourteen time periods. Counts in each time period were then divided by the maximum count in any time period to standardise all analyses (between a range of zero and one).

---

[9] See, for example, S. Sudman and N.M. Bradburn (1973), above, n.3, D.C. Rubin and M. Kozin (1984) Vivid Memories, 16 *Cognition*, p.81, W.A. Wagenaar (1996) My Memory – A Study of Autobiographical Memory Over 6 Years, 18(2) *Cognitive Psychology*, p.225, J. Wright and S. Morley (1995) Autobiographical Memory and Chronic Pain, 34 *British Journal of Clinical Psychology*, p.255, and P. Chapman and G. Underwood (2000) Forgetting Near-Accidents: The Roles of Severity, Culpability and Experience in the Poor Recall of Dangerous Driving Situations, 14(1) *Applied Cognitive Psychology*, p.31.

176

Finally, we fitted exponential decay and power function models to the data, using models proposed by Sudman and Bradburn[10] (equation 1) and Rubin[11] (equation 2).

Equation 1

$$r_0 = ae^{-bt}$$

Equation 2

$$r_0 = at^{-bt}$$

r_0 = retention rate

a = propensity to omit (i.e. percentage of problems reported)

b = rapidity of memory decay

t = time

In general terms, equation 2 tends to flatten more quickly, but generally produces a similar fit to equation 1. Models were implemented using simple non-linear regression models, constrained to prevent a-values greater than one. The non-time related propensity to omit events (a) applies where, for example, respondents choose not to report events, commonly due to the social desirability associated with an event. So, for instance, we might expect domestic violence to be relatively commonly underreported out of choice (a), rather than as a consequence of memory decay (b). However, we have no way of determining 'a' using our survey data. While we retained the term in our analysis, therefore, it was simply a measure of the tendency for the highest count to occur in the most recent time period and had no bearing upon decay. We fitted decay models for each problem type, broad strategy (collapsed into three categories), by monetary value of problem and by how important respondents stated their problem to have been to resolve (very important vs. all others).[12] In the last case, our analysis yielded little by way of meaningful results, as

---

[10] See above, n.3.

[11] See above, n.3.

[12] Details of an analysis relating to the type of advisers used by respondents was set out in chapter 3 of the main text.

the great majority of respondents reported their problems as having been 'very important' to resolve. For brevity, only results from the Sudman and Bradburn model are reported, as the Rubin model produced very similar results.

Fitted values (*a* and *b*) for each problem type, strategy, monetary value and stated importance are shown in Tables C1 to C4, along with proportion of the variance explained by each model (R^2). These R^2 values are particularly important, as the decay model fits some problem type data (e.g. immigration, domestic violence, unfair police treatment, homelessness) particularly poorly. Such problems show little or no evidence of memory decay and are most likely to be the most important or salient. Each group of analyses also has ranks corresponding to memory decay, with the lowest rank assigned to the category with the least decay. Some examples of relative memory decays are also set out in Figures C1 to C4.

Table C1: Problem Category

Problem Category	a	b (decay)	R^2	Rank
Discrimination	.81	.054	.19	8=
Consumer	1	.164	.89	18
Employment	.96	.123	.72	16
Neighbours	.88	.11	.51	14
Housing (Owned)	.81	.054	.18	8=
Housing (Rented)	1	.105	.71	13
Homelessness	.43	.033	.04	4
Money/Debt	1	.112	.81	15
Welfare Benefits	1	.14	.78	17
Divorce	.47	-.041	.27	1
Relationship B'down	.66	.051	.16	5=
Domestic Violence	.56	.051	.09	5=
Children	.77	.063	.20	10
Personal Injury	.95	.086	.63	12
Clinical Negligence	.92	.053	.42	7
Mental Health	.54	.075	.14	11
Immigration	.37	.013	.003	2
Unfair Police Treatment	.73	.027	.05	3

Table C2: Monetary Value

Problem Category	a	b (decay)	R^2	Rank (Alt)
To £200	.99	.209	.72	4 (3)
£201 to £1,000	.93	.122	.76	3 (2)
£1,001 to £10,000	.83	.058	.31	1
£10,000 and above	.65	.085	.22	2
(£1,000 and above)	.87	.066	.37	(1)

Table C3: Stated Importance

Stated Importance	a	b (decay)	R^2	Rank
Very	1	.105	.86	2
All other	.99	.104	.75	1

Table C4: Strategy

Stated Importance	a	b (decay)	R^2	Rank
Did Nothing	.97	.134	.83	3
Handled Alone	1	.133	.91	2
Sought Advice	.98	.068	.67	1

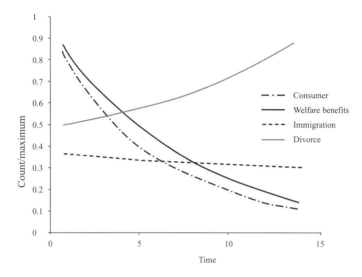

Figure C1: Memory Decay by Problem Category

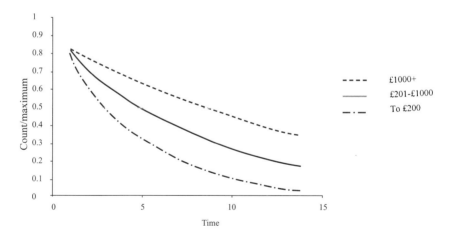

Figure C2: Memory Decay by Money Value

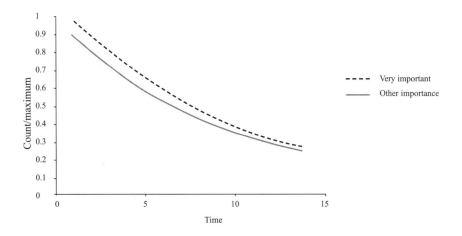

Figure C3: Memory Decay by Stated Importance

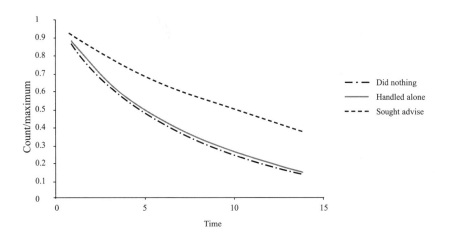

Figure C4: Memory Decay by Strategy